SADDLE UP

THE STORY OF A RED SCARF

BY

JOHN C. HEDLEY

A15 Publishing
PO Box 66054
Hampton, VA 23665
www.A15publishing.com

ISBN 978-0-9989005-4-4

THIRD PRINTING

REVIEWS

"*Saddle Up!* is an intimate and intense tale compellingly told. It provides an insight into the special bonds forged among and between members of a US infantry reconnaissance platoon in the heat of battle in the sweltering jungles and rice paddies of Vietnam, and provides a glimpse into the very soul of the small unit combat commander who led them."

Dutch Hostler
USMA '68

"Lieutenant Colonel (Ret.) John Hedley takes you deep inside a close-combat infantry unit in Vietnam in his first-hand narrative, "*Saddle Up*". Follow these hardened soldiers through some of the fiercest days of the Vietnam War. Fell the sense of camaraderie and unit cohesion that makes these men put their lives on the line for days on end. Gain an understanding of the shared danger and mutual respect that forges these men into a true "band of brothers". This riveting book provides clear insights into what makes men face mortal danger in war like none other on the market. Hedley's writing style will captivate you from the start. I challenge you to put the book down! Truly a superb testimonial to the American fighting man."

Ray Rhodes
LTC (Ret), US Army

"John Hedley literally wrenches his story of fighting in Vietnam directly from his gut. As an Infantry leader, he amply demonstrates throughout the story of his tour exactly what it took then and still, to this day, takes to instill in the men who comprise a unit a fierce loyalty and a strong will to successfully accomplish the harrowing missions that are assigned. As an author, he brings the sights, smells and sounds that accompany the adrenaline peaks and ebbs that become a continuous and familiar cycle to those who must confront the enemy face-to-face. The honing of a combat unit's discipline and keen instincts through highly effective leadership becomes familiar to those who have been in Hedley's situation. The fears that one must swallow and overcome are a great part of a combat leader's normal day as he struggles against a largely unseen enemy that appears infrequently, providing an almost surreal backdrop to the rising tensions prior to actual contact in battle. This internal conflict is brought to the fore in this author's highly accurate and extremely sound descriptions of his personal feelings. Through all of his story, John Hedley relates the admiration and love for the men who are in his unit. His steadfast attention to the smallest details of his warrior craft coupled with his all-consuming care for their welfare most certainly brought the majority of his unit back home from the horrors of this war. This book will enlighten those who reverently wish to follow in Hedley's footsteps as a small unit leader. The book should become required reading for all who wish to pursue a career of excellence in our American military."

Scott Vickers
USMA '68

"LTC Hedley's experiences can be summed up in the short phrase often seen in Vietnam amongst American troops. I am what others feared to be; I went where others feared to go; I did what others should have done.' Read the book and find the meaning in those few words."

Craig S. Carson
Infantry Company Commander in RVN, 1970-1971, 173rd ABN

"This book bleeds 110% of the raw emotion, stress, and brotherhood that can only be experiences by those who lived it. If you were one of the warriors who literally bled, sweated and cried over brothers lost and a war unnecessarily given away, John's experiences will be like a magnet that locks on to you at the first touch. Some thoughts that you thought were buried and long forgotten will instantly leap from the page...other thoughts that have always been there will seep from your memory as you read, like water being pulled from a sponge by a slow steady vacuum. Reliving the memories being evoked will make you laugh and smile, then weep and mourn with tears for lost comrades that were never fully shed.

For families it will give you a glimpse into the unknown life of the soldier you thought you knew and understood, loving him even more when you begin to understand what out war was really like. It will give you an adrenaline rush as you swell with pride over the man of valor and courage that your teenage son quickly became.

For future soldiers, it will steel your hearts to the reality of the value of hard training, loyalty and proper planning.

Finally, for the curious reader who doesn't even know a Vietnam veteran because of our nation's have separated we the people from the duty of shared responsibility, I pray that this book will motivate you to fins a way to serve the Republic that has given you more freedom than any country in the history of civilization.

The writer of this book and his Fox Force brothers, past and present, have paid the price for all of us to enjoy the freedom that we must all defend each and every day."

T. Allan Barnes
4th Inf. Division, FA

DEDICATION

This work is dedicated to the men of Fox Force (Current and Those No Longer with Us), the Reconnaissance Platoon of "E" Company, 1st Battalion 14th Infantry (Golden Dragons), 4th Infantry Division who served in the Central Highlands of South Vietnam, 1969-1970.
And
"The Dragon"
I have never had the honor to serve with a finer, more dedicated, more courageous group of men, nor have I ever been led by a finer commander.

ALSO

To A Very Special Honorary Member of Fox Force, Mr. Rockie Lynne, Friend, Comrade in Arms, Incredible Musician and Song Writer, Selfless Supporter of Service Members, Veterans and Gold Star Famili

TABLE OF CONTENTS

THE WEIGHT OF COMMAND

It's always the mission comes first…
and at times you feel blest and at times you feel cursed
as you pray for the best…
and prepare… for the worst.
And it's always the mission comes first.
And there's only so much you control.
It's the weight of decision that crushes the soul…
when you know that your soldiers will not go home whole…
for the war will relentlessly exact it's toll.
And the mind may forgive but the heart can't console…
because you got to live… past their final drumroll…
and the guilt of survival encumbers your soul.
But there's only so much you control.
And it all passes by in a blur.
But the bullets still whine… and the shrapnel shards whir…
and you are who you are… never more who you were…
as you wrestle the reaper's grim gray raconteur
who now batters with names of those you helped inter
and whose last whispered words were "I tried my best, Sir."
And you're bearing the scar of a provocateur.
But you are where you are… if not where you prefer.
And your mind may forgive but your heart can't concur…
for you know that's the tariff commanders incur:
a soul that can't rest…
and the rest you'll defer…
through a life full of strife
trying hard to aver
the decisions that cost…
the lives lost…
weren't in err.

And the truth is that you learned to cherish the rush…

and you yearned for the burn of adrenaline's gush.
And your mind hollers "Why?" …But your heart answers "Hush!"
for it cannot sustain what the memories crush
as they rumble and roil in unruly onrush…
those grim images caged in an aged underbrush.

And you're living a life that's both blessed and accursed
A full life… lived alone… but immensely immersed…
and intensely condensed… yet perversely dispersed…
with a hunger fulfilled… and a lingering thirst.
And the truth is you now know that isn't the worst…
yet as always the mission comes first.

And you know you can never atone…
For command bears its burdens alone.

Dutch Hostler, USMA '68

INTRODUCTION
Winter 2016 – 2017

This project has been more than seven years in the making. I started it as a means to preserve some of the history of the Reconnaissance Platoon known as Fox Force, E Company, 1st Battalion 14th Infantry, 4th Infantry Division in 1969 and 70 while serving in the Central Highlands of the former Republic of South Vietnam. I was fortunate to command that unit from August of 1969 until January of 1970.

As I began to write I expanded the time line somewhat to include my own history from before Vietnam until the end of hostilities in 1975. I had two primary objectives; to record our history for the families of my guys who served in Fox Force so they would know what their soldier had done during at least part of his time in that war. The other objective was to document some of my history for my own kids, driven by a deep frustration that I know so little of my own Dad's service in World War II or even before that.

The men of Fox Force were the finest soldiers that I served with in 24 years. As I look back on those days I marvel at how competent and professional those young men were. We were fortunate in that most of us arrived in the unit at about the same time so there was very little of the usual old timers versus new guy separation. The fact that most of us were "new guys" resulted in incredibly close bonds amongst all of us as we learned how to survive and accomplish our mission in the fires of infantry combat.

Most of my Fox guys were draftees but that fact did not make them any less competent, courageous, or professional than the volunteer Regular Army soldier. In every case that I witnessed, my Fox guys were much superior in their tactical knowledge and conduct than the battalion's line companies.

In addition to commanding the finest soldiers in the 1st Battalion, 14th Infantry, I was blessed with an incredibly proficient Non-

Commissioned Officer (NCO) chain of command. Without exception these leaders reflected the highest levels of professionalism and courage. My platoon sergeant, Staff Sergeant Jimmy Harris, is one of the finest men I've ever known. Although his Army experience before coming to Vietnam was limited to Army schooling; Basic and Advanced Individual Infantry Training, NCO Academy, Airborne and Ranger Schools; Jimmy was a born leader who was able to forge an incredibly close bond of trust and respect with the other guys. He served as the interim platoon leader in the gap between officers. Without his leadership we would not have been such an accomplished fighting force. When the going got tough I seldom needed to tell Jimmy what to do, he just knew instinctively and reacted without waiting for guidance.

My NCO squad leaders were cut from the same cloth. Robin Sneeden, Danny Williams, Ron Shewell, and Russ Simpson were all really great young men as well as incredibly proficient soldiers. These guys, working under Jimmy Harris, formed the real backbone of Fox. It has always been that way with the core and heart of the US Army, the Non-Commissioned Officers.

And a special note of admiration and thanks to my two RTO's (Radio/Telephone Operators), Charlie "Red" Siner and Alan "Buck" Buckelew. Just by the fact that they carried radios with the tell-tale antennas made them prime targets, for the enemy knew that good communications was critical to our survival and also, since they were both always within arm's reach of me, that the three of us constituted the unit's command core. Red carried the radio used to communicate with higher headquarters, air and artillery support as well as other units; Buck's radio was used to communicate with my three team leaders. Never once did I find either of them beyond arm's reach, even in the worst of times. Their role as an integral part of the platoon's command group also provided them special insight into what was going on and have made them invaluable sources of information as I've put this book together. Their jobs carried with them an extra measure of danger as well, and I'll always be grateful to them both for the incredible job they did keeping me in touch with everyone, and for keeping me alive.

Each of the soldiers of Fox Force was a phenomenal young man who always performed to the best of his abilities. I never heard dissent nor argument. Whenever I went to my bunkers to tell my guys to "Saddle Up!" they were ready to go, no matter the time of day or the mission.

The American infantryman or grunt is truly a noble creature. For alone among all of the others in the military, his mission is the most dangerous; to close with and destroy the enemy by close personal combat.

2

He stands with his rifle and courage at the very tip of the military spear. To accomplish his mission in Vietnam he lived in a primitive and dangerous environment, the likes of which had not been seen since some of the jungle fighting of World War II. The Vietnam grunt lived at a primal level, surviving on what he could carry on his back or find in the area. He lived and fought while exposed to Vietnam's three-month monsoon season, sometimes remaining wet for so long that he developed trench foot not seen since World War I. At other times he had to carry his 100 pound rucksack through rice paddies, jungles and up and down mountains in temperatures of 120 degrees or more, with close to 100% humidity; all the while having to stay alert for possible contact with the enemy at any time.

This was accomplished in some of the most difficult terrain and vegetation in South Vietnam. From the relatively flat land of the highlands to the steep and heavily jungled slopes of the Annamese mountains with an average elevation of around 6000 feet, the II Corps Central Highlands area was rugged and contained all kinds of critters disagreeable to infantrymen such as voracious mosquitos that carried malaria, incredibly painful stinging red ants, leeches, snakes, lizards, tigers, apes and monkeys as well as an incredible collection of birds.

One of the most loved of the lizards was the "Fuck You Lizard" as that is exactly what his voice sounded like. It was almost kind of reassuring to have that little guy around sounding off all night. Another favorite was the "Reup Bird" whose call sounded just like the two words that most Vietnam grunts despised.

Combat forges bonds among men that transcend all other relationships. It's different than love between a man and woman, or man and child; in many ways it's almost sacred and more basic. It's a bond of shared dangers, trust, respect and love among men who have shared the prospect of death at any minute. While patriotic movies and books will claim that men fight for their country and flag, which may be true initially and may be the prime motivator for entering the military during a time of war, once assigned to a unit and experiencing being shot at, the infantryman quickly realizes a quick change in primary loyalties to the band of brothers with whom he fights. When rounds begin to fly up-range at you it quickly becomes apparent that your survival to a large degree is dependent on those to your left and right, and that they in turn are dependent on you for their survival. The bonds formed during the all-consuming and sometimes terrifying experience of close combat are ever lasting and can very seldom ever be broken.

During the year in Vietnam War covered by this book, approximately 8000 young soldiers died and another 45,700 were wounded. Those are astounding numbers when they are considered in conjunction with the fact that by this time the US Army in Vietnam had begun to return home. In this one year we lost more Americans than in the entire 15-year span of the current wars in Southwest Asia, which now stands at around 6600. At its peak strength in 1969 there were approximately 543,000 Americans actually in country, about 10% of whom were in the field pulling triggers; the rest were in support activities; a tooth to tail ratio of one to nine. In 1969 the total number was reduced to 475,000 and by the end of 1970 there were 335,000. Over the course of the war about 2.5 million Americans actually had boots on the ground, today there are about 850,000 of us left, or only one third of those who served. Vietnam Veterans are dying at about the same rate as the World War II generation except that with us the predominant factor is probably not age but rather our exposure to Agent Orange.

The men of Fox came from a population back home that was becoming more and more stridently against the war; the hippy revolution was in full swing with its free love and marijuana culture gaining momentum. Parts of our cities had been burned down during racial upheavals. The nightly news was full of film of young men chanting "Hell no, we won't go!" as they burned their draft cards and the flag. Many of these same cowards fled to Canada to save their worthless butts. About a year after I returned, John F. Kerry, who would later become a Senator, US presidential candidate, and then still later Secretary of State, testified before Congress about the war crimes and law breaking of his former comrades in arms in the war zone. What a despicable excuse for a military officer and American!

The Paris Peace Talks were underway, and after a year the delegates were still arguing about the shape of the negotiation table. With that going on all who deployed to Vietnam during our time knew that it was a war that the country did not intend to win, but rather wanted to negotiate an "honorable" way out of. What kind of national "honor" is there but final and complete victory? Is there any wonder that there was an increase in disciplinary and racial problems in this environment; no one wanted to be the last to die in a useless war.

As I look back to my experience of over 45 years ago I'm amazed and somewhat unbelieving of the life that we led in those days. I also realize that I love my Brothers from Fox in a way that only another infantryman can understand. They are the finest men that I've ever had the honor to associate with and I was truly thankful and blessed to have served with them.

In places in this book I've used less than acceptable language, and have referred to our enemies as Gooks or by other disparaging names. The language reflects the true vocabulary and mind-set created in the war, and the pejorative name for the bad guys is a recurring issue found in all of our wars. Our soldiers throughout our history have referred to our enemies as Redskins, Injuns, Krauts, Huns, Japs, Chinks, Slopeheads, Dinks, Gooks and other non-politically correct names. We were raised in then typical, church-going, God-worshipping families, where we were taught that killing another man was a sin. Our young soldiers often found it difficult to pull a trigger on another human being, and the mental and emotional experience of gathering information from the bodies of those bad guys we killed, and finding pictures obviously of girlfriends, wives or kids, made that burden more personal and even heavier. The use of derogatory nicknames made the bad guy seem less than human and therefore lightened the mental burden of trying to kill him. Most of us found it difficult, at some time during our experience, to kill. Many of us carry lifelong mental burdens from having had to do so. With my language I've tried to be true to the climate we existed in.

I've found that putting these memories on paper has had a somewhat cathartic effect on dealing with my own personal demons and dragons. There have been many late nights spent on the computer trying to put some of this down through eyes filled with tears that seemed to come out of nowhere and for no reason. Listening to music like "Mansions of the Lord" from the movie "We Were Soldiers…" that I would sometimes happen upon while doing some research awoke powerful memories and feelings that I didn't quite expect or know how to deal with. Therefore, sometimes the effort to complete this project was helped along with a couple of fingers of a good single malt scotch.

I've tried in most cases to not make this primarily a tale of combat and body count, but rather to make an effort to reflect my own state of mind as a small unit leader, and to explain the reasons behind some of our missions and some of the decisions I made. I'm sure that I've not included every time that we had a firefight with either Viet Cong or North Vietnamese Army soldiers. I really want to explain the pressures and fears of a small unit leader who finds themself alone in combat with 25-30 men for whose lives he's responsible. Writing about some of these incidents has caused a lot of reflection about my own role with Fox.

Vietnam was in fact a war of killing, a true war of attrition, as our only measure of success was enemy body count, not terrain held or cities liberated. While we might fight like hell and expend numerous lives to take a certain piece of terrain, we typically left within a few hours or days and made that area accessible to our enemies once again. There were no front lines, just pockets of friendly terrain that we occupied as bases of operation. The enemy usually controlled the land between those pockets, at least during night hours when our close air support couldn't find them. There just was no really safe place for the American Grunt.

On the other side, the NVA in particular fought with a barbarity and ruthlessness not seen since the Imperial Japanese Army in World War II. The enemy's major motivator was to kill as many Americans as possible so as to influence the mindset of the population in the United States which they knew was now strongly against the war. This doctrine inspired them to walk battlefields after firefights and execute American wounded soldiers. It also motivated many of us to never be taken captive. Many Americans that I know vowed to save their last rounds for themselves. Additionally, many NVA units had men equipped with ropes and big hooks that enabled them to drag their dead and wounded off of the battlefield so that we wouldn't be able to see or count them. This served two purposes; it made the gathering of a body count, our measure of success difficult, plus it severely affected the morale of our guys who couldn't find "pay back" to balance the loss of their buddies.

In short, the year reflected in this book was a hell of a time, fighting a war half way around the world that we had no intention of winning, in conditions that can only be described as primitive and sometimes even sub-human, to say nothing of being incredibly dangerous. That the men of Fox served in such a dedicated and heroic way, even in the face of all of the negative influences, is testimony to the fact we were truly an exceptional Band of Brothers.

I was fortunate to loose only one man in Vietnam, with a possible second that we medevac'ed that I could not track through the hospital system, and had three or four wounded in combat. It's extremely sad to note that I've participated in seven funerals since we returned home and began to reunite in the year 2000. The first funeral was that of Ron Shewell who died between our first and second reunions. I was not able to attend his funeral due to work in Tokyo, but sent a letter to be read by Red Siner. Since that time we've lost Bob Beasely, Ron Classen, Bill Strate, Robin Sneeden, and two wives, Lois Robertson and Chris Buckelew. In addition, we learned of the deaths of two other Fox Brothers, Peaches and Chumley.

All who we have lost since the first reunion most probably died from Agent Orange related cancers or other Agent Orange issues. Now it's hard to believe that at that time we welcomed the use of AO and loved its effects because it stripped away foliage so that we could see the bad guys. Little did we even imagine in those days that AO was extremely toxic for us, and that its deadly effects could remain undetected in our bodies for decades. The seven guys who have passed away equal almost one third of the field combat strength that I had on any given day in Vietnam. Their deaths are combat deaths as surely as any of those whose names are on the Vietnam Memorial. In addition to those we've lost, several others of us have had AO related cancers but have been fortunate enough to survive. No Vietnam Veteran ever goes to the doctor by himself for he always has the specter of Agent Orange right alongside.

The other scourge of combat veterans is Post Traumatic Stress Disorder (PTSD); a term that I hate for that wound is not a mental disorder but rather a natural result of the horrors of combat that everyone experiences to varying degrees; we all come home with our own personal demons and dragons, it is just post traumatic stress. It's bad enough that young men have to experience first-hand the horrors of war, but for the Vietnam Vet the results of that experience were exacerbated by the fact that after the initial deployments we all went alone, and worst yet, we all returned home alone and so quickly that there was no time to process or deal with our experiences.

Our fathers went to war in World War II and Korea and usually returned home with the same unit unless they earned enough points to come home early. People may have changed due to wounds or death, but by and large they returned as a unit. That was one great aid to dealing with the trauma of war. The other was that they returned by ship with their buddies, giving them weeks to talk over events and to put their experiences in the context of everyone else's, and to mentally throttle down from the experiences of war. They went with buddies and came home with buddies. We Vietnam veterans however, had an entirely different experience. Except for those who deployed with their buddies in the initial unit deployments, we others went to war alone, with no support. Worse yet, we came home alone, and too quickly. For many grunts, they found themselves on their Freedom Birds just three or four days after coming out of the jungle. They had a quick trip of about 24 hours and then found themselves back in "The World," having to make their way home alone and without the support of friends or the time to decompress, with no welcoming bands and crowds to thank them for what they had been through. In addition, we came home to a country that loathed us, subjected us to incredible hatred and harassment, and thus made our readjustment even more difficult.

Many of the enlisted guys were draftees, and many of them got out of the Army the day of their return, or the next if they landed in the US at night; no friends, no Army. Many other guys had a few months remaining on their enlistment and returned to dispirited units in the States or even overseas beset with drug and race problems. The Vietnam Vets, the "short timers" in my first stateside battalion before I went to war were a tough bunch to deal with. As a Second Lieutenant Battalion Duty Officer I had to make my rounds at night armed with a .45 caliber pistol and accompanied by a staff duty NCO armed with a club. We had had an experience of a duty officer being thrown out of a barrack's second story window by a bunch of drunk or drugged-up "short timers".

Those of us who were "Lifers", officers and NCO's who were making the Army a career, had the same problems dealing with problem soldier "short timers". The stateside units were understaffed and overworked. With the coming end of the hugely unpopular draft the Army instituted a program called "VOLAR" (Volunteer Army) for enticing young men to voluntarily join. This was primarily a program of reduced standards and discipline. As a company commander I had to put beer machines in my barracks and allow soldiers to grow hair and mustaches to a length that a year or so earlier would have resulted in non-judicial punishment.

In addition, many veterans who stayed in the service felt that they had to hide on post with their wives and children because American society was so hostile to returning warriors. Some veterans of Southeast Asia didn't admit for decades that they had served in the military or that they were veterans of the conflict. Vietnam Veterans were even shunned in some of the organizations where veterans of other times had been able to find solace and support like the American Legion or the Veterans of Foreign Wars, because ours was not a real war and we "lost" it anyway. That has been a real blow to many vets who needed the support and acceptance from those very folks with whom they shared a heritage and experience. I have no doubt that the accumulation of these types of stresses has also led to a unique form of Vietnam Post Traumatic Stress.

The views and thoughts in this effort are mine unless directly attributed to someone else. I used the daily Battalion Operations Logs to help establish a time line and record of daily events. I got access to these logs relatively late in the writing process so I had to go back over what I had done to fill in many holes. The descriptions of events are described from my perspective and my memory. It's a proven fact that in combat, two soldiers fighting side by side may see or remember the event in an entirely different manner. One may not even see what his buddy next to him observed. My view and memory was also influenced by my responsibility as the platoon leader. It may be that some of my guys may remember some of the incidents described in this book in an entirely different format; I guess that's part of the fog of war. I've tried my best to remember my thoughts and fears, and to describe my feelings and decision-making process as clearly as possible. The responsibility for the lives of the guys of Fox was sometimes pretty heavy, but always foremost in my mind.

I owe a special note of thanks to Charlie "Red" Siner, who has been an incredible friend since we reunited at the first reunion. Charlie has been my go- to- guy when I needed to unscramble a sequence of events or couldn't remember specific details of that event. He has an almost a photographic memory and has been an incredible asset. On one visit he brought me copies of the maps we used in the Area of Operations around the Landing Zone (LZ) St. George and LZ Lois areas, and we spent several happy hours retracing our steps in several operations. I would not have been able to completely recount several of the incidents without his help. Thanks Red, for having my six as always!

I also want give a special note of thanks to some of my classmates, Scotty Vickers, Bob Hensler, Dutch Hostler and Brian Utermahlen. These guys are accomplished authors in their own right with skills far beyond mine, yet they devoted time to read excerpts of this work as it progressed, and provided help and motivation to assist me in getting this done. I owe a lot to those guys; they are true proponents of our class moto: No Task Too Great For '68!

I have to say some very special words of thanks to Margie, the love of my life and my soul mate. This has been a lengthy undertaking, and the dredging up of the memories has been very painful at times. There were incidents where I was so affected by what I was remembering that I retreated into my mental "dark space" for up to a couple of days, or exhibited the flash anger or sullenness brought on by my own demons, or even unstoppable tears. Throughout this entire effort Margie has been nothing but supportive, loving and understanding of all of my efforts and mood swings. I know that I could not have gotten through some of the bad and emotionally trying times without the comfort of her love. I will be eternally grateful that this phenomenal woman came into my life at an extremely dark and depressing time for me. She is living proof that even during the darkest of times that the sun will come up and shine brightly again. I love her more than words can express.

I sincerely hope that this book will prove to be worthwhile to my Fox guys, their families and to my family as well; if it is then "Mission Accomplished!"

"Courage is being scared to death… but saddling up anyway."
John Wayne

1 - REFLECTIONS ON WEST POINT
THE BEGINNING

I honestly can't remember the first time I thought about West Point; on the other hand I can't remember any time when I didn't think about West Point while I was growing up. I don't remember what initiated my interest; all I know is that I had wanted to attend the Military Academy for as long as I can remember. I wanted nothing more out of life than to graduate from USMA and to be a career infantry officer.

My Dad was not a grad although attending the Academy was his dream as well at an early age. Dad had essentially been an orphan after his Mom passed away when he was four years old and the family was living in Rochester, New York. My Grandfather, who had been a British merchant seaman, returned to sea after his wife's death and my Dad never saw him again that I know of, and never spoke of him to me except once when describing his childhood. There were an older brother and sister with whom he lived for a while until the older brother moved to New York City where he became an acclaimed opera singer, and his sister joined the United Nations and worked for UNICEF in Beirut for almost her entire life. My Dad was eventually taken in by a family who I came to know as my Aunt and Uncle, even though they were not blood relatives. I don't know when my Dad enlisted in the Army the first time nor why.

Dad did tell me that he tried three times to enter West Point from the Army as an enlisted man in the days when each Army Area had its own preparatory school. Dad was assigned to a First Army unit in New York City and somehow managed to go to the 1st Army Prep School at Ft. Totton for three years. The first year he failed the math entry exam. The second year he passed math, but failed English. The third year he passed all of the academics, but failed the weigh-in; he was too light. So he stuffed himself with bananas and milk shakes, as he told the story, went to another weigh-in, passed and received an appointment to, I believe, the Class of 1938 or 39. With this success he took some leave to go home and prepare himself for Beast Barracks. While there, excited about finally realizing his life goal, he received a letter from the War Department and was informed that his hard-fought-for appointment to West Point had been revoked because he would be a few days over the maximum allowed age limit of 22 on his class entry date.

This was a severe disappointment and Dad left the Army for a while. He worked for Otis Elevators and then somehow got the job as Chief of Security for the 1939 World's Fair in New York City where he met my Mom who, with her family, had come into the US from Germany through Ellis Island when she was just a little girl. She told us from the earliest days that her Dad had been the one that developed the recipe for what would become Hellman's Mayonnaise, but I've never been able to verify that fact. I don't know much of her background except that she had been quite a horsewoman until thrown in New York's Central Park, injuring her back. She had also lived in Hollywood and had been married to an early movie star. Sometime after they met, Mom and Dad were married in New York City. Also, sometime during that period Dad rejoined the Army; received a commission and served for many more years as an infantry officer before retiring and returning to the civilian world.

Evidently sometime during the war Dad had received a leave to go home, for I was born in July of 1945. I have no knowledge of my Dad's war time service; although I believe it was in the Pacific Theater. Despite many efforts on my part to get him to talk, particularly after my combat tour, he never would. And, unfortunately, my Dad's records were destroyed in a large fire in the records repository.

After the war ended Dad was assigned to occupation duty in Tokyo. My Mom and I went over by troop ship, the USNS General Rose, as soon as housing had been assigned for dependents. Dad worked in ATIS; the Allied Translator Interpreter Section for General MacArthur's Headquarters in Tokyo and had an office in a building across the street from a place where, many years later, I would work for eight years as the only foreigner in the Headquarters of Mitsubishi Electric Corporation. We then lived on a former Imperial Army Kamikaze base that is now Yoyogi Park in Tokyo, the site of the birthplace of Japanese aviation, much like our Kitty Hawk, and was within easy walking distance from an apartment that Margie and I shared for eight years. The parallels between my Dad's life and my own are striking.

My sister Sue was born at St. Luke's Hospital while we were in Tokyo, at that time staffed by American medical personnel. I do have a few memories of those days. I know that we had two Japanese live-in maids, one of whose name was Michiko. My folks corresponded with them for years after we returned stateside; I even tried to look one up during my own Tokyo assignment with no luck. I do also have a memory of riding around in a big red Ford; I don't know the year or model name. I also remember that my Dad smoked Lucky Strikes in those days, because if I could touch the pack in his shirt pocket I could hit him once; hence a "lucky strike".

After three years in Japan, we were assigned to Fort Benning, Georgia, which was then the home of the 4th Infantry Division. Ironically, I would serve in the 4th Division in Vietnam. We lived in brand new military housing; they were still pouring cement for the sidewalks. The smell of fresh cement today still takes me back to those days. It was at Fort Benning that I received my first electric train, an American Flyer; I've had a love affair with trains, real and model, to this day. During my military career I also served at Ft. Benning a couple of times and our daughter Marcia was born in the Army hospital there.

From Georgia, Dad was transferred to Germany when the division deployed there and shortly thereafter, to France. My Mom, sister and I rode another troop ship to La Havre where we joined him for a three year assignment. I believe it was on our first morning in France when I remember hot chocolate for the first time, and a crunchy, sticky breakfast roll known as an elephant ear. During that time we moved a couple of times, living in a small farming village named La Jarne where we lived in a farm house whose septic tank opening was in the living room; a fact we learned one night when my Mom was preparing for a large dinner party and the toilets plugged up. After a while in this remarkable place we moved to a farming village named Villandreau near Bordeaux. I have memories of riding to the base with my Dad in the morning to attend school, being held up by herds of cows in the road, and of my Dad making an official inspection of the two classroom school I attended on base. Our final home in France was in La Rochelle.

While in France, I ate bread and chocolate with my French friends after school; drank wine with dinner as there was little fresh milk available; and learned to shoot when I received a BB gun for a birthday while in Villandreau. I was taught to shoot by a tough WAC officer, Maxine B. Michl, who in later years was promoted to be one of the first six Army female full colonels. She was stationed in Washington, DC when I visited with her as an enlisted man at Ft. Belvoir, VA. She would later become the first WAC colonel to command the WAC Training Center at Ft. McClellan, Alabama. In Villandreau we lived in a very picturesque farmhouse, shared with and owned by a French woman who raised cows and guinea hens. I was frequently sent down the hill to the small river that bordered our home to pick fresh watercress.

The cows often ate my Mom's laundry off of the clothes line and I shot at the guinea hens with my BB gun; they jumped, squawked and ran around when I hit them; that was great fun. I guess this caused problems for my Dad as, unknown to me, the landlady gave some of the hens to her French neighbors as gifts and one of whom, much to my later consternation, broke a tooth on a BB. I heard that I became a pretty good shot at an early age as my folks loved to tell stories of the bottles of wine that I won at shooting galleries during the town festivals. Maybe that's why I was usually allowed to drink some with the dinner meal.

Dad retired from the Army while we were in France and we returned to the US on the *SS United States*. I have some fond memories of that ocean crossing, one of the most lasting being the taste of the beef bouillon served in mid-afternoon on the Promenade Deck where we sat in wooden deck chairs. It was an incredible trip; the ship had great restaurants and a neat movie theater where I saw the western *Broken Arrow*. It's really sad to see the level of neglect and decay in her these days. We pulled into New York Harbor and passed the Statue of Liberty, a memorable sight even for a nine-year-old boy. We initially lived in Carteret, New Jersey with my Mother's Mom and then moved to Rochester, New York, my Dad's hometown. I lived there until I graduated from Gates-Chili High School in 1963 and joined the Army. I guess I grew up with the Army in my blood.

Being a West Point cadet had always been my dream, but not one that was directly influenced or initiated by my Dad. It just happened. When he learned of this he was, of course, very supportive and we would drive once a year in the fall from Rochester to West Point so that we could watch a parade and see a football game. I was in absolute awe… West Point was my shining castle on a hill. I could dream of me being in full dress gray marching across The Plain in those gorgeous Saturday morning parades. Wow! I knew it was an important place when I had the chance to see President Eisenhower on one of those trips. We watched games in the days of the Army's "lonely end," Scott Carpenter, who never went into the huddle. Years later he would become famous in Vietnam for calling a US air strike in on his own position because he was being overrun. I would later have a similar experience.

My Dad had a couple of old Army footlockers in the basement of our home. One was his financial center, which contained envelopes for the cash which was deposited every month depending on his family budget allocation. When the cash ran out in one of the envelopes there was no more spending in that category until the next payday. The other footlocker contained military memorabilia I think; he only opened it once in my presence and it had disappeared by the time he passed away. One day he took me downstairs and opened the footlocker to show me a framed picture of a West Point cadet, probably a *Howitzer* yearbook picture. He told me that this was a picture of his best friend from his enlisted days at prep school who had been lost on Doolittle's raid over Tokyo in the early and dark days of WW II. I never saw the picture again and he never spoke of his friend again either. I wish that I could remember his name.

I took the civil service entrance exams for my congressmen during my senior year of high school to qualify for an appointment to West Point, but received only a 2nd alternate appointment, which never came through. I was devastated. I considered myself to be a failure; my dream now seemed to be unreachable. I determined then that I would enlist in the Army because I'd heard that there were appointments available for Regular Army soldiers. So an olive drab Army staff car appeared in my driveway the day after high school graduation (24 June 1963, my Dad's birthday) to take me to Buffalo, New York to be sworn in as a new recruit. All of us new recruits were then put on a train for Fort Dix, New Jersey, for basic training where I spent my 18th birthday.

I became a trainee squad leader with an armband with sergeant E-6 stripes because I took easily to the Army training and discipline. We lived in old WW II wooden barracks at the end of one of the McGuire Air Force Base runways. Our "big deal" was being allowed to go to one of the on-base beer halls after 4 weeks of training to drink 3.2% beer. No matter how much we drank we could never find a "buzz." I can honestly say that I really enjoyed most of the training that summer. I found that I really liked being a soldier and wearing a uniform.

Of everything that happened at Ft Dix, one event stands out in my memory. I think it was at the end of 5 weeks when we were eligible for our first overnight pass to go off base, most to Trenton, New Jersey. We formed a single line outside of the company orderly room and were to report to the company commander after being cleared by the First Sergeant at the door.

Our First Sergeant was a real character. He was a stocky and broad shouldered man with cauliflower ears, like maybe he was or had been a boxer. He was a Korean War veteran and proudly wore the blue and silver badge of the combat infantryman on his left chest. When we were subject to frequent harangues because we weren't training hard enough, he would point to the CIB (Combat Infantry Badge) on his chest and tell us that while it was blue and silver on the outside, it was blood red on the inside. The message was that we needed to pay attention in order to survive any future combat action.

When it came my turn at the head of the line I snapped to attention and reported, "First Sergeant, Private Hedley requests permission to see the Company Commander." The First Sergeant just stared at me and then snarled, "So you're Hedley... get out of line and come with me behind the orderly room." Boy did I get nervous. In those days it was not unheard of for NCO's to enforce discipline with a good physical ass whipping. When we went around the building I stood at a rigid attention, as the First Sergeant looked me up and down.

"Hedley, just who the fuck do you think you are?"

"First Sergeant, I'm Private Hedley"

"I know that dumbass; just what the fuck do you think you're doing?"

"First Sergeant, I don't understand."

"Did you write to your Dad and tell him that you weren't getting enough milk to drink in the mess hall?"

I had to think for a minute and then realized that I may have done that. In one of my letters home in response to a question from my Mom on how good the food was, I had replied that it was pretty good although we had to eat in a real hurry and not talk with anyone, and that we weren't allowed to refill our glasses, hence only one glass of milk per meal.

"Yes First Sergeant, I think I did."

"Well dumb shit, your Dad wrote a letter to the Commanding General of Ft. Dix and complained that his little Johnny wasn't getting enough milk to drink. And do you know what happened because of that?"

"No First Sergeant." My knees were really beginning to tremble. I couldn't even imagine that my Dad, a retired Regular Army officer, could do anything so stupid.

"You dumb shit! Because of your Dad my commander got a nasty note from the Commanding General, sent through the whole chain of command, advising him to stop rationing milk to his soldiers. Do you realize that you may have ruined my commander's career?"

"First Sergeant, I'm sorry, I didn't know . . . "

"God damn it, shut up!!" He looked me up and down with scorn running out of his now bulging eyes. "You sissy, do you really think that you can go to West Point? You go crying to Daddy about not enough milk. You fucking baby, you'll never make it; you're not worthy enough to go to West Point. West Point, you, what a fucking joke that would be! I ought to run you out of my Army and save everyone a bunch of trouble!!"

He then told me that as long as he was the First Sergeant that I would never get a pass, and told me to return to my barracks. Needless to say I was shocked that my Dad had done such a thing. Being a retired officer he should have known that shit, from any source, always rolls down hill. I never did see what was outside the gates of Ft. Dix.

During the in-processing and initial skill testing of basic training, I had been told about the Army's West Point Prep School at Fort Belvoir, Virginia. This was a school for Regular Army and Army Reserve soldiers who expressed a desire to go to West Point and were recommended by their commanding officers. So I took the qualifying exam, passed, and received orders to USMAPS (United States Military Academy Preparatory School) Class of 1964 at Fort Belvoir, Virginia. Once again I was following in my Dad's footsteps.

Another of the soldiers in that company would also go to the Prep School and ultimately become a West Point classmate as well. Now maybe I could realize my dream.

USMAPS was a rewarding experience; I now know that it was the only way I could have ever become a cadet. Math had never been my strong suit; USMAPS helped me to improve my ability so that I could raise my score on the math portion of the SAT entrance exams. The other invaluable reward of attending USMAPS was the opportunity to meet some of the finest guys in the world. We were all there for the same reason. While there was certainly some competition, there an underlying feeling that we would all work together to achieve a common goal. We all wanted to be West Point classmates. It was an inspirational time for me.

To this day I cherish those relationships, some of those guys are my closest friends, and some of those names can now be found on The Wall . . . so sad. On the happy side, one now lives just a few miles away, and another, who was also my roommate during Firstie Year, comes from Colorado with his wife to visit frequently. The three of us get together to remember old times, mutual friends, drink scotch and smoke cigars while enjoying the lake view.

I learned that I could also compete for a Congressional appointment while in the Army, so I decided to try that route again as well. On a snowy day, in the middle of a blizzard, I made my way to Washington to visit my congressman, Mr. Ostertag, who also sat on the Board of Visitors of USMA. I proudly wore my Army Dress Green uniform with the single Pfc. stripe, known as mosquito wings, which I had sewn on the night before. I guess that I must have impressed him as I later received a letter with an Appointment to West Point just as we were getting on buses to take our weekend orientation trip to USMA.

I was flying!

2 - FOUR LONG YEARS

The happiest and proudest day in my life up to that time occurred in early July of 1964 when I entered West Point with the Class of 1968. I had worked hard all summer to get into good physical shape. I drove down a day or two early with my parents and sister and we all stayed on post in the Thayer Hotel. I was nervous and scared, but so proud and so anxious to get started. On THE morning we all ate breakfast together in the hotel's restaurant and then moved outside where shuttle buses were parked to take us up to the gym where we would pass through the door into the rigors of West Point's Beast Barracks. I ran into a couple of my Prep School classmates and we decided that we would all ride together to start the great adventure. I waved good-bye to my folks and sister as the bus pulled away.

I remember almost every minute of the initial in-processing; reporting to the "Man in the Red Sash" multiple times, being yelled at by upper classmen who put their faces just inches from mine, leaving their spittle on my face from their yelling. We were issued bags of Army and West Point gear, fitted for dress uniforms and shoes, and issued our first cadet uniform, which we would wear later on that first day. I was assigned to the First New Cadet Company; where during the summer I received a memorable introduction to the Academy's well-earned reputation for hazing. We also received intensive basic instruction in dismounted drill, how to march, as we would need that skill later in the day to march to Trophy Point to be sworn in as New Cadets. That was an easy task for me because of my Army basic training experiences.

The West Point Class of 1968 was significant in the history of the Academy in several ways. We were the first of the large, modern classes that entered with a strength of over 1000 new cadets; previous classes had been limited to 750 and the entire Corps of Cadets numbered about 2500. The Corps was being enlarged to produce more officers because the Vietnam buildup was looming. With the entry of our class the corps was scheduled to grow to a total of around 4000. Many of us lived in the "old

West Point", the famous Central Area of barracks with numerous four-story stairwell divisions that had existed for over 100 years. I lived in the First Division that summer, and would spend my entire Plebe Year in the same room. We learned the old dismounted Squad Drill, which was infantry drill and ceremonies for parades that had existed since the Civil War. When we entered there were only two regiments, 1st and 2nd.

During our four years the Corps expanded to four regiments, with some cadets from the 1st Regiment being moved to become the core of the 3rd, and cadets from the 2nd moved to form the 4th. We were also the first class to be allowed to go home for Christmas leave; all previous classes "enjoyed" Plebe Christmas at West Point with those families that could visit. Ground was also broken for a doubling of Washington Hall, the cadet mess, and two new barracks wings, which would replace Central Area with the exception of the 1st Division, which would remain as a museum and reminder of the old days.

Late in that first day of our Beast Barracks, we were formed up in our new summer uniforms and marched behind the West Point Band down the main street around The Plain to Trophy Point for our swearing in ceremony. The day was gorgeous and sunny, and the music from the band kept us not only in step but also served to make our hearts beat proudly. While we were told to look only to the front and not "gaze around," I managed to see my family as we marched by, and saw the tears in my Dad's eyes, the first I had ever witnessed. Our first weekend at West Point was the 4th of July holiday, and my whole class stood in ranks outside of Central Area, presenting arms for a 50 gun salute to mark the importance of the day. I remember being really hot and sweaty, but also reveling in the fact that I was finally wearing a West Point uniform and paying respect to our country and to all of those who had worn the uniform before me.

My four years at West point were the best of times and the worst of times. I loved it and hated it at the same time. Beast Barracks, while challenging, was enjoyable as I was passing the test that would let me become a full-fledged cadet of the United States Military Academy. I had been pretty well prepared for its rigors by Army Basic Training. I had a Prep School classmate in the room across the hall in the First Division of Central Area Barracks and at night, after Taps, I would sneak across the hall and we would sit under his desk to smoke a cigarette and talk over the days' events.

The First Division was one of the four-floor stairwells in the old Central Area Barracks that had four rooms to a floor. The First Division was also known as the "Wheel House" because it had larger than normal, semi-circular rooms on the side facing the Plain that were the residences of the Brigade Staff during the academic year. In the basement was "The Sinks," an area including showers, toilets and storage areas.

Beast Barracks was in reality a "Beast". We weren't even Plebes yet, just New Cadets. We were forced to move around in a "brace" position, an exaggerated position of attention with our chin crammed back against our neck and our shoulders pressed as far back as possible. The upper classmen would always scream at you to produce more chins; i.e. "Cram your chin in meathead!" All movement was at a double time and we were made to square corners while running or during the few times that we were allowed to walk. We had to keep our eyes straight to the front. As a part of our new life that would stay with us throughout our first year, we were forced to memorize incredible amounts of primarily worthless, but sometimes useful, "Plebe Poop." As a matter of fact, we were issued a "Plebe Bible," a small gold covered book, *Bugle Notes* (I still have mine), that contained the traditional requirements, like the *Definition of a Cow* and how many gallons of water were in Lusk Reservoir up the hill near Michie Stadium. We also had to memorize a week's worth of mess hall meal menus, the movies for the week, the names of all of the upper classmen in our detail, the names of the marches for the parades, etc. etc.

Meals were an eating opportunity in name only. We sat in a brace on the front 2 inches of our chair with our eyes down on our plate while our chins were crammed into our necks as far as possible. This was the position of "sitting up" and was our normal pose. We could eat only when allowed to by an upper classman and had to take small square bites; i.e. move the fork vertically until it was on line with your mouth and then do a 90 degree turn to get the food into your mouth. We could take only small bites and had to chew them thoroughly. While chewing the fork was returned to the plate in the same 90-degree movement in reverse and our hands were placed in our laps. During "meal time" we could be challenged at any time to recite any item of Plebe Poop, and if we had a problem we were forced to "sit up" for the rest of the meal; that is, we were not allowed to eat. If we did well we might hear that very welcome instruction, "Take big bites smack head." While all of us were in great physical condition, we all lost weight during Beast due to the amount of physical exercise coupled with the scarcity of food. I remember one night sucking the toothpaste out of my tube because I was so hungry.

At some time, well into the summer of Beast, we were finally granted a long awaited privilege, permission to visit the "Boodlers" in the basement of the mess hall building. I'm not sure of the origin of the name, but the Boodlers was a snack and candy shop where we could buy all kinds of treasure like ice cream, candy, chips, cookies and other snacks. On our first opportunity my room-mates and I went to the Boodlers, loaded up on as much good stuff as we could carry or afford, and then scurried back to our room across Central Area with the hopes of avoiding any upper classmen. If caught, we were sure to be harassed long enough to cause our ice cream to melt in the August heat.

We successfully returned to the old First Division, ran into our room, and began to tear open the packages and stuff as much down our throats as we possibly could as quickly as possible; we had to have everything gone by a certain time. The devious upperclassmen, knowing full well what would happen after our first visit to snack heaven, timed the trip for relatively late in the afternoon. Because we rapidly stuffed ourselves with snacks and candy bars that our stomachs hadn't seen for six weeks, many of us became violently ill. That, however, was not an excuse to miss dinner formation. The march to the mess hall was like a punishment march, the route being littered by sick and gagging new cadets. The dinner meal wasn't a whole lot of fun either.

Many nights during Beast I lay on my bunk just thanking the Man Above that I was there. I don't ever remember feeling home sick, even on my 19th birthday – I probably didn't even realize the significance of that day given our rigorous training schedule.

For those of us who survived Beast Barracks, the eagerly anticipated end point was to participate in the Acceptance Parade held during Reorganization Week, or "Reorgy Week" as labeled by cadets. During this week the three upper classes returned to West Point from their summer training duties or leave, and the regular cadet companies were reopened and all prepared for the start of academics. With the end of the Acceptance Parade we became official Plebes and were accepted into the United States Corps of Cadets and assigned to a lettered company; in my case A-1 or A Company, 1st Battalion, 1st Regiment. During Beast we had out-numbered the upper-class cadre members; however in our regular companies the status was reversed and we found it a lot more difficult to avoid or hide from harassment.

A-1 had the reputation of being the hardest company in the whole Corps for Plebes. There were two regiments in the Corps, 1st and 2nd; the 1st was hard-core, the second was thought to be kind of loosey-goosey and not nearly as strict or military; at least by those of us in first regiment. 1st and 3rd then became the two strict regiments while both 2nd and 4th enhanced the reputation of being loose and not so military, particularly the 4th.

There were two memorable high points in our Plebe year. The first came in November at the annual Army-Navy Game in Philadelphia. The Navy had a hot-stuff quarterback named Roger Stauback who would later go on to NFL fame with the Dallas Cowboys. Army also had a superb, but lesser known, quarterback named Rollie Stichway. If Army won, historically the Plebes had been allowed to "fall out" until Christmas; that is, to not have to be in a constant brace position and also be allowed to eat normally in the mess hall. Army won that 1964 game against all expectations and so we all fell out until Christmas. This joyful event was followed by the other high point of that year, as the Class of 1968 was the first to be allowed to go home on Christmas leave. We would experience the traditional Plebe confinement later in the year for Spring Break. When we went to church on Christmas Day my Dad had asked me to wear my full dress cadet uniform which included a coat with tails and both the front and tails had lines of big round brass buttons. Imagine the noise everytime I sat down in a full wooden pew! I was really uncomfortable with all of the interest that I generated.

The time before and after Christmas was crammed with classes five and a half days a week. Since we were working on a Bachelor of Science in Engineering degree, we had math classes 6 days a week. I fought a constant battle with that department, normally residing in the "last section". In each course we were assigned to sections, and to seats within those sections, on an order of merit basis, those with the highest grades being in the first section and those of us barely hanging on in the last. Many times I sat close to the end of the section. On one memorable occasion after the end of semester finals, I found myself to be the only cadet in the classroom when academics resumed, all of my classmates had been "turned out", or had failed their math exams and were required to take a re-entry exam and pass it to come back to class. Failing that exam normally led to expulsion. On that first day the "P" or professor, a regular army officer, walked into the room. When I stood and reported that we were all "present or accounted for" he told me to sit down and then looked at me sternly. "Mister Hedley, I sure as hell don't know how you managed to pass that exam, but congratulations."

At the end of Plebe year we were "recognized" after the Graduation Parade during June Week. At this time we officially became accepted as full-fledged members of The Corps, and were allowed to call upperclassmen by their first names. After the parade, the Plebes in each company formed into a single line. Each upper classman would pass down the line of Plebes and introduce himself with his first name and a handshake after some last minute harassment. I still have my cross belt's

23

breastplate that was dented by a couple of rifle butts. I had made it; Plebe year was OVER!

The academic years would prove to put a little tarnish on my shining castle. My lack of math prowess was a constant challenge during all four years. We could be graded in each class each day, which called for an incredible amount of studying and cramming if you were not among those naturally gifted with academic ability. While some classes varied by the day of the week, not math – which we had to suffer through for all 6 days for two long years! After classes ended on Saturdays during the fall, we had to "ping" (run) back to our rooms to prepare for a full dress parade. All the way back we would chant "Odin! Odin!" Odin was the Norse God of Rain, and we chanted his name in the hopes that the heavens would open up and we wouldn't have to fall out for the parade. After the parade we ate lunch and then went to Michie Stadium to watch a football game if played at home. Saturdays was also the day of the S.A.M.I. (Saturday AM Inspection), or "Sammy," a full room inspection. It was not unusual as a Plebe to return to your room to prepare for the parade only to find it in complete disarray with contents of drawers and closets thrown about. These had to be squared away before we could enjoy any freetime.

I had my ups and downs with the tactical department and other academic departments as well. The absolute low point came during one of our periodic physical fitness test requirements my yearling year when I passed out during a rope climb on the infamous Indoor Obstacle Course, a gut-wrencher that we had to run at least once a year for a grade. I don't remember how that happened. I only remember suddenly being on the mat on my back instead of on the elevated track. This was the beginning of the darkest days of my life. I had always believed myself to be in great physical shape. I never had any physical problems while growing up, to include while playing sports in high school, during Army Basic Training and at Prep School.

However, that all changed after my first year. To this day I don't know what the catalyst was for my developing problems, maybe it was the intensity of the program, I really don't know. Due to failing the PE test, I was "turned out" at the end of first semester Yearling year. Being "turned out" was a form of short suspension; if you passed a re-entry exam you could be reinstated to your class with no lost time. West Point, with its high levels of testosterone, was not a good place to have issues with physical fitness. Eventually I was "found" (separated) when I failed the turn-out exam, which included the same obstacle course, as well and had to move out of A-1 into the Boarders Ward. This was a dark and dreary area under the Guard Room in Central Area that was reserved for cadets who had been found to not measure up to the standards of the Corps of Cadets in any number of aspects; academics, physical fitness, adaptability to the military life style, low peer ratings, etc. We were kept separate from our erstwhile classmates, even being marched to the mess hall after the regular meals where we ate by ourselves. We were truly no longer a part of The Corps.

I don't remember ever having been so depressed. After all of the hard work to get an appointment, and after having survived the rigors of Army Basic Training, Beast Barracks and Plebe year, I had now failed. I wasn't sure if I was going to be able to go home and face my family. In 1965 cadets who flunked out of West Point were normally kept in the Army and assigned to a unit as an enlisted man. As time went on these guys quickly found that their first assignment was in Vietnam. Former cadets were not allowed to attend anything like OCS or ROTC to earn a commission at a date earlier than the graduation date of their former class.

While undergoing my separation physical at the cadet hospital, I met an officer and surgeon (Dr. Robert Geer) who would, it would turn out, save my career a couple of times; it was he who administered the final separation physical exam. In the conduct of that exam he could find no physiological reason for my arm strength stamina problems. I had discovered during a second attempt at the obstacle course that my arms suddenly went completely numb, thus losing my ability to grasp anything, causing me to fall off of the rope or the chin-up bar.

One afternoon I was summoned to his office where he told me that he'd discovered that I had a major—and until that time undetected—birth defect which interfered with the major nerves and blood flow to my arms and muscles when my arms were raised. This defect literally cut off the blood flow up my arm while pinching the nerve at the same time. He asked if I really wanted to stay at West Point. Of course there was only one answer to that question. He then told me that I would have to probably undergo a couple of, in those days, experimental surgeries that might not be successful.

With his help I was reinstated to the Class of '68, and began what was to be two years of surgeries at Walter Reed Army Hospital in Washington, D.C., long hospitalizations there and back at West Point, and tough studying to keep up with academics from both Walter Reed and the West Point Hospital. There was also intense physical rehabilitation and training because I had to meet all of the physical fitness requirements in order to graduate and be commissioned in the combat arms. I also had to maintain my academic proficiency throughout this time, even from the

25

hospitals. Although turned out in PE, I was never turned out in an academic subject even with all of the time away from a formal classroom. Although not an easy process, I'd made it.And I owed this chance to realize my dream to Doctor Geer.

During the fall of our First Class year all of the local car dealerships held a car show in the field house. Traditionally, they also made us really good deals in regards to price. The dealers knew that they would never have to worry about maintenance or warranty problems as we would all spread to the four corners of the country and beyond after graduation. My proud purchase was a 1968 Firebird 400, burgundy red with a black vinyl roof. It also sported a 4-speed manual transmission which I had never had an occasion to learn to drive before that purchase, and a new invention called an 8-track stereo that played large tape cassette versions of popular record albums. I taught myself to handle the intricacies of a standard transmission on the hills of West Point, and never burned out a clutch nor rolled backwards down a hill into the car behind me!

Spring Leave of Firstie Year was the first time we were allowed to drive those beautiful new cars even though they had been delivered a couple of weeks earlier. Until the official OK to drive, we would trek up the hill after class to our parking lot above Michie Stadium just to put the key in the ignition, start the engine, and inhale that heady new car smell. I practiced my gas and clutch coordination by moving the car a couple of feet forward and backward. The first day of spring leave was like the start of a LaMans race, seven hundred of us set loose in our new hot cars to run around the countryside. Most family members on post probably stayed inside that day, and I'm sure that every New York and New Jersey policeman possible was on duty to keep us under control. Some time that spring my buddy Bob Hensler and I, he in his '68 Pontiac GTO, and me in my firebird, were tearing up the Garden State Parkway when we were caught by a state trooper. Fortunately he noticed the cadet parking stickers on our bumpers and threatened to turn us in to the administration at West Point; he advised us sternly that an action like this could ruin a military career. When he determined that we were sufficiently scared he smiled, told us to be careful, and let us off with a warning. What a relief!!

What phenomenal freedom!! In those days we were not allowed to drink on the campus or within 15 miles of the front gate. There was, at 15.1 miles south on Route 9W, a hangout famous in the Corps, Snuffies Bar. As can be imagined this was a very popular place whenever we could get into our cars and get off post. Tragically we lost two of our classmates in an auto accident shortly before graduation as they were returning from a stop at Snuffies.

I eventually successfully met all of the graduation qualifications to include all of the physical performance requirements, selected Infantry as my branch of service, and experienced the most incredible sense of achievement imaginable when I received my West Point diploma on June 5th, 1968. During this time I had also again mastered the PE test that had been my downfall Yearling year, and did so with an extremely high score. I have never been so proud of an accomplishment. Graduation was the second time I saw tears in my Father's eyes. Later that day my Dad administered my commissioning oath of office and I was now officially a Regular Army 2nd Lieutenant of Infantry.

Like many of my classmates, I had also volunteered to go to Vietnam at the earliest possible time, in my case to the 4th Infantry Division in the Central Highlands of South Vietnam as my Dad had also served in the 4th. "Duty, Honor, Country" were part of my soul and there was no other viable option. The mission of USMA in those days was to produce combat arms officers to lead young soldiers, and as my country was at war there was no other option for combat arms 2LT's in my mind. I'm not sure that these were conscious thoughts, but there was really no other option for me. I knew that the good folks of the US of A had spent a lot of tax dollars on my education, and it was now my time to give back.

After graduation we had a wonderful two-month leave until we had to report to posts around the country to begin our official officer training. I drove my new car to Ft. Sill, Oklahoma to visit a former roommate who had dropped out during our Yearling year. What incredible independence. Also during this leave my Dad took me on a tour of all of the old harbor defense forts in New York harbor to include Ft. Totten, Ft. Wadsworth and others. It was at these installations where he had served as an enlisted man and where he had also attended the Prep School for three years. We stayed in non-air conditioned BOQs and drank warm scotch in paper cups at night out of a bottle that he had brought along while we swatted mosquitoes that entered through the gaping holes in many of the screens.

After this memorable summer I reported to Fort Benning, Georgia for the Infantry Officers Basic Course, Ranger and Airborne schools. As I was working out one day on the pull-up bar to get ready for some of these schools I began to experience some familiar sensations; weakness and numbness in my arms. The situation worsened over time and I got really scared, particularly because of the rigorous training that I was facing. So I went to Martin Army Hospital, ostensibly to get a check-

27

up of my surgical scars, but in reality to see if there was a new problem. I was once again filled with the hard feelings of dread and apprehension, just as I had been at school when I was moved to the Boarders Ward. Little could I guess that years later my daughter would be born in the same hospital.

When I went to the Surgical Clinic whose name did I see but that of my savior from West Point, Dr. Geer; he was now the head of the hospital surgical department! I asked to see him and we had a great reunion. I confided my thoughts that my original problem had re-occurred; that my surgeries at Walter Reed had not really solved my problem. After some exhaustive testing he confirmed my fears, the bones had regenerated, and he made two suggestions. I could accept a medical retirement from the Army—as a brand new 23 year old 2nd lieutenant—or I might possibly be offered a commission in a non-combat arms branch. Neither of those options was acceptable to me after all I had been through, so the doctor suggested a new surgical approach, which he would personally perform. I spent three months undergoing two major surgeries and then about three to four months of physical therapy and training while assigned to the 1st Battalion 29th Infantry in the 197th Infantry Brigade on Fort Benning. Once again I was able to meet all of the requirements and retained my Infantry commission.

During the fall of 1968 I met a woman who would become my first wife. We dated for a while and were married in the winter of 1969. It was a quick, whirlwind romance; fueled in part by the knowledge that I was soon going to war and wanting to experience as much of life as possible. Although we started off well, things began to deteriorate after I returned from Vietnam and we were eventually divorced after seven years of marriage and two sons.

Although the marriage didn't work I was blessed to meet her Dad Jimmie; a man that I loved almost as much as my own father. He was a member of a special Army amphibious engineer group that went ashore on D-Day ahead of the first landing wave to destroy beach obstacles. That day he received a Silver Star, a Purple Heart and a battlefield commission to 2nd Lieutenant. He fought through the war as an engineer officer and ended as a Captain. He had great fun, as he loved to tell me, liberating German wine cellars.

After the war he was RIF'ed, (reduction in force), back to his highest senior enlisted grade and continued to serve. When the Korean War started he made a combat jump with the 187th Regimental Combat Team. Jimmie had an eagle tattooed on his chest; the wing span went from nipple to nipple. At times, he would take off his shirt and make his eagle fly by flexing his pecs! He was a great soldier and a superb man.

After his daughter and I divorced, I remarried after several years and was eventually reassigned to Ft. Benning. During that assignment my daughter Marcia, "Penny" was born. Even though they were no longer technically my in-laws, I was welcomed back into my former in-laws family with my new wife and child; Jimmie used to love to hold Penny on his lap. While I was on that assignment, Jimmie contracted lung cancer, which quickly spread. He died on Father's day, shortly after we had been reassigned to the Inspector General School in preparation for becoming the IG of the 5th Infantry Division and Ft. Polk. I still miss him today.

I think that I managed to make it through all of these hurdles because of my training at West Point where I had learned that I could do far more than I had ever thought possible. My view of West Point when I entered was certainly that of a romantic, concentrating primarily on the good aspects and on the lofty ideals instilled in all of us: Duty, Honor, and Country. By the time I graduated that image had been temporarily blurred somewhat by the ordeals and issues that I had faced; but even with that maturation of image and view, I have never, ever lost my love of our motto and the incredibly valuable lessons and concepts that I learned while at the Academy. They have been the bedrock of my life ever since. Duty! Honor! Country! West Point had not only tested me in ways that I would have never have imagined or experienced anywhere else, but it also gave me the tools, pride, courage and training to face later, even more intense tests and persevere. So while I've encountered a lot of scary things in my life since those days, deep, deep down in my soul I've known that I could conquer any fear and successfully meet any conceivable test.

West Point in those days operated on an attrition model. Since the mission of the Academy was to produce officers for the Combat arms (Infantry, Armor, Engineers, Artillery and Signal Corps) we were subjected to tight disciplinary standards, a very strict honor code, and incredible daily stress. The goal was to weed out anyone who could not operate under a high stress level with the thought that if one could not handle the stresses of West Point, then one could certainly NOT handle the stress of combat. This system had worked well for over 150 years, producing outstanding officers who led our Army through all of our wars up to and including Vietnam. My class lost about 30% of our number before we graduated with 705 new officers.

Today, with the acceptance of women in The Corps, who at that time could not serve in the combat arms, the mission of the Academy changed from producing officers for the combat Army to producing "leaders of character". In conjunction with this event, a new policy replaced the old attrition model; the buzz word now is "developmental". This has resulted in a change to many of the standards of our day and a strong emphasis in retaining as many cadets as possible, even those who might violate the Honor Code, or those who otherwise might have been dismissed for academics, discipline, physical fitness and or other standards. This has resulted in an entirely different atmosphere at West Point, a good or bad change depending on oust ne's point of view.

I graduated with an at-the-time unrecognized feeling of obligation, both to the country and to the Army. I was a member of the Long Gray Line, and as such had a duty to serve my country and to lead her soldiers to the best of my ability. Perhaps I had been brain washed, but I sincerely carried those beliefs. I had watched the TV series *The Long Gray Line,* had read a series of fictional books, by Colonel Red Reeder, about the life of an Army football player—Clint Lane —and his journey through the four years at the Academy. I had finally walked that hallowed ground; had persevered through some tough issues and graduated. I now assumed the same responsibility as all of those who had gone before. West Point had truly become a part of who I was and whatever I was to become.

I was eventually deemed fit for combat duty by the medical staff at Ft. Benning and received my somewhat delayed orders to go to Vietnam. Since I had a little time I went to Panama to attend the Army's three week Jungle Warfare School. That was quite an experience and introduced me to guys who I would later see in Vietnam. While there I had the unique experience of swimming a poncho raft across the Panama Canal. One night, during a night navigation course, I found out the hard way about Black Palm Trees. I reached out to steady myself at one point and found my hand pierced by 4 long barbed spines, much like porcupine needles. To remove them I had to break off the barbed point and then pull them back through my hand. The medics got hold of me immediately after we finished the course to clean the wounds to prevent a potential serious infection.

After a short trip home to Fort Benning to say a final good bye to my wife, I caught a plane for San Francisco where I would go to Travis Air Force Base for my ride to Southeast Asia. I linked up there with a couple of other guys who were also en route to the war zone and we had one hell of a "last night in the world" time. I don't remember much of it, where we stayed if we did have a hotel room, or the trip to Travis the next day for that matter. Somehow we successfully in-processed and boarded the correct flight when the time came. I do remember sitting in a hallway in the departure lounge, wondering how my stomach would survive the flight.

Eventually our flight number was called and we all boarded the plane. My buddies from the night before and I shared a row of three seats by the window. During the long flight there wasn't much chatter or laughing after about 30 minutes into the trip. When we weren't sleeping or recovering from the excesses of the night before, I think we were all alone with our private thoughts about what awaited us at the end of the journey. Some few guys on board were going back for a second or third tour, and they talked quietly among themselves. The rest of us sat quietly, consumed by wonder and fear. The stewardesses tried to ease our thoughts by engaging in conversation, but it was a solitary trip even though there were a couple hundred guys on that airplane.

Like most inexperienced guys going to war I had my share of fears and doubts. I wondered how I would handle the rigors of combat, would I be a coward? What does it feel like to be shot, or to shoot another person? Would my wife want me back if I lost an arm or leg or if I was horribly disfigured by an explosion? How would I fit into my new unit, handle the responsibility for men's lives? Did I know enough; damn I wish that I had listened better in some of the classes I had attended! My mind churned almost as much as my gut. Unlike in previous wars where the Army had gone to the combat zone by ship, affording days or even weeks to get adjusted and mentally geared up for combat; because we flew we had only a day. That caused us to go through a tortuous transition in a very short time. Also, in earlier wars soldiers deployed to the combat zone with units in which they'd served for a couple of years and with the guys with whom they trained during that time. For us going to Vietnam, aside from the initial unit deployments, ours was a lonely trip as we were sent as individual replacements, expected to work well with seasoned combat vets when we reported to our units as new guys.

We stopped in Hawaii and Guam for refueling en route to the Republic of South Viet Nam. While on the ground we were tightly controlled and not allowed the freedom to explore the base. I guess I now know why; the military authorities just wanted to make sure that we all got back on our plane. I don't remember much of Hickam Air Base as we were there early in the morning. I do remember looking at a lot of B-52's on Guam and beginning to realize that I really was going to go to war.

While the flight up to arrival in Guam had been kind of unreal in many ways, when we lifted off from Guam and the pilot announced that our next stop would be Vietnam, a new sense of reality began to settle in. If possible, the plane was even quieter on that last leg as we settled deeper into our seats and pulled our heads in a little. That might have been an unconscious preparation for the bullets we knew would soon be coming our way. I think that even the returnees were soberly considering what lay before them. We were all about to embark on a really momentous experience, one that would change all of us in many ways for the rest of our lives.

During the final leg our flight my thoughts turned to the Farewll Speech by General MacArthur to the Corps of Cadets in 1962, which has been a real inspiration for me from those early days until today.

GENERAL DOUGLAS MACARTHUR'S FAREWELL SPEECH TO THE CORPS OF CADETS, MAY 12, 1962.

This speech was delivered from the elevated "Poop Deck" of Washington Hall, the mess hall, and General MacArthur spoke from the heart without any notes or script. It has become one of the most revered addresses in the history of West Point. General MacArthur had just been presented the Sylvanus Thayer Award, West Point's highest for service to the nation.

General Westmoreland, General Groves, distinguished guests, and gentlemen of the Corps. As I was leaving the hotel this morning, a doorman asked me, "Where are you bound for, General?" and when I replied, "West Point," he remarked, "Beautiful place, have you ever been there before?"

No human being could fail to be deeply moved by such a tribute as this, coming from a profession I have served so long and a people I have loved so well. It fills me with an emotion I cannot express. But this award is not intended primarily for a personality, but to symbolize a great moral code - the code of conduct and chivalry of those who guard this beloved land of culture and ancient descent. That is the meaning of this medallion. For all eyes and for all time, it is an expression of the ethics of the American soldier. That I should be integrated in this way with so noble an ideal arouses a sense of pride and yet of humility which will be with me always.

Duty, Honor, Country: Those three hallowed words reverently dictate what you ought to be, what you can be, what you will be. They are your rallying points: to build courage when courage seems to fail; to regain faith when there seems to be little cause for faith; to create hope when hope becomes forlorn. Unhappily, I possess neither that eloquence of diction, that poetry of imagination, nor that brilliance of metaphor to tell you all that they mean.

The unbelievers will say they are but words, but a slogan, but a flamboyant phrase. Every pedant, every demagogue, every cynic, every hypocrite, every troublemaker, and, I am sorry to say, some others of an entirely different character, will try to downgrade them even to the extent of mockery and ridicule.

But these are some of the things they do. They build your basic character. They mold you for your future roles as the custodians of the nation's defense. They make you strong enough to know when you are weak, and brave enough to face yourself when you are afraid.

They teach you to be proud and unbending in honest failure, but humble and gentle in success; not to substitute words for action; not to seek the path of comfort, but to face the stress and spur of difficulty and challenge; to learn to stand up in the storm, but to have compassion on those who fall; to master yourself before you seek to master others; to have a heart that is clean, a goal that is high; to learn to laugh, yet never forget how to weep; to reach into the future, yet never neglect the past; to be serious, yet never take yourself too seriously; to be modest so that you will remember the simplicity of true greatness; the open mind of true wisdom, the meekness of true strength.

They give you a temperate will, a quality of imagination, a vigor of the emotions, a freshness of the deep springs of life, a temperamental predominance of courage over timidity, an appetite for adventure over love of ease. They create in your heart the sense of wonder, the unfailing hope of what next, and the joy and inspiration of life. They teach you in this way to be an officer and a gentleman.

And what sort of soldiers are those you are to lead? Are they reliable? Are they brave? Are they capable of victory?

Their story is known to all of you. It is the story of the American man at arms. My estimate of him was formed on the battlefields many, many years ago, and has never changed. I regarded him then, as I regard him now, as one of the world's noblest figures; not only as one of the finest military characters, but also as one of the most stainless.

His name and fame are the birthright of every American citizen. In his youth and strength, his love and loyalty, he gave all that mortality can give. He needs no eulogy from me, or from any other man. He has written his own history and written it in red on his enemy's breast.

But when I think of his patience under adversity, of his courage under fire, and of his modesty in victory, I am filled with an emotion of admiration I cannot put into words. He belongs to history as furnishing one of the greatest examples of successful patriotism. He belongs to posterity as the instructor of future generations in the principles of liberty and freedom. He belongs to the present, to us, by his virtues and by his achievements.

In twenty campaigns, on a hundred battlefields, around a thousand campfires, I have witnessed that enduring fortitude, that patriotic self-abnegation, and that invincible determination which have carved his statue in the hearts of his people.

From one end of the world to the other, he has drained deep the chalice of courage. As I listened to those songs of the glee club, in memory's eye I could see those staggering columns of the First World War, bending under soggy packs on many a weary march, from dripping dusk to drizzling dawn, slogging ankle deep through mire of shell-pocked roads; to form grimly for the attack, blue-lipped, covered with sludge and mud, chilled by the wind and rain, driving home to their objective, and for many, to the judgment seat of God.

I do not know the dignity of their birth, but I do know the glory of their death. They died unquestioning, uncomplaining, with faith in their hearts, and on their lips the hope that we would go on to victory. Always for them: Duty, Honor, Country. Always their blood, and sweat, and tears, as they saw the way and the light.

And twenty years after, on the other side of the globe, against the filth of dirty foxholes, the stench of ghostly trenches, the slime of dripping dugouts, those boiling suns of the relentless heat, those torrential rains of devastating storms, the loneliness and utter desolation of jungle trails, the bitterness of long separation of those they loved and cherished, the deadly pestilence of tropic disease, the horror of stricken areas of war.

Their resolute and determined defense, their swift and sure attack, their indomitable purpose, their complete and decisive victory - always victory, always through the bloody haze of their last reverberating shot, the vision of gaunt, ghastly men, reverently following your password of Duty, Honor, Country.

The code which those words perpetuate embraces the highest moral laws and will stand the test of any ethics or philosophies ever promulgated for the uplift of mankind. Its requirements are for the things that are right, and its restraints are from the things that are wrong. The soldier, above all other men, is required to practice the greatest act of religious training - sacrifice. In battle and in the face of danger and death, he discloses those divine attributes which his Maker gave when he created man in his own image. No physical courage and no brute instinct can take the place of the Divine help which alone can sustain him. However horrible the incidents of war may be, the soldier who is called upon to offer and to give his life for his country, is the noblest development of mankind.

You now face a new world, a world of change. The thrust into outer space of the satellite, spheres and missiles marked the beginning of another epoch in the long story of mankind - the chapter of the space age. In the five or more billions of years the scientists tell us it has taken to form the earth, in the three or more billion years of development of the human race, there has never been a greater, a more abrupt or staggering evolution. We deal now not with things of this world alone, but with the illimitable distances and as yet unfathomed mysteries of the universe. We are reaching out for a new and boundless frontier. We speak in strange terms: of harnessing the cosmic energy; of making winds and tides work for us; of creating unheard synthetic materials to supplement or even replace our old standard basics; of purifying sea water for our drink; of mining ocean floors for new fields of wealth and food; of disease preventatives to expand life into the hundreds of years; of controlling the weather for a more equitable distribution of heat and cold, of rain and shine; of space ships to the moon; of the primary target in war, no longer limited to the armed forces of an enemy, but instead to include his civil populations; of ultimate conflict between a united human race and the sinister forces of some other planetary galaxy; of such dreams and fantasies as to make life the most exciting of all time.

And through all this welter of change and development your mission remains fixed, determined, inviolable. It is to win our wars. Everything else in your professional career is but corollary to this vital dedication. All other public purpose, all other public projects, all other public needs, great or small, will find others for their accomplishments; but you are the ones who are trained to fight.

Yours is the profession of arms, the will to win, the sure knowledge that in war there is no substitute for victory, that if you lose, the Nation will be destroyed, that the very obsession of your public service must be Duty, Honor, Country.

Others will debate the controversial issues, national and international, which divide men's minds. But serene, calm, aloof, you stand as the Nation's war guardians, as its lifeguards from the raging tides of international conflict, as its gladiators in the arena of battle. For a century and a half you have defended, guarded and protected its hallowed traditions of liberty and freedom, of right and justice.

Let civilian voices argue the merits or demerits of our processes of government. Whether our strength is being sapped by deficit financing indulged in too long, by federal paternalism grown too mighty, by power groups grown too arrogant, by politics grown too corrupt, by crime grown too rampant, by morals grown too low, by taxes grown too high, by extremists grown too violent; whether our personal liberties are as firm and complete as they should be.

These great national problems are not for your professional participation or military solution. Your guidepost stands out like a tenfold beacon in the night: Duty, Honor, Country.

You are the leaven which binds together the entire fabric of our national system of defense. From your ranks come the great captains who hold the Nation's destiny in their hands the moment the war tocsin sounds.

The long gray line has never failed us. Were you to do so, a million ghosts in olive drab, in brown khaki, in blue and gray, would rise from their white crosses, thundering those magic words: Duty, Honor, Country.

This does not mean that you are warmongers. On the contrary, the soldier above all other people prays for peace, for he must suffer and bear the deepest wounds and scars of war. But always in our ears ring the ominous words of Plato, that wisest of all philosophers: "Only the dead have seen the end of war."

The shadows are lengthening for me. The twilight is here. My days of old have vanished - tone and tints. They have gone glimmering through the dreams of things that were. Their memory is one of wondrous beauty, watered by tears and coaxed and caressed by the smiles of yesterday. I listen then, but with thirsty ear, for the witching melody of faint bugles blowing reveille, of far drums beating the long roll.

In my dreams I hear again the crash of guns, the rattle of musketry, the strange, mournful mutter of the battlefield. But in the evening of my memory I come back to West Point. Always there echoes and re-echoes: Duty, Honor, Country.

Today marks my final roll call with you. But I want you to know that when I cross the river, my last conscious thoughts will be of the Corps, and the Corps, and the Corps.

I bid you farewell.

DUTY! HONOR! COUNTRY!

3 - WELCOME TO VIETNAM

I landed in Vietnam on July 9th, 1969, my 24th birthday, after a long and tiring trip across the Pacific from California. I'm sure that we were served several meals during the journey but I have no memories of eating; although I think we were served steak and a baked potato as our "last meal" before arrival. I remember that my intestines were too tied up in knots caused by apprehension over what we were facing when we got to our destination. There was no alcohol served toward the end of the flight as I remember, although a couple of the returnees kept lifting brown paper bags to their mouths. They were the only ones on the airplane talking and laughing for parts of the flight. You could almost feel and smell the tension on that airplane.

As we crossed the coast of South Vietnam, the Captain came on the PA to tell us to look down at all of the bomb craters. The land was incredibly green, filled with rice paddies and big round holes, which we assumed were the bomb craters. There were small villages and rural towns scattered across the landscape. He also told us that we would make a quick approach at a sharp angle and tight spiral to decrease the likelihood of receiving ground fire. We were to deplane quickly as he had to refuel and load up with guys going home. He didn't want to stay on the ground any longer than was absolutely necessary. I remember a sad look on the faces of the stewardesses as we deplaned. They said *"Good- bye and good luck; see you on the return trip."*

As I walked out of the door of that airplane two sensations smacked me hard in the face that would stay with me for my entire tour. One was the unbelievable brightness of the sun, with its accompanying blast furnace heat and humidity that almost physically pushed me back into that plane. The other was a unique and pungent aroma; I wasn't sure of the origin of the odor at first. We learned in the next few days that there were no sewers where we were going. Instead we used outhouses that were one, or two, even three and four holers that contained sawed-in-half 55-gallon drums under cutout holes. We knew we were in civilization when the holes sported real western toilet seats, reducing the chance of splinters in the butt, and there was a roll of real toilet paper sitting close by! I found that there was nothing quite like sitting next to your buddy on a stinky crapper to forge close friendships. Every day the drums were dragged out from under the seats and some poor bastard, Vietnamese if possible, poured kerosene over the odiferous mass, and then threw in a match.

In order to ensure that most of the mess was burned, this poor guy had to stand over the barrel and stir its contents with a 2 x 4 until it was completely consumed. The combination of the kerosene and burning matter produced thick black clouds of greasy smoke with an intense, never-to-be-forgotten odor. I can't even imagine the reaction of the family when the "shit stirrer" returned home at night!!

As we came off the plane we were quickly loaded on to buses for the trip to the 90th Replacement Battalion at Long Binh where we would receive our orders. The bus windows were covered with wire mesh, which the driver said was to keep hand grenades from being thrown through the glass or openings. We all soaked in the strange sights, sounds and smells of South Vietnam as we rode through the city streets, tensely waiting for a bad guy to shoot at us, or to hurl a grenade at the bus. Fortunately, nothing like that happened. I remember having an intense urge to pee, but knowing there was no recourse until we arrived at the "repo depot". Even though the top halves of the windows were open it was incredibly hot inside that bus, adding to the unsettled nature of a lot of our stomachs.

After arrival at the replacement center we were assigned bunks in barracks that consisted of 3' wooden walls topped by screening that went to the tin roof. Outside the wooden walls were blast walls for protection against incoming mortar and rocket rounds; these consisted of 55 gallon drums filled with sand and topped by a couple layers of sand bags, spaced about three feet from the building's side. The 55 gallon drum industry in the US must have been rolling in dough – blast protection and shitters! Inside, the bunks were double stacked with thin mattresses and, if you were lucky, a beat up and greasy pillow. The aisle was lined with butt cans, empty cans filled with sand to be used as ash trays. I don't remember sheets or blankets, especially since the last thing needed at night in July was a heavy wool GI blanket. The interior really reminded me of the WW II era barracks I had lived in while in basic training at Ft. Dix years earlier.

There was a small, ramshackle officer's club nearby where we could gather to drink beer and smoke endless cigarettes while waiting to hear our names called at one of the two daily formations, morning and noon, to identify names listed on manifests for transportation to units throughout South Vietnam. Officers didn't pull details so we had nothing much to do but worry, drink, think and imagine. That situation was not necessarily good or conducive to easy sleep and a care-free attitude. We looked suspiciously at all of the Vietnamese workers, wondering if any one of them was carrying a hand grenade that would be tossed in our direction. I remember being surprised that so many were allowed on base. This was also my first introduction to "hooch maids," local ladies that were hired to clean the barracks, shine boots, and wash, starch and iron jungle fatigues for the permanent rear echelon party. The younger and better-looking ones also performed other services for nominal fees, or at least so I was told.

During the time in-processing at Long Binh, we FNG's (Fucking New Guys) were constantly subjected to the catcalls and jeers of the "Old-Timers" who were processing to go home; "You'll die in Vietnam," "Hey, FNG; ya got your body bag?" Fortunately they lived in other barracks. I looked in awe at those hardened combat vets, particularly those wearing CIBs, awarded to infantrymen after living through 30 days of combat against an armed enemy force, and wondered if I could ever be up to the task of leading guys like these. They were lean, tanned and tough looking to a new guy. Many had distinctive headgear, and few were in complete uniforms. Those manifested for a return flight on any given day were offered clean and new jungle fatigues, or many wore khakis so they could wear their medals and especially their CIBs.

Once in a while some officers on the way home would come into the officer's club for a couple of drinks. There was a definite air of confidence, even cockiness, about them that set them apart from the rest of us sitting around in our brand new, still-stiff jungle fatigues and black jungle boots. Usually they started out sitting by themselves, talking and sharing war stories. But inevitably we new guys would find a way to approach them and would then bombard them with all of the questions that were on our minds. We developed a belief that if these guys could survive then maybe so could we.

After a couple of days my name was finally called at a formation for a flight to my new unit. While I had volunteered for service in the 4th Infantry Diivision, I had tried to have my orders changed to the First Cavalry Division before arrival in Vietnam. The First Cav had been developed as the Army's first airmobile division and had been equipped with a large number of helicopters to ferry its grunts around the country. This was exciting new doctrine and I wanted to be a part of it. However, the crusty old sergeant running the formation told me in no uncertain terms that I was going to the 4th! The division had just been involved in heavy combat, had suffered many officer casualties, and by damn that's where I was heading. "Get your ass over to the 4th Division formation lieutenant!" I boarded a plane that afternoon en route to Camp Enari, the HQ base camp of the 4th Infantry Division near Pleiku in the Central Highlands, an area known to the Army as II Corps.

We were bused to a military airfield for the trip up-country to our new unit. The plane was a USAF C-130 transport plane with 4 turboprop engines; very noisy and drafty. If you were lucky enough to be one of the first on board, you could find space on the web-strapped seats that pulled down from the inside fuselage of the aircraft. If you weren't lucky, you sat on the floor or varied cargo that the plane was also carrying. There were no seatbelts or smiling stewardesses on this flight. It was hot inside with a strong smell of hydraulic fluid and aviation gas, combined with the smell of many sweaty bodies. These aromas didn't help our already unsettled intestines inside that hot and humid airplane. I also noticed a couple of holes in the fuselage, which I assumed had been caused by ground fire. "What if you were sitting right there when that hole was made?" I remember sweating so much that I felt as though I had just come out of a shower.

"Would I be good enough? Would I be a coward? Holy shit, what had I gotten myself into?"

These were the endless questions that circulated through my mind on that flight. I knew that I was getting close to that ultimate test for a warrior; I would soon have to "see the elephant" . . . combat.

After landing at Pleiku Air Force Base we were trucked to Camp Enari. Upon arrival we were processed into the Division Replacement Company and underwent three or four days of orientation, training and familiarization. We learned about the division's organization, its standard operating procedures (SOPs), the terrain of our area of operation (AO), radio procedures and a refresher on combat first aid. II Corps was in the Central Highlands in the northern half of South Vietnam, an area marked by many steep mountain ranges and thick, triple canopy jungle. It was some of the toughest terrain in the world, tortuous enough to severely test even those in the best physical condition. We also went out to the rifle ranges for intense training to make sure that we knew how to use our weapons. I had to qualify with both the M-16 rifle and the .45 caliber pistol. We were briefed on the differences between the Vietnamese people and the Montagnards who were the primary residents of our area. These were two distinct races, somewhat similar to white Caucasians and American Indians of early US history.

Much like in our early frontier days, these two groups were in almost constant conflict with each other, with the Vietnamese looking down on the "Yards" as uncivilized jungle-living savages. I would eventually find myself in Montagnard villages back in the depths of the jungled mountains where we were probably the first westerners, probably even the first non-Montagnard, whom the natives had ever seen. I can only imagine their reaction to what we looked like and all of the gear that we carried. I can also only imagine their reaction to the sight and sounds of helicopters, the hissing radios and other strange gear that we carried, and to the sounds and explosions of various weapons during firefights.

I soon learned that these "Yards" were fierce fighters themselves while using only a blow gun or simple crossbow. Montagnard women were usually bare breasted and quite a sight for guys who had been in the jungles for months without seeing many women. However, there was an unwritten caution passed among all of the combat grunts; don't mess with any of these ladies or you might not make it 50 meters out of the village. Blow guns and cross bows were extremely deadly, silent weapons in the hands of male villagers.

The final exercise of the school was a patrol into "Indian Country"; out into the bush where Charlie might lurk. This was an operation into areas actually patrolled by the VC, in some cases these teaching patrols had been fired on. Maybe because this was my first time "outside the wire" I have sharp memories of the terrain and of my feelings. I found it was very difficult to walk with an asshole that is tightly puckered up with fear. Fortunately not a shot was fired at us and all went well.

From the Replacement Company I was assigned to the 1st Battalion, 14th Infantry; the "Golden Dragons," and reported to their rear support area and the Battalion S-1 or Adjutant, on Camp Enari. I was assigned a bunk in the same kind of building as the ones at the Repo Depot, but the officer's BOQ "Hooch" at least had one- or two-man rooms and a kind of shower at the end of the building which consisted of an Air Force wing tank filled with water and heated by the sun. Dangling from the tank was an assortment of hoses and showerheads. There was even a real mess hall that served real food and the reconstituted milk that was not as good as what we had at home but nonetheless delicious when compared with the dirty water from stagnant rice paddies.

Guys coming in from the field for admin appointments or R&R found the mess hall to be a welcome relief from their usual C rations. The REMFs (Rear Echelon Mother Fuckers) did nothing but bitch all of the time about having to eat "such crap". Life was really tough and demanding for those guys who never went into the field or heard a shot fired in anger, and the BN mess sergeant had a really tough job keeping those gourmet diners satisfied.

While there I processed into the battalion, received some orientation on its organization and operating procedures, and was issued my field gear to include an M-16 rifle. After a short time in the field I traded my M-16 for a CAR-15, essentially a shorter barreled carbine version of the M-16, which also had a telescoping butt and a higher rate of fire. This weapon proved a lot easier to handle during those times that I had to use it while talking on the radio.

Finally came the big day, I had completed all of my "new guy" training and orientations and was scheduled to ride a re-supply convoy of 4 trucks from Camp Enari about 30 clicks SE to Firebase St. George, the jungle home of the 1st of the 14th. As I was the only officer on the convoy I would be its commander for the 24-mile trip. I think the date was July 22nd; I had been in Vietnam for 13 days.

Holy shit!! I didn't realize how anxious and nervous I was until a sergeant came up to the window of my lead truck just before we were due to leave. I had had some problem getting comfortable because of the sandbags on the floor and against the door, and the bi-pod from the M-60 machine gun that some soldier had resting on the cab's canvas top right over my helmet. "L Tee, ya know ya fergot yer bullets. Even John Wayne needed bullets." He snickered as he handed me the two bandoleers of magazines that I'd left on the ground when I grabbed my gear to go. I heard some laughter from the troops in the back and thought that I was really off to a shitty start on my combat career. What kind of a West Point combat leader was I going to be?

The trip through the Vietnamese countryside proved to be uneventful, much to my relief. The road was populated with old trucks, colorful old buses crammed with people and livestock, farmer's carts and wagons pulled by an assortment of livestock and other US military vehicles. The road itself was rough with potholes and general disrepair leading to an extremely bumpy and twisting ride. The road passed through a couple of villages which were noisy and filled with Lambrettas, three wheeled motorcycles with a small cab in the front which belched incredible amounts of exhaust smoke. There were small stores, restaurants and houses that lined the dusty highway across a ditch which ran each side of the road that was used for sewage, garbage and whatever. Many of the buildings looked really comical as they were built from coke or beer cans that had been cut and laid out flat on the walls. The sides of the roads were lined by kids waiting for candy and cigarettes to be thrown from the trucks, and women trying to sell cold cokes, beer or other "goodies." "Hey G.I., you numba huckin' one, you want buy cold Coke?" Sometimes the kids yelled that we could have "boom – boom" with their virgin mothers or sisters for "one dolla". It was incredibly hot and dusty in the cab of that truck even with the windows rolled down.

It was a really interesting trip for a newbie, even though I was constantly on guard for the expected grenade through the truck window or the sniper round that would find its way into one of the bodies in the truck. It was a relief to finally pull off the highway and jolt over a dirt track towards what was obviously an American firebase surrounded by bunkers and concertina wire. This was Fire Support Base St. George, home base of the 1st Battalion, 14th Infantry Regiment; 4th Infantry Division, the Golden Dragons.

As I climbed down from the cab, thankful to be able to stretch and take a deep breath, and thankful to still be alive, I was directed to the company command post (CP), a buried conex container covered with sand bags and sprouting a couple of tall radio antennas. I met my company commander and after a few minutes of introduction and conversation was assigned as the platoon leader for 1st Platoon, Charlie Company, call sign Apache 6. His RTO called down to the 1st Platoon to send up the Platoon Sergeant. When he arrived there was a short introduction and then he took me over to the bunker line to what would be my CP.

Fire Base St. George was situated right on one of the major NVA (North Vietnamese Army) infiltration routes from Cambodia into the Central Highlands and its purpose was to house an infantry battalion and a direct support 105mm artillery battery of six howitzers. In our case there were only 5 tubes as one had been lost in a recent fight. The battalion's companies roamed the countryside looking for bad guys and their logistical support such as bunker complexes. The mission was to interfere with, and stop if possible, NVA units coming into Vietnam off of the Ho Chi Minh Trail, which passed through Cambodia to our west. The NVA were officially known as the PAVN, or People's Army of Viet Nam. As I remember, enemy contact was almost a daily occurrence somewhere in our AO (Area of Operations).

The ground of the entire firebase was scraped raw red dirt. During the dry season it created clouds of dust whenever vehicles or people moved over it. During the rainy season it became a glutinous red mud that could practically suck the boots off of your feet. St. George's outer limits or perimeter was designated by three fences of razor wire that consisted of three rolls each, two on the bottom and one on top. These rolls were tightly staked down at short intervals to insure that they couldn't be easily moved or penetrated. There were gates on both the north and south sides. The northern gate was near the Battalion Commander's (BN CO) hooch and briefing tent and was known as the VIP gate; the other on the southern side was the one used by the troops. It fed into an open area where we boarded the helicopters that took us out into the countryside. Outside of the VIP gate was a small helicopter landing pad outlined in white rocks that was used by high ranking visitors to the battalion.

In between the fences we put out "tangle foot," single strand razor wire that was zigzagged back and forth over the open area at varying heights to prevent anyone from walking or crawling between the wire fences. Scattered throughout this area were "trip flares," small ground-staked magnesium flares with a pin that was attached to a trip wire that was anchored some distance away. If someone tripped one of the flares it would go off and provide instant illumination as well as a warning that something was in the area that shouldn't be. We also hung cans filled with rocks or empty shell casings in the wire that we hoped would rattle if disturbed.

At one point some enterprising guy, either in the rear or in the US, thought that we could aid security by putting geese in the areas between the fences. The theory was that they would raise a huge racket if someone tried to penetrate the defenses as they were thought to be very territorial. After a couple of nights of little sleep because of their horrible racket as they got caught up in the fence or tangle foot, they suddenly disappeared. The delicious aroma of roasting goose drifting over St George told us of their fate.

Completing the perimeter defenses, we put out claymore mines 10 yards or so in front of the bunkers and buried some "phougas" containers. Phougas was a variant of napalm that remained in a primarily liquid form rather than the gel of napalm. The claymores were small anti-personnel mines about six by ten inches that could be aimed in a specific direction by extending their two sets of short legs and sighting through an aperture on the top of the mine. One side was labeled "Front Toward Enemy" so that we wouldn't put them in backwards! They were essentially shotguns as they consisted of three hundred or so ball bearings backed by a solid sheet of C4 explosive. When fired by an electric detonating device connected to a hand plunger by a long wire, they were devastating to anyone within range. The phougas was poured into 55-gallon drums that were buried in the perimeter. The detonator was a white phosphorous grenade with a long wire attached to its pin. Pull the wire, release the pin, and there was an instant inferno that was spread over a pretty large area by the explosion of the grenade, which lit the contents. Being almost a jelly, it caused horrendous burns as it would literally cling to anything it landed on and generated its own oxygen.

Inside the last roll of wire and tangle foot were the perimeter bunkers. There were probably about 15 or so that provided the major defensive and sleeping areas on the perimeter. On St. George these were either semi dug-in, or completely above ground. I never did learn why they weren't dug into the ground thereby providing a low silhouette to folks outside the wire. There was one bunker assigned per infantry squad, so six or seven guys lived inside. They were constructed of sand bag walls and timber or PSP (pierced steel planking), roofs covered with more layers of sandbags. PSP had originally been designed in WW II to be linked together to form temporary aircraft landing strips. The tops were from three to eight or so feet above the ground level.

Sometimes the walls were made of artillery ammunition boxes that were filled with dirt and then sandbagged. Troops tried to make the insides as livable as possible. One way was to line the inside of the sand bagged walls with parts of wooden ammo crates from the artillery. Some enterprising troops passed a blowtorch over the wood; the flames would darken the grain and thus give the interior of the bunker a look somewhat like it was covered with pine paneling.

Many of the bunkers became infested with rats over time. They would come out at night and scurry over your body while searching for food. One solution to that scary problem was, of course, to shoot them. But since you didn't really want to discharge your weapon inside of your own bunker, some enterprising G.I.s developed "soap rounds" for .45 caliber pistols. For this purpose, the lead bullet was pulled from its shell casing and half of the black powder in the casing was dumped out. The shell casing was then pushed into a bar of hard G.I. soap, creating a soap bullet. These could be fired in the bunkers and had enough force to kill a rat without destroying anything else it might hit.

The bunkers had a six to eight foot high chain link screen about three feet in front of them known as B-40 screens. B-40's were the Russian or Chinese rocket propelled grenades (RPGs) favored by the bad guys. The warheads were often shaped charges which would funnel the molten metal of the warhead into a hot stream and force it through the wall at almost supersonic speed. These warheads were developed to penetrate various thicknesses of steel in order to kill a tank. We hoped that an incoming round would hit the fence and detonate rather that penetrate the bunker and then go off. The sand bag walls would then hopefully absorb the blast and shrapnel with minimal damage to those inside. The bunker entrances were normally in the rear and protected by another sandbagged blast wall to stop shrapnel from rounds impacting inside of the perimeter.

The bunkers on most of the perimeter were connected by trenches and two man fighting positions dug in at varying intervals behind a low sand-bagged wall normally three or four sand bags high. This constituted our primary defensive line if subjected to a major ground attack. The bunkers also had a couple of firing ports in the front. The firebase was always manned by one of the rifle companies on a rotating basis when in for a stand down, a time to rest and refit. The company consisted of three infantry platoons plus the 81mm mortar platoon, which had their own area toward the center of the firebase near the company command post bunker. Most platoons had responsibility for three or four bunkers. The others were manned by the recon platoon when they were not in the jungle and a collection of headquarters admin people such as clerks, cooks, supply guys, etc.

Inside of the outer perimeter were two other major areas. One was the position of the 105mm direct support artillery battery from the 1st BN., 29th Field Artillery, assigned to fulfill that function for the 1st of the 14th. When I arrived they had five towed artillery pieces (one had been lost on a recent combat operation) plus their own admin support, ammunition and command bunkers all surrounded by another fence of razor wire. Outside of their wire but within the outer perimeter were the rest of the bunkers and tents used by the other battalion personnel such as the BN HQ, the tactical operations center (TOC), supply, medics, transits, mess, etc. There were several general purpose (GP) medium tents with their 55 gallon drum blast walls used by the medics, transits, supply, and one called a BOQ (bachelor officers' quarters) tent for officers. There was also a mess tent with an eating area covered by tarps for protection against the sun or rain. On any given night there were probably 150 or more guys manning St. George.

There were makeshift showers and outhouses scattered throughout the area as well as many 105mm shell canisters buried in the ground at about a 30-degree angle. The lower end was buried in a hole that had been lined with rocks and sand. These were "piss tubes" that were there for an obvious function. We had several of the Air Force wing tank showers. As we had no females on the firebase there was no modesty. It was not unusual to see naked G.I.'s going to the shower with only a bar of soap and a green Army towel. This was to be my home until some four months later. I later discovered that was an awfully long time to be in one place.

At first sight, as I climbed out of my truck cab after a thankfully uneventful trip, St. George was a depressing, foreign, barren moonscape. I wondered to myself how guys could live like this in such a primitive and foreboding atmosphere. Because it was July, the earth was dry and hard packed, and every step raised a cloud of fine red dust. As I got acclimated and spent more time there, it truly did become a familiar home and a welcome sight as we either flew or walked back in after an operation.

I was in back of my new platoon CP bunker meeting my platoon sergeant and squad leaders shortly after my arrival when the radio squawked and I was told to meet the CO at his CP and to get my guys saddled up and ready to move. I couldn't believe it, here I barely knew the names of my NCOs' and which squad they led and I was going out on a mission? I went to the company CP and learned that I would go about 15 clicks down the highway by truck to secure a Montagnard village that had been attacked the night before. Intel reported that the VC might be back again tonight and the village had requested assistance.

Here I was, in command for all of two hours, and I was going to be sent on my first mission far away from other American forces. God damn, there was a lot I needed to remember. And how would I pull this off in front of 30 combat seasoned veterans who would look at this new officer with a real jaundiced and critical eye? I know I was sweating from more than just the heat. This was a real burden for those of us who were untested and assigned as leaders to combat experienced units. This system really sucked. I guess my company commander figured that this would be a good way to break in an FNG, throw him in the deep end and make him swim.

I had the platoon assemble so I could check to ensure that each man had the proper gear and weapons. I could see them watching me with great suspicion; who was this FNG? I gave them a short briefing on the upcoming mission and details about all of the support functions that we could expect. After that was over I told them to "saddle up," grab their gear and put on their rucks. We moved out through the gate in the wire to where the trucks were waiting. I climbed into the lead cab and secured the radio handset from my RTO who was standing in the truck bed right behind the cab. I waited for the designated start time, called the company CP, told them we were moving, and told the driver to head for the highway and turn left. The trip took about an hour as I remember and was uneventful. We passed through several small Vietnamese villages and traveled with many Vietnamese trucks and motor scooters. There didn't seem to be any rules of the road other than the fact that all drivers stayed generally to the right hand side and the biggest vehicle always won any disagreement over who would occupy what space at what time.

Upon arrival at the designated village we unassed the trucks and formed a hasty perimeter in some secondary underbrush close-by where we could watch the road and a major intersecting trail which came through the village. After making sure that we were set and secure I took my RTO (Radio Telephone Operator) and PLT SGT (Platoon Sergeant) into the village to see what was going on and had a quick and brutal introduction to the atrocities of war. The VC had eviscerated the village chief's pregnant wife and had hanged her upside down from a tree. I was told that the baby had been left hanging by the umbilical cord until removed by one of the villagers that morning. The chief and some of the other village elders to include the local schoolteacher had been executed and their bodies thrown down the only well in order to make the water non-potable for the villagers. The VC had threatened to return the next night if the village did not give in to some demands, which I don't remember ever hearing about. The villagers were panicked and demanded that I protect them if the VC did reappear.

As dusk was approaching I got together with my platoon sergeant and we decided on some good defensive positions for the night just outside the village. I remembered that I had so much to do and check on: were the individual positions adequate; were we taking advantage of cover and concealment; did we have interlocking fields of fire; was ammo distributed correctly; did I have observation posts (OPs) in the right places; could they get back if they had to; should I register defensive fires; did I have adequate commo with my squads and with higher (higher headquarters, in this case my company CP at St. George); were my automatic weapons in proper locations, was my CP in the best possible place; did my guys understand light and noise discipline; plus what the hell was I going to do if the VC did come back? And, last but not least; who the hell was I to tell these hardened combat vets how to set up a defensive perimeter? I settled down with my RTO, Zeke, to survive my first night in the field. My mind was racing and I knew that there was no way that I was going to get any sleep that night.

I thought back on all of the training and classes at various schools during and after West Point, and began to realize that the responsibility for men's lives in combat is the most awesome responsibility anyone could ever shoulder. When I was finally put into a position with that responsibility, I found it to be far heavier than I had ever imagined. I always put the welfare and safety of my soldiers in the forefront of my planning and thought process, even though I realized that I might some day be in a position where I could not put those requirements as my highest priority. Here I was, in my first night in the BN, and I was already in the field and totally responsible for the lives of thirty or so young Americans in a decidedly hostile area. That was a heavy load; I don't think that there is anything else quite like it. And so it began.

DUTY! HONOR! COUNTRY!

4 - FLEAS

I really didn't sleep a wink in that little circular night defensive position that first night - I was too nervous and too unsettled about what I was going to do. I did think back about all that I had learned, about how different this place was compared to my comfortable room in East Barracks at West Point. What an incredible transition. What would I do if the VC did return that night? But the more I thought about it, the more convinced I was that I had been pretty well prepared. And not too surprisingly I found that I was really enjoying the challenge and experience.

The VC did not return. The sun came up over the jungle in the morning accompanied by roosters crowing and the smell of burning wood cooking fires. The animals; chickens, dogs and pigs, began to scurry around on their morning business. I knew that I was in a truly strange place as the villagers began to stir. A man came down the log steps out of his hooch to take a leak; he squatted beside a fence post and carefully covered himself with his hand. A bare-breasted young woman wearing only a skirt came down the ladder next; she just walked into the middle of the path, spread her legs while standing there, and relieved herself while curiously looking at us. Wow! Some memories like this will be with me forever.

Later that first full day we moved into the remnants of a nearby small triangular mud fort that had been built by the French years before; we were just off National HWY 14, a major north-south route through the highlands. We dug new bunkers, put out concertina wire, tangle foot, ground flares and claymores. We were pretty far from St George and would be resupplied only sporadically by truck and maybe a helicopter if we were lucky. We were to be there until the 28th with a mission of training the local Popular Force guards on marksmanship and basic techniques of defending their village. My job was to ensure that this new position was properly prepared and to coordinate a game plan with the local guards on actions to be taken in the event that the VC, or the NVA, returned.

Several times during our days there we were probed at night by the VC, accompanied by small arms or automatic weapons fire or mortars, but we never received a major attack and fortunately didn't suffer any casualties. Any time that we experienced suspected enemy action or movement at night I called for illumination rounds from the artillery at St. George. These were parachute flares that lit at a pre-determined height and then floated down, swaying from side to side with an eerie whistling noise, which was to become all too common during my tour. The swaying of the flare caused the ground shadows to constantly move, which could easily feed the imagination that there were a lot of bad guys out there. While manning that little fort was my first real combat assignment, I did have one very memorable personal experience. As in any other profession, there are rights of passage to becoming a real combat soldier. One of those steps was the first time you went out into the woods to take a crap, all by yourself.

It took a couple of days for the urge to hit me strongly enough that I could no longer ignore it. Who the hell wants to leave the perimeter by themselves, walk into the woods far enough for privacy, drop your drawers and then take care of business? When the time came for me I told everyone that I was going out of the wire, and to please not shoot me when I came back. I carried an entrenching tool to dig a hole for my deposit, my weapon –locked and loaded – and a small package of toilet paper from my C rations. I can now tell you that there is no more vulnerable feeling in the world than squatting with your pants around your ankles while looking in every treetop for a VC sniper. I thought about how embarrassing it would be for my parents to get a letter from the Department of the Army:

> Dear Mr. & Mrs. Hedley, I'm sorry to inform you that your son John was killed in action while taking a shit. He died bravely while valiantly trying to pull up his pants.

I do remember squatting with my back against a tree (I would NOT be shot in the back), with my pants around my feet, with my weapon locked and loaded while I scanned the trees and treetops. I had gone far enough into the tree line to not be visible from our position, but not so far that I couldn't get back quickly if I had to. I was in such a hurry to get finished and out of that vulnerable position that I didn't want to waste the time trying to open the toilet paper, which could be difficult because of the way it was taped together, I just reached down and grabbed some leaves, never taking my eyes off of scanning those trees. Only a couple of hours later did I realize that in those leaves must have been a colony of fleas or ants!! I was in agony for a couple of days until, on the advice of one of my medics I smoked them out over a fire (I'll leave the detailed description of that act to your imagination). This was certainly one of the untold hardships of war and not one of my finest moments! How would John Wayne have handled this problem?

> Dear Mr. and Mrs. Hedley, I'm sorry to inform you that your son John was wounded when he attempted to smoke some insects out of his ass while squatting over a hot fire and was severely burned.

Upon returning to St. George on the 28th after about a week guarding the village, we had a one-day stand down to repair weapons, clean up, draw fresh jungle fatigues and get some sleep. The refit time was very short, we left St. George again at noon on the 29th to move to a new village to conduct the same type of training for the local guard force. The duty was not real exciting but it was relatively uneventful as far as contact with any bad guys was concerned. We returned to St. George on August 6th. We left at about 2 PM to go to firebase Weigt-Davis to add to their defenses for the night. Weigt-Davis was primarily an engineer firebase but our battalion 4.2-inch mortar platoon was collocated there as well. We spent the night on their bunker line and returned to St. George the following afternoon.

I went out into the jungle on a couple of missions with all of Charlie Company. My first experience with a helicopter combat assault occurred on August 11th when the company was combat assaulted into a new area of operations. This was a really interesting and educational experience for me. I learned that the platoons were broken into "chalks" of five to eight men for each bird. The number of GI's was determined normally by local weather conditions and the height of mountains that we had to fly over. Fortunately my platoon sergeant and squad leaders were very experienced in this procedure and all I had to do was look observe and learn. Our PZ (pick-up zone) was LZ (landing zone) St. George; our LZ was some clicks (kilometers) into the jungle. LZ's could be either hot (enemy shooting at us) or cold (no enemy reaction). Fortunately for my first experience the LZ was cold.

Humping in the field was a real experience; I had never been so hot, miserable or dehydrated. At times I wondered if I could keep up with the younger guys who had all acclimated themselves. I sometimes became dizzy and disoriented for a short time. The heat and humidity were incredible, especially while carrying a hundred pounds of equipment and weapons. How was I supposed to live and fight in that environment?

During those operations I learned a lot about navigating in the jungles and mountains of the Central Highlands. The terrain was infinitely varied, at times steep and covered with triple canopy jungle, at other times open and rolling with rice paddies or barely forested terrain. Here and there were small villages or sometimes even a larger cluster of several "vills." There were a lot of streams (blue lines) to cross, often on single log bridges. Navigating these was a real trip with weapon and a rucksack on your back. One thing that really surprised me was how beautiful the countryside was. I often thought that it would make a great tourist destination if only there wasn't a war.

I learned during these times to carry only those parts of the C-Rations that I liked in order to lighten my load, as well as the value of commercial hot sauce and garlic salt which were sent from home and allowed us to vary the taste of our meals. One other necessity was packages of Kool Aid, which helped to mask the taste of the water that we had to purify with terrible tasting little pills inside of our hot plastic canteens. Sometimes we had to take our water out of rice paddies after pushing green sludge out of the way. That could be even more disconcerting after the first time you saw a water buffalo use the same paddy as his personal slit trench! I also learned why everyone carried as many canteens as possible, a bare minimum of three, and celebrated with the troops when we were issued two quart canteens which were at first a little awkward to carry, but did allow us to carry more water.

It was incredibly hot and humid and I was constantly trying to wipe the sweat from my eyes. I learned why all of the grunts carried a GI issue OD bath towel around their shoulders, their hump rags or boonie rags. Boonies referred to any area outside of a firebase or town; humping was the act of moving through the terrain; sometimes we went into the boonies on a two-week hump. The towel acted as a pad to cushion the pain of the heavy rucksack straps on your shoulders, and the ends were used for wiping our faces. Many guys carried bottles of weapons oil and mosquito repellent in the bands that held our cammo covers onto our steel pots.

My first experience in the field lasted six days. We replaced "D" Co because they had lost two men the previous night to a tiger attack!! And that's where we had landed! Fortunately this was a relatively quiet hump with little sign of the enemy or tigers for which I was extremely happy. I felt that I had all that I could do to acclimate, the terrain, life at a very primitive level, and the constant fear of enemy contact. We returned to St. George on the 16th with only the major excitement caused by a tiger nearby on the night of the 14th.

To call in helicopters for an extraction we needed to "pop smoke"—this entailed throwing a smoke grenade of some color into the LZ to mark a spot for the bird to land which also served to help them judge the wind direction. When we threw out the smoke grenade we never identified its color, but rather had the pilot respond and identify what he saw, "Roger, I see goofy grape" (purple). We had learned that if you threw something out and told the pilot that you had thrown purple, then a couple more purples could also appear, thrown by the bad guys who were monitoring our radios, in an effort to lure the bird into heading for the wrong one and thus into a killing zone.

We remained at St. George for about a week. During this time we continued to work on our positions, conducted some training, and ran patrols during the day and set ambushes at night. This was a pretty quiet and peaceful time.

This was to be my world for the next year. There were many challenges to be faced when waking up in the morning; would there be contact with the bad guys, were my guys taking their required malaria pills, did we have enough ammo and everything else that we needed, would we have enough water, would I be able to keep up, was I going to be able to navigate correctly and always know where I was? Would I do the right thing when we were shot at? The life of a small unit grunt commander was not going to be easy.

DUTY! HONOR! COUNTRY!

5 - FIRST BLOOD

Most of my missions during my first couple of weeks in the battalion were pretty forgettable; I didn't experience a lot of heavy combat. We encountered an occasional booby trap and were sniped at a few times by some VC farmer who had a weapon and maybe two or three rounds of ammunition in his pocket. Sometimes he even smiled and waved from the rice paddy he was working in as we passed by. After we had gone out of sight, Nguyen (A common Vietnamese surname that we applied liberally to any local) would retrieve his hidden rifle and follow after us and take a couple of pot shots. He was generally only a nuisance and seldom hit anyone, but once in a while he'd get lucky and cause a casualty. The primary effect on us was psychological, making us feel that we could never let our guard down nor trust any native. Each time we were shot at we would drop our rucks, deploy, and maneuver to get the guy shooting at us. You just never knew how many bad guys were out there. Sometimes we were successful, often times as not the sniper would quickly hide his weapon after firing his couple of rounds and go back to tending his paddies, smiling and waving at us as we looked for the culprit.

We spent countless hours "humping," dealing with the incredible weight on our backs and the stupor caused by the heat, looking for signs of the enemy and becoming increasingly bored, which was a very dangerous state of mind. You naturally became less alert, less tuned in to what was going on around you, less vigilant and more lethargic from the heat. Many times these mental lapses caused by the heat and lack of action proved to be very dangerous, as inevitably this was when you would find the bad guys, or worse yet, they would find you. Many grunts will tell you that Vietnam was hours of horrible boredom sprinkled with minutes of sheer terror.

During this same time there were several reports of convoy ambushes on Highway 14, the major logistical route from Pleiku to Ban Me Thout. This was the main supply route of St. George. The situation was becoming so dangerous that our operations shop requested air cover for supply convoys along the route. Around this same time the Battalion Operations Center received a directive that would haunt some of us in the future.

This Div. has had 14 weapons accidents by 14 Aug. (I assume that was a tally for the month up to that date.) *This represents a 55% accident increase over the July reporting period. Four accidents occurred on 13 and 14 Aug.*
Such a record can only indicate a relaxed emphasis on accident prevention resulting in a totally unacceptable trend which will be immediately acted upon by all commanders.
All addressees will insure safety orientations are conducted with all troops in all areas of unit operations within 72 hours within receipt of this message.
Conduction (sic) *of individual weapons safety, buddy guard watch teams, grenade safety and the critical requirement of double checking. Adherence to every positive safety procedure in delivery of all types of fires will be stressed.*

A second directive was received on policing the battlefield:

Police of the battlefield, your attention is directed to the referenced message. The police of the battlefield include vehicles used in transportation of combat troops. Recently, claymore mines, LAW's, small arms ammo, and grenades have been found in vehicles after troop movement.
All commanders are reminded that it is a command responsibility to insure that the police of the battlefield is complete to include vehicles.

Reading this directive long after the fact really struck me as being ridiculous when directed at a battalion commander.
Another message from division was also received at the same time:

Recent information from POWs, Hoi chans, and documents captured throughout II Corps indicates the enemy is planning another high point (of activity) *commencing on the 19th. This date is the anniversary of the National Revolution. The enemy can be expected to conduct stand off and sniper attacks similar to attacks on 11 and 12 Aug. Commanding General desires appropriate action be taken against expected attacks.*
It is likely that the enemy plans to employ 140mm rockets against Pleiku, Kontum, Nha Trang, Oasis and Camp Enari
On the 19th the BN TOC received the following advisory from the CG:

Recent enemy contacts by LRRP teams has revealed units not reacting quickly enough to provide significant aid to teams in contact, or to exploit possibilities of such contact.

Slow reaction to enemy contact endangers lives, lowers morale of unit, and deprives us of the opportunity to destroy the enemy. The key to success of this concept will be repeated aggressiveness and overwhelming employment of reaction force. The reaction force will include Air Cav. Each brigade will designate a quick reaction force. This reaction force of a platoon size element will be on one minute notice and no more than 15 minutes. Troops with organic ARP element and armed with mechanized infantry bns will lighten to explore contacts. Designated DS artillery batteries will be able to deploy firing platoon on short notice. Commanding General desires that reaction force will be designated in all plans summary. Upon reaction, platoon will be ready to move to assembly area point and follow up contact. This to be passed to all BN COs and Company Commanders

The 19th was an extremely busy day in the Battalion Area of Operations with A and B companies both reporting contact along with two LRRP teams. Three enemy soldiers were killed during these operations.

On the 28th the Battalion Operations Center received a very interesting message from the Brigade Commander, Col. Warner.

> 1. *The number of initiated contacts has reduced sharply in the last 10 days. Reduction has been accompanied by reports of US units failing to engage the enemy element. The Bde mission of defeating the enemy in decisive combat remains the same. I believe the enemy is still here and tactics need a hard look. 2. COs at all levels are encouraged to conduct aggressive tactical operations capitalizing on surprise and greater mobility. Effective immediately each battalion size unit will conduct a minimum of one night operation a week, involving night movement and occupation of acceptable ambushes along blue lines and trails. COs are encouraged to conduct (a) a stay behind element, (b) element on standby for a prepared C.A, (c)a C.A with multiple LZ's, (d) saturation patrolling at night. Good hunting. Col. Warner.*

I don't believe that any units in the 1/14 INF were avoiding contact. The directive to conduct at least one night operation a week was particularly egregious. This simple order showed no thought given to the actual tactical situation, the types of terrain and vegetation in each battalion's area, or the battalion commander's intent or concept of an operation. Stumbling around at night for the sole purpose of stumbling around at night was extremely dangerous and not necessarily mission effective in triple canopy jungle. In addition, we had no night vision devices like every modern soldier now has attached to their helmet.

Again that night the Operations Center received the following from Brigade:

1. *BDE CO will attend a conference on Sunday on small unit tactics and small unit night operation tactics. 2. Request your comments, suggestions and variations on small unit tactics. 3. Submit no later than Saturday via radio or courier.*

I vividly remember the first time I was engaged in a serious fire fight; it was also an occasion when the Battalion Commander and his Command Sergeant Major (CSM) decided to accompany me for a day. No stress there! The Battalion CO was an officer whom I would come to admire greatly, and would be lucky enough to link up with again some 40 years in the future. This was my first meeting with him and it had to be on a patrolling operation! He told me to pay no attention to him and to just do my job—he wasn't there to interfere, I was in command. He said that he and the CSM would be happy to help out if I needed them to pull triggers; just tell them where to go and what to shoot at. The fact that they would hump with grunts in the boonies gave them a firsthand look at an outfit's actual capabilities; an invaluable opportunity to judge the skill of both the men and the leadership. Only in this environment where the possibility of combat was always present could a real judgement be made. Lieutenant Colonl Vic Robertson was a real soldier's soldier.

By this time the company commander had developed some confidence in my ability to handle myself in the jungle and he would sometimes split the company in half; he'd take two rifle platoons in his unit and give me the mortar platoon, without tubes, as a small additional maneuver element. This was the situation for the upcoming day.

I guess that I had been in the battalion for a couple of weeks. We conducted a helicopter borne Combat Assault (CA) out of St George early in the morning of August 21st and were inserted into a cold LZ. Our mission was to try and track an enemy formation and to locate a reported hospital.

After everyone jumped out of the birds we formed a hasty perimeter to get a feel for the area and to determine if we had been detected. We also checked to insure that there were no injuries sustained in jumping off of the birds like sprained or broken ankles, and to make sure that everyone had the equipment they needed. We then formed up into our movement formation and moved off the LZ.

As we were moving into our assigned area, we entered a densely jungled streambed. Because of the triple canopy, it was as dark at noon as it would have been at 1900. The jungles in II Corps were mostly triple canopy, very little light filtered down to the jungle floor. Mother Nature had enabled the trees to cope with less light in the second and third layers, and collectively, the overhead was extremely thick, completely covered the area, and blocked all view of the sun and sky – eerie at times. Normally it was so thick that sounds were masked or distorted, making it difficult to determine the direction of the sound of small arms fire or artillery air bursts if you were trying to triangulate a position. The triple canopy also made it impossible to pinpoint your position for friendly air support using smoke grenades. You could pull the pin and throw the canister, but the smoke could drift for a long distance before finding its way up and through the overhanging canopy. The pilot couldn't be sure of your exact location.

In most areas the underbrush was also exceedingly thick. There was an abundance of ferns, small bushes and what we called "wait a minute vines" that were somewhat like climbing rose vines. They grew in thick tangles and were populated with an enormous number of small thorns that would lock into your jungle fatigues, web gear and even skin. They were horrendous, very difficult to get out of if you were snared. Plus the humidity was trapped under the layers of jungle canopy so that the trees and bushes constantly dripped moisture.

It was a distressing, creepy and scary place. In this type of area the enemy could lie concealed only a couple of yards, or even feet away and never be seen. Even if he opened fire it could be very difficult to pin point his location.

We were moving cautiously along the stream, hugging the banks while moving over large slippery rocks interspersed with boot-sucking mud, when my point man opened up on someone he had seen ahead of us. I later found out that he couldn't tell if it was VC or NVA. As the men were getting down to secure our position and I was moving up to the point we began to take fire from AK 47s from a couple of locations, we had probably run into an NVA unit. This was a lot different than dealing with a local village sniper.

Shit! Here it was; my first real test and God, in the form of the Battalion Commander was watching my every move. I thought of nothing except getting to my point man to learn what he had seen. I grabbed for the radio handset to let higher know I was in contact and that the Battalion Commander was with us. My RTO and I ran in a crouch to where my point element had hit the dirt. There were rounds zipping all around us; this was the first time I realized that the enemy used green tracers as opposed to our red ones. They just seemed to float… Some made strange cracking noises, which I later learned were the ones going by close to my ear. My heart was thudding and I was gasping for air due to the exertion in the humid air and the fear. Adrenaline was pulsing into my system and sweat was poring down my face making it hard to see.

I suddenly knew that I had a guy hit because I heard the yell for "Medic!!" Oh shit, my heart beat tripled, I knew that call meant one of my guys was shot. I ran over to find one of my soldiers bleeding from an arm wound, it wasn't serious. I just had my first introduction to the cloying, kinda coppery smell of fresh blood. The medic had the situation well in hand, bandaged him, and the soldier continued on. I don't think that he ever pursued a Purple Heart.

The firing eventually stopped. We made a hasty check of the area, found no enemy bodies but a couple of blood trails, some of them had been hit. We reformed and continued cautiously up the stream for another hour until we saw a waterfall that looked to be about thirty feet high in the distance. As we moved forward, the stream banks got higher and steeper. Eventually we got close to the falls. I ordered a halt to take a break for lunch on the riverbanks. While still incredibly humid, the air was cooler here thanks to the mist generated by the falls.

Because I didn't want to be caught by surprise, I decided that I needed a security presence on the high ground above the falls. I led one of my squads with a gun team (M60 machine gun) on a climb beside the falls until we reached the top. This would act as an observation post, OP. The going was tough as the bank was steep and the underbrush thick. In some cases we pulled ourselves up by grasping at roots or rock outcroppings, hoping we wouldn't lose our grip and fall. When we reached the top we were soaked with sweat and totally out of breath.

After we had caught our breath the squad leader and I selected a good position about fifty yards beyond the falls. We selected a location with enough secondary growth to provide some cover and concealment but affording good observation of the surrounding area, thus ensuring some degree of security. I went back down to the rest of the two platoons. They had moved into the jungle on the steep banks on either side of the stream so as to not be visible to anyone on the high ground. They shook off their rucksacks and dug into them for some cans of Cs. Several of the guys refilled their canteens from the cold, clear stream. I needed some time to think about what we were going to do next; climb the bank and continue our hump, or backtrack to where the slope wasn't as high or steep. There was a good chance that our earlier firefight had alerted a larger NVA unit.

As we were taking the break, a couple of the guys were exploring the falls and discovered a cave entrance behind the running water. One of them dashed over to me and excitedly informed me of their find. I got a squad together and we climbed up to investigate. As we cautiously entered the mouth of the cave, alert for any enemy soldiers hiding inside, it soon became obvious that we had uncovered a fully stocked NVA hospital. There were several rooms which included a surgical suite and a couple of wards with bamboo beds. There were some bloody bandages piled in the corner of one room that looked fairly fresh. There was also a good supply of medical gear as well as assorted cooking pans in a kitchen area that had a vent that went up to the surface. Our first mission had been successfully completed with this discovery.

In what appeared to be a storeroom, we also discovered a couple of footlocker-type boxes that we carried outside to investigate. We opened one and found that it contained, among other things, several lacy black bras and panties. So there were either nurses present or this place also served as a "comfort station" for war-weary NVA troops. Needless to say my guys got pretty excited about this find, wanting a bra or pair of panties as a unique souvenir. I presented the Battalion Commander with a pair of the panties; forty years later he still had them! I really wanted to make a good initial impression by giving him something to remember me by! It was quite possible that the NVA we encountered earlier were a guard or care-taking force for this hospital.

The Daily Staff Journal for the 21st listed the following items removed from the cave:

- Hammock frames for up to 100 people that looked as though they had been used the evening before.
- 4 NVA packs and 4 pair of NVA pants.
- 12 Chi-com grenades, I NVA gas mask, 6 socks, 1 NVA canteen, Ho chi Minh sandals, 2 pair of underwear, 3 hammocks, a couple of first aid kits.
- A lot of medical gauze, sewing kit, 2 pouches of tobacco, 1 US ammo pouch, 6 blasting caps.
- Papers, charts maps, codes, blood stained clothing (without bullet holes)

There were a lot of smaller caves in the area as well, plus six fresh latrines with three-foot diameter logs as seats. The entire area looked as if it had been freshly used up to the 21st. With these finds indicating a probable and recent sizable enemy force, we all became hyper vigilant.

As we were admiring our find of lingerie and letting our imagination run wild, all hell broke loose on top of the falls. I could hear M16s and my M60, also AK 47s and RPGs going off. I grabbed my weapon and ammo, told the closest guys to follow me, and started up the cliff side. I yelled at my platoon sergeant to get the rest of the guys into good secure and concealed positions, and to be prepared to reinforce me should I call for him. I cannot adequately describe the feeling of urgency and the "rush" that comes at such a time when trying to cover difficult terrain while trying to get to some of your guys who are in contact. When I got to the top my lungs were bursting and I couldn't see from all of the sweat streaming down my face. All I wanted to do was stop, but my guys were being shot at. We collected ourselves and moved forward cautiously, but quickly, scanning the underbrush for any gooks.

I saw my M60 gunner, a tall, strapping guy, standing buck-assed naked in the middle of the stream firing furiously while screaming for more ammo. His ammo bearer was hiding behind a big rock, too scared to move forward to resupply his gunner. I moved up beside him, smacked him in the helmet with the butt of my CAR 15, and screamed at him to "*MOVE!*" as I pointed to his gunner who was running for the bank and swearing furiously at his ammo bearer to get that "god damn ammo up here!!" The little guy took off like a scared rabbit and helped the gunner feverously reload the gun.

I took the rest of the guys I'd run up the hill with on a flanking movement around where I determined most of the enemy fire was coming from. The adrenaline was rushing and there was incredible noise. There was the sharp smell of gunpowder that hung close to the ground; it burned my eyes as much as the sweat that was pouring into them. I was breathing so hard I could hardly talk. I could hear the pounding of my heart in my ears; my eyes were watering; and my main thought was that I needed to do whatever it was to make sure I didn't lose anyone. I could see fleeting figures in the dense underbrush, men in khaki wearing pith helmets. During that mad dash I took my first aimed shot at another human being; he went down. He was an NVA soldier scanning the underbrush and looking for a target, his head exploded in a red mist. I don't remember any emotional reaction but immense satisfaction, my first kill. I can still see that guy as though it were yesterday.

Finally the enemy broke contact and disappeared into the jungle, dragging any dead and wounded with them. That was one of the frustrating things about this war; the enemy normally took their casualties with them so that you couldn't have the satisfaction of seeing dead ones. They knew that a confirmed "body count" was the US unit's measure of success. Often the best you could find was the ubiquitous blood trail left as dead and wounded soldiers were dragged away, or spilled by walking wounded as they made their escape. No satisfaction; kinda like the title of a popular song by the Rolling Stones, *Satisfaction,* that often played in the Weapons Room in the gym at West Point when we went for a hamburger and shake: *"I can't get no… satisfaction"*. I looked for but couldn't find the body of the NVA soldier that I knew I had killed.

After the contact was over I called my security team together to find out what had happened, and why my machine gunner was completely naked while on guard! It turned out that several of my guys had been taking advantage of the cold and clear stream to get cleaned up when the NVA approached. They had literally been caught with their pants down, kind of embarrassing for a seasoned US combat infantryman. Even so, they had seen the NVA first. The NVA soldiers were obviously not expecting to encounter any Americans as they were moving in a loose formation with their weapons on their shoulders or being carried loosely at their sides. The enemy soldiers, 10 or 12 of them, were probably returning to the hospital cave for the night and hadn't heard the earlier gunfire due to the blanketing effect of triple canopy jungle. They were talking, joking and laughing which allowed my guys to get the drop on them. That could explain why I suffered no casualties, we luckily caught the NVA totally by surprise and their return fire was hasty and ineffective. My guys had no idea of how many NVA they may have hit but naturally claimed a few because of the blood trails.

As things quieted down I grabbed my squad leader and furiously chewed his ass. I was angry but awfully relieved when all of my guys were present and accounted for with no holes in their bodies. How could he have let his guys be caught in such a compromising position? Didn't he realize that there could be enemy soldiers in the area, especially after our earlier firefight?

He was really embarrassed as he was one of the oldest and most experienced guys in the unit in regards to time in country and in combat. After I finished yelling at him he promised to never ever again get naked in Indian Country! I told him to secure the area again as the rest of us would soon climb up to join him and continue our mission and try to track the guys we had just fought with. After I rejoined the rest of my unit at the foot of the falls the reaction set in. During the contact and dressing down afterwards I remember being a little scared, and incredibly pissed off at the bad guys for screwing with us while I had the Battalion Commander in my formation, and at my guys for being so stupid. As I sat down to take a break and get my breathing under control my hands started to shake, I couldn't light a cigarette. I tried to hide the shaking and it took a while before it disappeared. There was no way I could take a much-needed drink from my canteen. I found that incredible amounts of adrenaline flow through your body when you are being shot at, and that "adrenaline drain" afterwards was a very uncomfortable feeling.

We had a "thing" about the NVA—they were kinda regarded as superb soldiers by most American grunts in the area. The Viet Cong, or VC, both local and main force, were primarily local farmers, although some of their units were pretty good, and not usually heavily armed,. This was particularly true of the "Main Force VC" as opposed to the local guerilla groups. The main force guys were in organized units, much better equipped and trained than the real local guys, but still no match for a US unit. They had their designated areas of responsibility and did not go back to their villages at night.

The NVA, on the other hand, were well trained and outfitted regular troops, much better equipped and much more aggressive. The VC would usually melt away after firing a few shots, or a B40 rocket or two. The NVA regulars would usually stand and fight if we were in a smaller than company sized unit. They had learned from experience that they were normally no match for a full American infantry company with all of its organic firepower and access to formidable support like artillery, armed Army helicopters and jets from the Air Force or Navy. To account for this inequity their tactic was to get as close to you as possible so that you didn't dare use the fire support available as you stood a good chance of killing your own guys. They refered to this tactic in their manuals as "grabbing the enemy by the belt". This move could make for some pretty intense combat. They were certainly not supermen in my experience, but you could generally expect a pretty good fight if you crossed their path.

The rest of the day was pretty quiet. After we had removed all of the maps, documents and other potentially valuable intelligence from inside of the hospital, we bundled it all up and filled a couple of NVA rucksacks so that it could be sent to the rear for evaluation on our next resupply bird. We moved up the cliff side by the falls and cautiously followed a couple of the blood trails. The Battalion Commander and CSM left us when we found a suitable PZ for his bird. When the blood trails petered out we patrolled the general area, hoping to regain contact with the NVA we had chased from the falls. While we periodically saw signs of their presence we never re-established contact with them. The final toll for the operation that day was one US slightly wounded, and, we suspected, several NVA killed or wounded.

We eventually found a good place for a night laager and set up our perimeter, ate chow, and prepared to get some much needed sleep. I was exhausted from the adrenaline surges of the day. I'd also climbed up and down that damned waterfall cliff three times. Around 2130 we heard movement to our northwest at an estimated 100 meters away, I called in some artillery. Again at about 0200 we had a trip flare set off and I called in some illumination rounds. We saw nothing; so much for sleep. The remainder of the night was quiet. It was obvious from the fresh signs at the hospital area, our contact that afternoon, and the sounds that evening that the NVA were still in the area, and more importantly, they knew we were in their area.

Early the next morning we spotted four or five guys in green fatigues carrying ruck sacks about 600-700 meters away down in a valley. We called in some artillery and put rounds right on target. At about 1100 we were fired on by five guys carrying AK-47's dressed the same way as the guys we had seen earlier in the morning. We returned fire and I called in some gunships. It was my first experience with the new Huey Cobra, which stayed on station for about 45 minutes. Later that day, at about 1800, we spotted two files of armed soldiers numbering about 25 in total about a click to our northwest. I called in artillery hoping that we could score some kills this time.

Shortly thereafter we set up our night laager defensive position. The night was pretty quiet until about 0215 AM when one of my guys reported seeing a flashlight only about 60 meters away. Since no American soldier would use a flashlight I called in some Willy Pete (white phosphorous) with an unknown result. Most of us were awake for the rest of the night.

It was during this operation that I began to understand the feeling and effects of fear. There is not much that can be scarier than sitting in triple canopy jungle at night with about 40 guys and not able to see any further than ten. Do this after a couple of days of substantial enemy sightings and a couple of nights of hearing movement around your position and your anxiety level grows. You feel all alone even though you know your buddies were close. In this case I knew there were a lot of bad guys around and they were obviously tracking us; we had evidently stirred up a hornets' nest with our actions at the cave hospital. What we found there was firm evidence there were a lot of enemy soldiers in our area. You sit in the jungle; all of a sudden you hear a lot of strange noises, not the normal jungle night sounds, and your eyes begin to play tricks on you. In this case your imagination can begin to run wild as you picture lots of tough, little NVA soldiers crawling through the jungle to attack your position, determined to kill you and all of your folks.

As the commander you realize you cannot allow fear to get the best of you, you absolutely have to maintain self-control so you can do your job if the situation turns to shit. Plus you absolutely cannot afford to let your guys know you are afraid, as that feeling can be very contagious. So you think about the training you've received and mentally run through possible enemy actions and what you can do in the event any of them occur. Even though you may be personally scared to death, you need to face it and continue to do your job, taking advantage of that fear to make sure you've thought of every possible contingency and that you've got a plan to face any situation. Some years later I ran across a John Wayne quote that kind of summed it all up; "Courage is being scared to death – but saddling up anyway."

As the night ended and the sun came through the canopy we quickly ate a meal, packed up our gear, saddled up and left that night's position at about 0830. We moved carefully and quietly in a northwest direction, alert for anything that could be out there. After a few hours we spotted 3 guys dressed in black carrying AK-47s about 75 meters away. We opened fire and the enemy ran away in a southwesterly direction without returning fire. When we swept the area after the contact we found one enemy KIA and one pack; my first actual enemy body count. I will have to admit to a smug feeling of satisfaction. Again at 1045 we spotted 10 to 15 individuals in green fatigues carrying weapons. We engaged them with small arms fire and gunships. We found no enemy KIA when we swept the area but did find several blood trails once again. That night, after moving into our defensive position, one of our ambushes reported movement so close to them that they engaged with small arms and then returned to our perimeter. Once again I called in artillery to make sure the bad guys kept moving away from us.

An hour later another of our ambushes spotted lights coming towards them. When they were within 50 meters the ambush blew their claymores and engaged with small arms as they broke contact and returned to our perimeter. Once again I called in artillery on their suspected position. A half hour later we had more enemy movement close to our perimeter and I called in more artillery. It was obvious that the enemy knew that we were in their AO, and were probing us to pinpoint our location. I told my guys not to fire their weapons unless absolutely necessary. I fully expected a determined assault given all of the enemy movement; fortunately they did not try to attack our main position.

That same afternoon another 1/14 INF unit removed about 50 packs from the hospital cave area as well as about 150 pounds of rice. The packs were evacuated to the Brigade HQ and the rice was destroyed.

That night we received instructions from our battalion operations center to search a nearby draw and then to move out on a patrol. I was to leave 15 men behind in our night laager area in the hopes that we could catch the guys who have been trailing us. If that didn't produce results they were to rejoin our main body and continue to move slowly while "attempting to make contact through stealth."

At about 0600 that next morning we had movement straight ahead of us. After firing a couple of illumination rounds, we had movement again in another part of our perimeter. Once again I employed illumination with negative results. After we broke camp and started our patrol, we spotted two guys about 100 meters out. They were wearing green fatigues and soft caps. One was carrying a rifle, the other what looked like an RPG rocket launcher. They were moving away from us to the northeast. At 1930 we spotted six guys with weapons and rucksacks. I fired some artillery at them and they fled in a northeast direction. Again at 2130 one of my ambushes spotted six guys dressed in green once again with weapons and rucksacks. The ambush engaged them with small arms and withdrew into our night defensive position. Once again I covered their withdrawal with artillery. At about 0030 another of our ambushes reported movement at about 100 meters. An illumination round showed us nothing. At about 0150 the same ambush reported more movement about 100 meters.

I considered pulling in all of my ambushes and called the artillery guys and asked them to stand by with high explosive rounds since we had already fired a registration round with the illumination. We had no further movement so I left everyone in place for the remainder of the night. We left the position at 0920. With all of the activity of the past couple of days I learned that the CG had directed that we put out several 15-man ambushes that night, in coordination with the rest of C Co who was instructed to do the same in an effort to saturate the area and hopefully engage a lot of NVA. In the morning we were to start a sweep towards St. George. Upon arrival at St. George we were to be given a stand down for care and cleaning of weapons and equipment.

We closed on St. George at around noon on the 28th. It had been quite a week; starting with the discovery of the cave hospital followed by some heavy patrolling, ambushing and enemy contacts. It had been quite a learning experience for me as I had had my first real test as a small unit infantry commander. I had become pretty adept at calling in and controlling both artillery and armed helicopters. These new found skills would really pay off in the future. I had become much more confident in my ability to lead soldiers in combat, and in controlling my personal fears. I had also developed some personal operating procedures. I determined that I havd to do anything I could to safeguard the lives of my soldiers by employing abundant amounts of artillery and helicopter support.

I must also admit that I experienced a pleasurable adrenaline rush when in contact, almost a feeling of being high. It was a great sensation I found I enjoyed, a lot. I was finally doing what I had been trained to do for all of those years.

I think this also caused my soldiers to have confidence in me and my abilities. I had my first introduction to my battalion commander, the "Dragon", which was to come into play in a way that I couldn't even imagine. The battalion commander, Dragon 6 (The 14th Infantry was known as the Golden Dragons), as I said, was a guy who I really respected. He was every inch the Regular Army officer and commander. LTC Victor M. Robertson Jr. was from South Carolina and was a graduate of The Citadel.

Little did I know that I was about to have another encounter with the Dragon, one that would change my life forever.

DUTY! HONOR! COUNTRY!

6 - WELCOME TO FOX

One day, after returning to St. George from an operation with Charlie Company, I was walking on a path that led past the Dragon's lair, the home of LTC Victor M. Robertson Jr. I don't remember what I was thinking about, probably nothing important, when I heard someone call "Lt. Hedley!" I didn't recognize the voice as I turned around to see The Dragon standing at the entrance to his hooch.

"Yes Sir."

"Lt. Hedley, please come here"

"Yes Sir" I answered and started walking over to him. Holy crap, what now? I thought to myself. What had I done to warrant this personal attention from the Battalion Commander? Then I remembered that Dragon and his CSM had accompanied me on the mission where we found the NVA hospital behind the waterfall. Shit, what had I done? We had had a couple of contacts with the NVA that day and maybe I had done something wrong. Was I about to be relieved before my combat tour even got started?

I nervously walked up to LTC Robertson and saluted. He asked me to enter the tent with him, which I did, then stood at attention in front of the field desk that was in about the center of the room. The Dragon walked in behind me, sat on the stool behind the desk, and told me to be at ease and sit down.

I don't remember what I sat on, maybe a bunk. I was getting more nervous as I sat and looked at him, Dragon had a face that could be, in turn, welcoming or fierce; I couldn't tell which one I was looking at. After a minute he reached into a desk drawer and pulled out a bottle of scotch, Johnnie Walker Red as I remember. Now what the hell was going on; was he going to have a drink while he chewed on my ass?

"LT Hedley, do you like scotch?"

"Yes sir." I answered, thinking maybe this guy was cool and was going to give me a drink as he terminated my career, maybe an effort on his part to make it a little easier for me to deal with what was coming.

He poured some scotch into two glasses, gave me one and then sat back as he looked at me with a kind of neutral look on his face. Now I was really beginning to sweat. After all of the preparation, all of the time at West Point, was my military career about to come to a sudden end? Was I about to be court martialed for something that I'd done, or not done, in the field? Dragon then started asking me questions about how I was doing, did I like the battalion, and was I learning a lot.

What was I going to say? Fine sir, yes sir, and yes sir, all the while wondering where this was going? Would I like more scotch . . . , hell ya, you betcha!
Finally he said that he'd get to the point. He'd been reviewing the records of all of the lieutenants in the battalion, had accompanied several of them in the field, and had decided to select me.
For what . . . I wondered?

He wanted me to leave Charlie Company and take command of the battalion's recon platoon, Fox Force. Holy shit, me, Fox Force, no friggin way!! There was no way I was ready to take responsibility for those crazy guys and go to the field to get into contact almost every time out, no bloody way!

After taking a gulp of scotch that burned all of the way down, I managed to say "No thank you, sir." Wow, this was really something; Dragon was plying me with scotch to take the most dangerous job in the battalion for an infantry lieutenant. The most prestigious to be sure, but damned sure the most dangerous I thought.

Why not" he asked? I told Dragon that I didn't think that I was ready to assume that kind of responsibility or those kinds of missions. I didn't think that I'd been in country long enough, or had been shot at enough times, I really wasn't sure what my reaction would be to a really dicey situation if I was on my own.

Dragon sat there looking at me for a minute and then finally said OK. He asked me to think about his request and then dismissed me. HOLEE SHIT, me take the recon platoon? There was just no way I could do that, I just wasn't ready for that kind of responsibility in a shooting war!!

A few days later, after another operation with Charlie Company, I made the mistake of walking past Dragon's hooch again. This time it was, "John, come in here please!" "Yes sir!" As I entered his tent and saluted him as he sat behind the field desk, he asked me to sit down again. Oh man, what now . . . ?

Dragon looked at me with his stern face as reached into his drawer for the bottle of scotch and two glasses, poured the whiskey and handed one glass to me.

"John, do you remember the conversation that you and I had about a few days ago?"

"Yes sir, I do."

"Do you remember what I asked of you?"

"Yes sir, I do." Oh crap, what now? Was I in trouble because I'd told him no? Now what was going to happen?
I soon found out.

"John, have you thought of my request that you take over Fox? What do you think now?"

"Well sir, I still don't think that I'm ready for that kind of responsibility."

"Well John, I do; last time my offer was a request; this time it's not. Let me get Staff Sergeant Harris in here and have him introduce you to your new command." There was obviously nothing that I could do now; there would be no more requests.

While certainly a scary proposition, I was being handed a plum of an assignment by The Dragon! Command of the battalion reconnaissance platoon, composed of the best soldiers in the entire battalion, was an incredible honor that I really didn't feel worthy of accepting.

The Fox guys were special; the whole BN looked at them with a certain amount of fear, a lot of respect, and awe. Other guys in the chow line would stand aside and let the recon guys in their red scarves go first if they showed up to eat. Anyone stupid enough to go into the jungle wearing a bright red scarf . . . But, this started one of the most enduring sets of male relationships that I would ever have. The camaraderie of men who have shared close combat together in our situation is like no other imaginable.

As I was preparing to take over Fox, I did some serious thinking. I was certainly a little apprehensive about taking command of the most aggressive unit in the battalion; I wondered if I was up to it. But I found that I had a growing inner confidence. I was now a legitimate combat infantryman, having been awarded the coveted CIB by the Battalion Command Sergeant Major, Command Sergeant Major Jasper Wiggins. He was a great guy and wanted me to have his original CIB that was issued to him during the Korean War. Unlike the modern ones made from a piece of stamped metal, this was made of sterling silver. It was the only one that I wore for the rest of my military career.

I had been shot at, and had not failed my men or myself. My company commander had enough faith in my abilities to give me half of the company to command, in my own AO, on a couple of missions. I had seen men killed and wounded, and I had killed as well. I believe that West Point had prepared me well for the requirements of combat command. The four year "system" had placed a lot of stress on us in many ways, weeding out a lot of guys who couldn't handle the challenge, and developing those who could. I had been challenged and had persevered. The system had provided the basics; the rest was up to each individual Academy graduate.

By this time some of the wetness behind my ears had dried, and I had become as comfortable as possible with my responsibility for men's lives. I had trained for years to be a combat leader and finally really was one. I found that I enjoyed the feeling of command, that I was pretty good at the basics, and that there was a sense of fulfillment to be doing that for which I had trained, and doing it fairly well. In reality, I was really enjoying myself!

While I was somewhat nervous about the prospect of joining Fox; the Fox guys must have certainly been nervous about my becoming their platoon leader. As Buck, my RTO, recounts:

We were back at St. George when a strapping young officer, first lieutenant John Hedley introduced himself as our new Platoon Leader – our Six
My view was that he was at the same time honored and a bit frightened (Right on!!) *to be taking over the helm of our unit. We had a tremendous reputation as a fighting unit and our red scarves added to our legend.*
We were a bit nervous as well, as we learned early on that he was a graduate of West Point and hence a career officer. Our initial concern was that he would see leading us as a vehicle to enhance his career by putting us in harms' way needlessly.

So, obviously, each side, the men of Fox on one end, and me on the other, would be trying each other on for size. I knew, that with this kind of specialized and extremely cohesive unit, that I had to earn these guys' trust and respect They weren't going to accept me easily. Buck went on:

However, John was open to learning how we were so effective. Jimmy and the rest of the CP (of which I was now a member as an RTO) shared our lessons
- *To be silent all the time in the field*
- *To keep our distance from each other (4 meters)*

- *To keep off trails*
- *To never walk in a valley*
- *To stay on the ridgeline of the mountains*
- *To be better guerillas than the NVA*

While I had been in the battalion only a little more than a month, aprehensive about leading Fox Force and undoubtedly still had my greatest tests ahead of me, deep down I was pretty confident that I could handle Fox— and hopefully do it well. I believe that I took command of Fox sometime in early September. After assuming command, I learned that life there would be extremely challenging as we were almost always in the field, and almost always on our own. That revelation came quickly.

DUTY! HONOR! COUNTRY!

7 - THE RED SCARF

One of the major reasons that I'm writing about my experiences is to provide a legacy to all of the families, the kids and grandkids of this special group of soldiers. They need to know about their fathers and grandfathers. This band of brothers formed an association with each other that is difficult to describe. The emotions involved in the memories and our current circumstances are a mixture of pride, respect and love among men, a deep and emotional binding of the hearts and minds and souls of men who have together experienced the thrills, losses, joys and sadness that come from serving together in the ultimate crucible of infantry combat. The emotions that are forged by depending on each other for our very survival builds a spirit that lives forever in the hearts of those who have experienced it.

The name "Fox Force" originated sometime in 1967 or 1968. The battalion commander evidently decided that he needed another maneuver element, in addition to the authorized organizations and weapons, which made up Headquarters and Headquarters Company, and A, B, C, and D as the line or combat companies. E Co was a field support company consisting of the battalion support platoon, the 4.2" Mortar Platoon, and other elements. In a quest to have more maneuver unit fire power, the CO authorized an additional organization which would, by progression, be called F or Fox. Since another company was not authorized, the organization became known as Fox Force, with a strength of 70-80 soldiers.

Fox was absorbed into E Co, as the HHC Company, the normal home of the recon platoon, was located apart from the battalion in the Division rear at Camp Enari. Even up to shortly before our time, Fox consisted of maybe 60 guys. By the summer of 1969 the strength had dwindled to around 25 to 30, the name stuck, and Fox Force became the battalion recon platoon. The name, strength and organization described here remained the same until the division returned home late in 1970.

Command of Fox Force has been one of the seminal experiences of my life. A command like this is the dream of every young infantry officer, particularly in a combat environment. Somehow I was blessed to be given this opportunity, and as a result became associated with some of the finest men I've ever known.

The guys in Fox were young and mostly draftees and had been thrown together into the unit as individual replacements. This was normal during Vietnam. Those units that initially deployed at the beginning of the war were sent to combat with a trained and cohesive organization that had been together for a while. Because the normal Vietnam tour length was 12 months, replacements were sent into the combat zone on an individual basis and the original units were kept in country and not rotated home until the end of hostilities.

This policy led to many problems both for the old guys and the new ones. The new guys were normally extremely apprehensive because they had to join a unit that was already combat experienced, and had already formed those cliques and bonds found in all combat units. It was tough to break into that kind of an atmosphere. The old guys were often reluctant to accept the new ones as they could be a threat because of their inexperience. Also, many of the old guys had lost friends to combat, disease, accident or normal rotation and were very reluctant to form new relationships.

By chance, the bulk of the men who I would command arrived in the unit almost at the same time, giving a cohort-like esprit a chance to develop. I joined them a couple of weeks later. These guys were FNG's together, taught by the experiences and leadership of the old guys who really wanted these new guys to learn quickly because of the unique environment in which they operated. Because of their inexperience, the new guys couldn't be counted on to do the right thing and thus could cause the wounding or death of the old guys who had their own bonds and their own brotherhood, and who were so close to going home. The FNG's had to survive the roughest and most dangerous rites of passage imaginable, they had to pass the test of being shot at and responding correctly; to both not risk their own lives and more importantly, protect the lives of their buddies.

Once in Fox, this collection of individuals, inexperienced and apprehensive, had jelled into the most effective and efficient field unit I have ever seen. I don't know how to explain the process, but we quickly became devoted to each other and extremely proficient in the art of small unit warfare in the jungle. Maybe it was the nature of the missions;

normally on our own as a unit of no more than 25 to 30 soldiers including two medics.

Fox normally operated deep in "Indian Country," at the very edge of normal communications capability or sometimes even beyond. In that environment those who could not adapt were quickly identified and transferred out, often at their own request. Those who remained became a select bunch, men who knew that their lives depended 100% on the actions of every other individual. The men of Fox were as good at their mission as any unit in Vietnam, probably better than most.

Over time the bonds among us grew, as did our capabilities as a fighting force. We moved though the thickest jungle extremely quietly; we depended on stealth for survival. This was a remarkable skill when you consider the average Fox soldier carried 110 pounds in rucksack and gear, and wore a steel pot as well. Every soldier was extremely careful about where each boot was placed, and moved overhanging or clinging brush out of the way as quietly as possible. In most cases speed was not essential, survival was. We had to see them before they saw us.

The one item of issue that we did not wear in the field was the "flak jacket". This was an armored vest, the forerunner of what our servicemen and women in the mid-East now wear. It was made of a material that would supposedly absorb shrapnel but was of little use against small arms fire. They were hot, heavy, cumbersome, and of extremely questionable efficiency, so none of the grunts of the Golden Dragons wore them. Every once in a while on the firebase we had to put them on when a visiting senior officer came around, for appearance sake only. Most guys, however, would grab them only at night when subjected to mortar or rocket attacks. We also sat on them in convoys or sometimes even wore them when in a vehicle. But most of the time they were totally useless.

This was the organization that I joined as Fox 6 (my rado call sign after I joined the unit) after a few weeks in country. "Six" became my nickname with these guys, and I still wear it proudly today. Many of my memories from this time are blurred; I can't remember clearly the sequence of some events or many of the details. But I clearly remember how amazing it felt to be accepted by this bunch of wild warriors.

Fox Force was a really hardcore type of unit. The guys were afforded all kinds of deference from the admin types on the firebase, and even other combat experienced grunts because of their reputation for craziness and the fact that they made contact with the enemy almost every time they left the firebase. When I joined the battalion at St. George, we sat astride one of the major NVA infiltration routes into the South from

Cambodia. As a consequence, the infantrymen of the Golden Dragons experienced much more combat than other units of the 4th Division that operated in other parts of the Central Highlands. Fox Force had more contacts, more enemy KIA, fewer friendly KIA than any other unit in the battalion. This was a healthy reputation to begin with.

Combat engenders all kinds of emotions, for some there is a real high, some feel an overpowering sense of aggression and anger that someone is trying to kill them or their buddies. However, underlying those adrenaline inspired emotional states is another – fear. Fear can be all pervasive and debilitating if the soldier gives into that feeling, but most learn to cope with it and use it to their advantage. As "Buck" Buckelew recounts when describing one of his first missions; *Day two, we were walking in high grass when a sniper fired at us. I hit the ground and would be there today if the order to continue had not been given. I must say that being shot at is a truly unique experience. Something deep inside you (that you have never felt before) takes hold of you – FEAR like you have never experienced, at least I had not. I think that it affects everyone differently – for me it was necessary to control this natural fear; to dominate it until the battle is finished. This got easier over time, but it was always with me.*

I don't know of anyone who didn't grapple with this emotion, starting on the flight to Vietnam. Every warrior wonders how he will react when the rounds come up range. I know that every time I gave the order to "saddle up" I had a tightness in my gut, not just for my own safety but for that of all of these incredible guys that I was responsible for. Most of us experienced some degree of at least apprehension every time we went into the jungle, for most of us fear was not a motivator when things got dicey, or if it was we dominated that feeling and controlled it, as Buck observed. For me, when the action was complete and the adrenaline began to drain I suffered some of the after effects of controlling my fear as demonstrated by occasional outward reactions like badly shaking hands. Fear was there, but it never ever dominated my actions or thoughts when in a firefight.

Many years later I learned some interesting statistics from my battalion commander. During that conflict, the benchmark for success was enemy body count. We did not conquer and hold terrain on a permanent basis, we would secure an area, maybe build a fire base to support operations, and then tear it down and move on to another location. There were no front lines as in other wars; consequently there were no safe rear areas either. Normally the division bases were fairly secure because of their size and the large number of soldiers assigned, but even here the grunt was not safe from mortar, rocket, artillery, or even ground fire and sapper attacks. There were few places where a soldier could really let his guard down.

Our mission was to find the enemy without being seen, but in the worst case we assumed the traditional one of the infantry; to close with and destroy the enemy by close combat. During the last 6 months of '69, reliable sources indicated that 1-14 Infantry probably had the highest kill ratio among all of the battalions in country. During that time the ratio for all free world forces was 3.54 to 1 – them versus us. The ratio for 1-14 was 68 to 1; if you add in the effects of our direct support artillery and attached units the ratio went to about 120 to 1.

To further add to the mystique of craziness that surrounded Fox, all the guys in the unit wore bright red scarves, even in the field when on combat operations. Talk about craziness! Wearing the scarf in the jungle was almost like a dare to the bad guys; "here I am, get me if you can". The scarf had to be earned, its wearer tested by a combat incident or two, until a scarf was given without ceremony or acclaim. That event was an acknowledgement of the wearer's proven ability to add to the effectiveness of, and protect the integrity and lives of the team. I was told that the enemy had a bounty on our scarves, $10,000 for any enemy soldier that could kill one of us and get hold of the scarf.

The scarf had been awarded to Fox before any of us arrived by a local Regional Force/ Popular Force Vietnamese platoon. These units were not part of the Vietnamese regular armed forces, but more like a local national guard-type militia that was organized and supported by the regular establishment, and that operated in the area from which it drew its soldiers. RF/PF units varied greatly in their effectiveness and discipline, some being very poor, others being very effective. The one in our area was exceptionally good and had a reputation for fierceness in combat.

Their platoon leader had been a lieutenant in a regular Vietnamese Army unit that had fought with the French against the Viet Mihn before the French defeat at Dien Bien Phu. He was rumored to have been wounded some twenty times over the years. Rumor also had it he seldom carried a weapon in the field, but rather was armed with an old swagger stick that he had been issued when fighting with the French, and a large knife. This platoon wore red scarves as their unit identifier, with the same bravado as they would later be worn by the recon men of the 1st of the 14th.

At some point before my arrival, the Vietnamese unit and Fox operated together on a dangerous mission, which resulted in a lot of heavy contact. The US guys fought with bravery and fierceness, supporting their Vietnamese comrades as they did each other. When this operation was over the Vietnamese awarded the Americans their red scarves as a valor award in recognition of their accomplishments, their bravery and their fighting spirit and skills. From that day on the scarves were proudly worn at all times by the men of Fox Force while in Vietnam, even during combat operations in the jungle. That tradition has been carried on until today; we wear our scarves when together and at other special times. Members have taken their scarves into surgery for Agent Orange related cancers, and have had them present in their hospital rooms as they recover, and all who have passed away since those days go to their graves wearing their scarves as well. When one of our number is in a difficult situation such as surgery, we coordinate a pre-determined time when his brothers across the country wear or hold their scarves and raise a toast of good luck to the one in need. The scarf has become a tangible symbol of the intangible emotions that bind us all together, just like my West Point class ring that bonds me to all of my classmates. It has become a symbol of almost magical or religious quality that is closely guarded by all of us who have earned the right to wear it; a very select few. The scarf is a mark of pride and association that is revered by our family members as well.

This then was Fox Force, the unit with which I would experience some of the most memorable incidents in my combat tour. Fox is a true family of which I am extremely proud and protective, a unit whose guys and families today are held together in an emotional bond that defies adequate description.

Command of Fox would teach me many lessons that I have carried through the rest of my life. One is the old adage that you can't tell a book by its cover. When I took over command and was introduced to all of the soldiers of the recon platoon, I made some hasty mental assessments about some of the guys who may not have fit my image of what a United States Army combat soldier should look and act like. Some gave me the impression that they might not be trustworthy in the field because they fit a stereotypical image of the American youth of the 1960's.

Fortunately for me we were sent on a mission shortly after I assumed command and before I could make what time would have proven to be some stupid decisions. Almost without exception I had been given command of some of the finest combat soldiers in Vietnam. I learned that the maybe questionable outward appearance of some of these guys was really just an outward manifestation of what made them so special. They did not conform to any conventional standard in a lot of ways because we were not a conventional unit. We operated in ways and on missions that most other units could not perform. These guys were unique.

I think that in Fox I really learned the art of small unit leadership. There are several different commander types, particularly in the junior officer and NCO ranks. There was the "hard-core" type of commander, aloof from his soldiers and unaffected by their daily life issues, concerns or problems; and there were also those who tried to command by being "one of the guys", those who were afraid to perform their difficult responsibility of command and tried to hide from that burden by acting as a peer buddy to his soldiers and thus not directly assuming the commander role. There was also the "John Wayne" commander whose sole objective was to earn hero medals for himself, often at the risk of the lives of his soldiers. The successful commander was one who evidenced sincere concern for the welfare of his soldiers, never asked them to do anything that he wouldn't do himself, developed a bond with his men but never one of over familiarity, and who unquestionably assumed responsibility for mission accomplishment while looking out for the welfare of his soldiers. Not afraid to make a decision that would put his soldiers in harm's way, but never, ever doing that needlessly or for personal gain; he always led from the front. I tried my best to follow this last model.

Fox was organized into three teams plus my Command Post (CP). Our team organization was different than that of a typical rifle platoon squad. All three teams were organized so that each was about equal in personnel strength and firepower. Each team had a two man M-60 machine gun team, a bloop (M79 grenade launcher), and a PRC 25 radio. The PRC 25 or "prick 25," or its improved version the PRC 77, was normally found only in platoon or company headquarters, not down at the squad level. But we needed the additional "commo" capability because of the stealth with which we were required to operate, and because often we did not have line-of-sight visibility of everyone's location at all times. The radios came equipped with both a short whip and a long antenna; the longer one providing a greater range of capability than the short one. The long ones were only used when we were stationary because they were too cumbersome for use while moving through thick jungle. Each team was normally composed of 6 to 8 guys.

In my CP I had two RTO's, one to carry the radio for my internal Fox communications, and one to carry the radio with which I communicated with everyone else. The CP also contained two medics and my platoon sergeant. I eventually sent two guys back to the rear to be trained as snipers and kept primary control over them although sometimes they moved with one of the teams rather than with my CP.

My RTO's, Charlie "Red" Siner and Al "Buck" Buckelew were two very special soldiers. The bad guys learned how to determine who our officers or senior NCO's were just by their actions. Another give-away was the proximity of a radio. The leaders, and their RTOs, were prime targets for quick elimination for obvious reasons. While we tried to camouflage our roles to some degree by not wearing rank on our uniforms and hiding the radios in the RTO's ruck sack, the antennas were a give-away. When in contact it was the RTO's duty to stay close to his commander in order to facilitate communication, they could not spread out and many times couldn't seek cover. Small unit leaders and their RTOs often had a very short life expectancy. Red, Buck and I were either extremely lucky or had incredible guardian angels as we escaped some pretty close combat without a scratch among us.

When we moved during the day it was almost always in a wedge formation; with one team ahead of my CP and the others out to each flank. My medics were generally with me but sometimes moved with one of the other teams. The point team provided the point man and slack man (#2 in the lead formation), and the flank teams provided flank and rear security. With my CP in the center I was able to move easily with my RTOs to any point in the formation if needed. We had a lot of firepower with an M60 up front and one on each flank.

We always moved as slowly and carefully as possible. We normally moved through vegetation, avoiding roads, trails and large open areas unless it was absolutely necessary to cross them. This sometimes occurred when there was thick vegetation or the terrain was filled with rice paddies. When in the open we were widely dispersed so that we covered as much area as possible with as little risk of multiple casualties from one explosive round as possible. There was never any unnecessary chatter, playing of transistor radios, or "smoking and joking" in the field. These guys could move through the thickest jungle with the renowned quiet attributed to the American Indian. Of particular importance, I never detected the use of marijuana by my guys in the field. That could dull alertness and put all of our lives at risk. And I can't personally attest to its use in the rear either, although there are certainly stories that only my guys could tell!

One admirable result of the ability to move quietly was that we were never ambushed. Conversely, we were successful because we always caught the bad guys by surprise. The Fox guys reacted almost instinctively to sighting of the bad guys or to actual contact. At night we tried to be equally as quiet and stealthy. We seldom moved into a night laager position until it was almost dark. When we went to ground we never dug in because of the noise that would generate. We fortified our positions as best we could by moving fallen trees, rocks and other items around to give us cover and concealment. Also, we always tried to set up for the night in thick vegetation so that we would have a chance to hear any enemy activity before they could find us. I normally had each team put out a two or three man listening post (LP) at night at a site on a likely enemy avenue of approach. The mission of an LP was to provide early warning of enemy movement or activity potentially directed against us in their team's sector. The LP's were normally placed in locations where they had a good field of view or close to trails so they could monitor enemy activity. I never had to worry about any of my guys falling asleep while on a guard shift. Many times we were also directed by our battalion HQ's to put out ambushes. Design and implementation of a successful ambush was a unique skill in its own right. Sometimes the whole platoon would set up an ambush; sometimes an entire team would perform the function. A safe ambush set-up required at least a team to provide enough guys to provide security as well as initiate contact on any enemy force that came into the ambush kill zone.

At night we set up in as circular a position as we could, with the teams on the line and my CP somewhere in the middle or as close as possible to the most likely enemy's avenue of approach. My two RTO's were close at hand, my platoon sergeant normally on another part of the perimeter and my medics spread on the line as well. We used two or three man positions and always had at least one man awake in each position at all times. We would have everyone awake an hour or two before dawn. That was a popular time for the bad guys to strike, they figured that the US unit's guard would be down after a quiet night and everyone would be preparing coffee and food, if not still asleep.

If we were in a secure enough area, and definitely if at all possible during the monsoon season, we tied up "poncho hooches" to sleep under. We spread our ponchos out by tying them to vegetation so that they were just far enough off the ground to be able crawl under for protection from the elements. These were always single man hooches, we tried to spread out as much as possible at night like we did during the day.

Probably the most important factor in our success was the quality of my NCO chain of command. Every soldier was absolutely superb at what he did, but the NCOs, including my platoon Sergeant Jimmy Harris, and team leaders Robin Sneeden, Danny Williams and Ron Shewell, were the backbone of the organization and excelled in their responsibilities. This has been the case throughout the history of the US Army; it's an attribute that has set us apart from all other armies in the world with the possible exception of the Brits. It was extremely apparent to me in Fox. My guys were phenomenal, I never doubted that they would and could carry out all instructions in the most professional of ways, dedicated to mission accomplishment but mindful of protecting their soldiers' lives as well. I also knew that if anything happened to me my guys would be well taken care of by their sergeants.

Jimmy Harris, was a case in point. He received his E5 stripes by attending a six-month NCO academy at Fort Benning. A school known somewhat derisively as "Shake and Bake" school; it made NCO's out of inexperienced new soldiers. He then went on to airborne and ranger schools, being promoted to E6 after award of his Ranger Tab and less than a year in the Army. His first real assignment was Vietnam and Fox Force. He was so good that he was the acting platoon leader before I arrived. He and I just clicked; it was a natural pairing of personalities that provided the leadership core of Fox. I searched for him countless times between 1970 and 2000; being finally reunited with this superb soldier and man was one of the happiest moments in my life. He is truly my brother.

My team leaders were either promoted up through the ranks in Vietnam, or in one case I had another graduate of the "shake and bake" system. These great guys, most of them draftees, served in the greatest traditions of the US Army and its NCO Corps.

At one point, before my arrival, Buck had been selected as the battalion's soldier of the month because he was a college graduate. This was a stateside morale motivator that was carried over into the combat zone, at least for a while. Buck was told that he would have to return to Camp Enari, to compete at the brigade and finally division level. If he won it all, he'd be able to go home for a week.

That same day I rode the supply truck back to division and was met by the Top Sergeant (First Sergeant). *He gave me a manual to study and asked for my sizes as I would need a new starched uniform and polished boots. To win this honor one needed to answer a barrage of questions* (from a board of senior NCO's) *about one's MOS and the weapons used; and one had to look great, with polished boots and starched uniform. I beat out some soldiers for Brigade honors and then came in second for division honors but was awarded a three day in-country R&R trip. It was pretty strange to be given an R&R opportunity after being in the field for less than one month; but I'm in the Army now and I have to go with the flow.* After his R&R, which is another story that he wouldn't share, he returned to the battalion after taking a little sight-seeing side trip for a day to see how the Navy lived. *My only regret was that I had been required to polish my boots and now they were like new. Any self-respecting Vietnam combat infantryman wanted his boots to be scuffed and brown in color (to match the local soil) which was a clear marker of experience and time in country.*

Buck was a prime example of the quality of the men of Fox. They stood head and shoulders above everyone else in the battalion.

When we left the firebase we were normally equipped to spend five or six days without resupply. The last thing you wanted if you were trying to stay undetected was a helicopter flying into your position. If neccessary, we could live off of the land, there were normally villages available where we could find food. In the central highlands water was seldom an issue, there was an abundance of streams and rice paddies. At one point the battalion commander wanted to make a point that his troops were too laden down to be effective in the heat and humidity of the jungle. So he invited the brigade commander to come to St. George where he could prove his point.

The battalion commander selected several men from Fox as we were preparing to depart on a mission, and had each man weigh his gear on a set of scales. While the load totals varied somewhat the average weight was 110 pounds. Most of that was made up of ammo, food, and water, there were very few extras. Some guys carried toilet articles beyond a toothbrush; some carried a favorite book or special family mementoes.

One critical area of resupply was the need for clean and dry clothes. This was particularly critical during the monsoon season, a period of almost constant rain. For a while we seemed as a battalion to be following the monsoon across the country, so we stayed wet. Mid-September to mid-October was a really wet time period. Little sores or scratches would fester and become infected and swollen because they stayed damp. Boots and uniforms would literally begin to rot. It was not unusual for soldiers in Vietnam to come down with trench foot as in WWI, the skin and flesh of your foot would literally rot off. One Fox soldier, Russ Simpson, suffered such a severe case of trench foot that he could no longer wear combat boots and was reassigned to the 106mm recoilless rifle crew on the firebase. Several pairs of clean and dry socks were more important than clean trousers or shirts.

Another key factor that made us what we were was our commander and mentor, Lieutenant Colonel Victor M. Robertson Jr, the DRAGON. LTC Robertson was one of those unique personalities and individuals who come into your life only on rare occasions, and we were blessed by such an occurrence. Vic was every inch the southern gentleman, and every inch the professional soldier. Dragon had an air of confidence and professionalism. And like every successful combat commander, the Dragon cared deeply for his men. I think he took a special liking to us because he knew that he could count on us to do what he needed. He used us as a real recon element, not just another small maneuver unit.

Dragon was always at the wire to give us "God speed" when we left on a mission, and if at all possible he was there to meet us when we came back. He did special things for us like making sure we were never short-changed on beer, and from time to time had commandeered enough chicken or steak so we could have a good old American cookout.

Dragon was a special commander and is a very special man. He frequently sent us out on hairy missions, but always took care of us when we returned. In the last few years, after we re-established contact with him, he has never missed a reunion, nor did his bride Lois until her untimely death. I sometimes look around at reunions, seeing Dragon, a goodly number of my guys, their wives, girlfriends and kids. And now we have grandkids as well. It is my heartfelt prayer that after all of us Fox guys are gone, that our families will still get together once in a while to appreciate each other and to think of us.

This was Fox Force, who we were and how we operated, and what we have become. Little did we realize that the bonds that were forming during 1969 would be strong enough, and important enough to each of us, that would foster the family camaraderie that we were to enjoy thirty years later when we first started having reunions in 2000. The initial reunion was held with seven or eight of us attending, plus a couple of the families. It was a weekend of crying like I've never before experienced. The emotions engendered by finally seeing each other again after 30 years are indescribable. The family members were also caught up in the emotions of seeing their husband/father cry, maybe for the first time, and they too were deeply affected. We had an admin meeting beforehand and one of the wives was detailed to man the phone to the front desk to ensure that we had enough Kleenex! At that initial get-together we agreed to meet every other year, but when that time finally arrived we knew that a two-year gap was just too long. We then decided to do it yearly. In addition, over time we have found reasons for guys-only get-togethers between the scheduled reunions like an annual pheasant hunt in Nebraska and a Spring fishing trip to Florida.

While we were proud of our reputation within the battalion, and very proud and protective of our red scarves, there was no way that we could realize just how much this association would become a center of our lives in the future. This Fox family now incorporates our wives, children and grandchildren, the wives and families of guys we've lost since our return, and most certainly the wonderful people of Humphry,

Nebraska and the surrounding area. Our wives talk frequently, and the older kids sometimes get together on their own. It is a truly wondrous thing.

As I talk with my guys now, I think that I was accepted into their brotherhood and as their leader because I sought their counsel and advice on almost all issues, but in the end always made the final decision myself and accepted 100% responsibility. The nature of our missions made that an almost required prerequisite for successful command. I was not as good a point man as my seasoned grunts. Had I tried to assume that responsibility I would have put my unit's safety in jeopardy, and would have placed myself in the worst possible position to exercise control over combat operations. But I knew that I could do the job if I had to, and I think that gave me the confidence to trust others in this most dangerous of tasks. Before we left on a mission I always tried to talk with my platoon sergeant and team leaders to get their input on how we needed to accomplish our objectives. If required I never hesitated to listen to any soldier who had an opinion, and many times found them to be wiser than I. But there was no doubt in anyone's mind that I was the one responsible for whatever did or didn't happen, or that I had the best interests of my soldiers always in my mind.

Now, at this time of life, I have more time to remember, and to realize how lucky I am to have commanded a unit like Fox Force, and to have those incredible guys and their families as a permanent part of my family. It is normal, I think, for all of us to wonder at one time why we were placed on this earth, and what value did we bring to our surroundings. I now think that my destiny was to command Fox Force, and I learned at the end of our first reunion that I had accomplished my life's mission during that time in SE Asia. As I was leaving Stag's back yard to go to the airport to fly back to Japan, one of the wives came up to me with tears in her eyes, gave me a huge hug, and whispered in my ear "Lieutenant Hedley, thank you for bringing my husband home."

DUTY! HONOR! COUNTRY!

8 - A NEW EXPERIENCE

The month of September, my first in Fox, was a busy and eventful time for Fox. The battalion duty logs for this time period reflect a lot of activity. We spent the 3rd at St. George and most of the 4th. After I had met and talked with all of the guys to include my team leaders and two RTO's we moved out of St George about 3 PM to go to the Plei Do Lim area of operations.

That night the battalion director of operations, S3, sent to Brigade a detailed summary of enemy activity in our area since the end of July. Enemy units had been sighted almost every day in groups of four or five up to a platoon sized unit of about 45. Most of the movement appeared to be going west to east, or from Cambodia. The sightings included VC, Main force VC and NVA, many equipped with new equipment and weapons. The general mission of these enemy forces appeared to be the transport of food, equipment and medical supplies to establish caches along streams and rivers.

The NVA and VC units appear to have had support from all of the villages in our area who supplied early warning of our movements, guides to these enemy units, and food supplies. The NVA, in particular, appear to be very relaxed as they moved across the countryside, as they often were seen to have their weapons at sling arms and not at a ready position. The battalion suspects that the NVA are from the K-1 and K-2 battalions of the 95B NVA Regiment. We also suspect that the H-15 Main Force VC Battalion has moved into our area of operations. The Majority of enemy soldiers whose packs have been captured appear to have been in South Vietnam since 1964 and therefore should be well trained and experienced.

Because of this information the 1st of the 14th was going to conduct extensive Reconnaissance in Force (RIF) operations throughout our area of operations. A and C companies moved into the field with some platoons setting up blocking positions along water features while others conducted RIF's and cordon and search operations. Each company was to be accompanied by a scout dog team. Fox was to conduct RIF operations to the SE of Plei Do Lim in concert with RF/PF units.

On the 5th another part of Fox, the Rat Patrol, left St. George en route to Dragon Mountain. En route they were fired on by two .30 caliber machine guns and one .51 caliber on an American ¾ Ton truck on the highway. They returned fire with their M60 machine guns and proceeded on to Dragon Mountain. The 60's weren't much of a match for the far heavier .51 caliber of the NVA. The bulk of Recon spent the night in the field near Plei Do Lim while putting out two ambushes.

On the 6th the ambushes closed on the night laager at around 0900 and the platoon continued our RIF operation. We received sniper fire around noontime but nothing further developed. That night we again laagered in the Plei Do Lim area and sent out two ambushes. The following day we returned to St. George at 1500 for a short stand down.

On the 8th we were alerted that we would depart on the 9th for a three day RIF to the north of St. George. We returned to the firebase at 0650 on the 11th and practiced night movement techniques that night beginning around 2100.

On the 11th D Company had two soldiers killed by a tiger.

On the 12th a liaison team from CONARC (Continental Army Command, responsible for equipping and training the force) visited to check up on the battalion's use of our only night vision equipment; the Starlight Scopes. These scopes collected ambient light that would enable us to see more clearly at night. Heat sources showed up as much brighter green. These scopes were pretty large and unwieldy and thus didn't have much use in the field, particularly in triple canopy jungle although they were of some use on the firebase. We left St. George at 1730 that day on another RIF operation.

On the 13th of September we left a night laager position early in the morning and continued on our mission. Evidently there had been some enemy activity in our area as we left a stay-behind element when we left the night's position to see if we could catch any enemy that might be following us.

At 1115 one individual wearing green fatigues, a soft cap and carrying an M-16 entered the area, spotted the stay-behind, and opened fire. I remember hearing the fire; we were probably a couple of hundred or so meters away. With the sound of contact we reversed course and rushed back to the stay-behind's position. I remember an incredible sense of urgency as we threw ourselves on exceptionally thick secondary growth and bamboo in an effort to break a trail. This was one of those moments when my guys were engaged with the enemy and the rest of us needed to get back to them immediately. At that time I don't think we knew the size of the enemy force; it was only natural to think the worst, my guys were being engaged by a large number of bad guys. We were not too concerned about security due to the thick vegetation as we concentrated on rotating guys up front to break brush as others tired out. When we linked up and regrouped we learned that there had been one enemy soldier who had fled to the southeast. We carefully followed in the same direction and came upon a small village with one particular young man suffering from what appeared to be muscle cramps and still breathing hard. In a hooch we found a green fatigue uniform and hat but no weapon. We detained him and searched the area hoping to find the M16. A and C companies were also finding evidence of a strong enemy presence in the same general area. Both units found bunker complexes containing an assortment of NVA gear and evidence that the complexes had been recently used.

On the 14th C Company heard growls believed to be from a tiger.

On the 15th of September the battalion received an order from the Commanding General. Any enemy caves or cave complexes were to be painted so as to be visible from the air. Looking back, I'm not sure what that meant. How do you paint a cave? That afternoon was eventful. At about 1430 we engaged two bad guys about 600 meters away; they fled to the north. Almost immediately thereafter we engaged two more who also fled north. Two more followed and while they were fleeing north, we dropped them. While we were sweeping the area after the contact we found an assortment of US and Chinese equipment as well as some bags of rice. We also found several fighting positions that looked as though they had been recently used. A further search discovered two heavy blood trails with drag marks; we claimed two enemy KIA. That night after setting up a night laager we received about 20 rounds of incoming M16 fire with no casualties. Also that night fire base Weigt Davis, site of our 4.2 inch mortar platoon, received incoming mortar and small arms fire.

The next day we returned to St. George for a 24-hour stand down before being attached to D Company for another operation to the northeast of St. George. On this day B Company lost a soldier while trying to cross a one-log bridge. He slipped and fell off and the weight of his gear took him under. Rivers were running deep and fast because of the monsoon season. Sometime during this period we found tiger tracks inside our perimeter. Evidently the cat walked across our position without being detected and without bothering anyone.

On the 18th we were back in the field and conducting a recon mission. At around 1730 we engaged four NVA wearing black berets, black clothing and carrying AK47s about 150 meters to our southwest.

After the contact we swept the area finding blood trails and drag marks. Not finding the enemy we moved into a night laager about dusk. The next day we were to recon the Ia Agun River searching draws and ravines in the area for an enemy force reported to be in that area. At about the same time A Company engaged a sizable enemy force not too far from us. At the end of the contact they claimed seven enemy KIA and four WIA. A sweep of the area showed a lot of blood and heavy blood trials. Our recon the next day was to find the force engaged by A Company. We didn't find anything and returned to St. George on the 19th.

On the evening of the 20th, battalion reported to brigade that we had conducted classes on night movement, actions under flares, and crossing danger areas earlier in the month. After the classes half of the platoon conducted night missions, the other half was to do the same the next evening. The concept of the operation was that we would recon likely sites for night ambushes from a distance during the day and then move in after dark. If no results in a given period of time we'd move in the darkness to another ambush site. We ran a night mission in the vicinity of Plei De Lim area on 2-5 September and again in the northwest portion of the battalion area of operations (AO) on the 12th through the 15th. I remember moving during night operations as being extremely high stress. We had not been trained to fight at night as a general rule.

The decision to practice night movement was an effort to deny the enemy free movement during the hours of darkness. There was a common saying among grunts in Vietnam, "The night belongs to Charlie." They were generally more familiar with the terrain, particularly in the case of Viet Cong units. They could move a lot more freely and used trails or roads instead of through the brush, which was a lot noisier and more difficult. Also, unlike today's modern military, our only night vision capability was our eyes. US troops were reluctant to move at night. While Ranger School taught the basics, few soldiers had the opportunity to attend that course. We did do some night ops in the Infantry Officers Basic course to include a night land navigation course, and did practice the basics at the Jungle Warfare School in Panama, which I attended en route to Vietnam.

The nights in Vietnam were scary enough. It was difficult to move in darkness except on trails due to the thickness of the secondary growth in the jungles and filled rice paddies in the lowlands. At night it was imperative all effort be made to move silently, difficult to do in the terrain and vegetation, particularly when wearing a steel pot, which Dragon 6 insisted that we wear, instead of a soft patrol cap. I would have much preferred the full-brimmed "boonie hats." They were a lot quieter and presented a more irregular outline than the standard steel pot, making it more difficult for the enemy to find us.

The major factor that made any attempt at night movement dangerous and almost impossible to do quietly was the terrain and vegetation. It's tough to move through triple canopy secondary growth when you can't see where you're going. It's impossible to move quietly. In addition, given that no light from the moon could get to the jungle floor, it was impossible to see holes or ravines before you fell into them. That being the case the only way to move effectively in the darkness was to use the trail network. And as soon as the gooks figured out what we were doing we'd be the target of ambushs. I was really glad when the mandatory training came to an end.

We moved back into St. George on the 20th for a stand down for care and cleaning of equipment and an inspection of our feet by the surgeon.

On the 27th Will was killed at St. George.

DUTY! HONOR! COUNTRY!

9 – FRIENDLY FIRE

The 27th of September, 1969, is a day that will haunt my memory for the rest of my life. On that day I lost one of my soldiers, Specialist 4 Will De Long, to friendly fire, the result of horsing around with weapons on the firebase. A commander is taught from his earliest training that casualties are an expected result of war, particularly for the infantry. Never easy to accept, deaths in action, while difficult and sad, are understandable if they are caused by enemy action and anything other than bad command decisions. But to lose someone in your outfit, one of your soldiers whose life is entrusted to you as the CO, to a stupid mistake can never be accepted or rationalized…ever. This is a commander's greatest fear, to lose a life to an accident; I've lost two, one in a combat environment and one in a stateside training environment. I believe the memories of those two soldiers, whose lives were cut short due to tragic incidents, will haunt me until the day I die.

Will was only 19 years old and from Enon, Ohio. His tour in Vietnam started about the same time as mine did, in June of '69. Will was a happy and carefree young soldier, known for the khaki beret he frequently wore. He was married and the father of two sons. Will was well liked by the other guys and was particularly fond of our platoon mascot, the boy monkey named Sue, those two were never far apart.

I had taken command of Fox in early September and had been on several missions by the end of the month. The Fox soldiers were superb in the field, however I had noted we sent a lot of bullets down range in a firefight without the expected results. There were several possible causes for that anomaly, probably the most likely was we could fire on "Rock & Roll" or fully automatic. When in contact, with their rounds flying around you, the first instinct is to put your selector switch on "automatic" and send as many return rounds down range as quickly as possible; in that mode the weapon will fire for as long as you pull the trigger; a 20 round magazine could be emptied in a matter of seconds. Needless to say, aiming carefully does not always accompany this action.

I had been troubled by this observation and decided that we would do some marksmanship refresher at the earliest opportunity. I talked this over with my platoon sergeant, Jimmy Harris, and we decided since we were on a short stand down, we'd conduct some training on the morning of the 27th of September before it got too hot. Training would be mandatory for everyone and would be conducted using each soldier's assigned weapons; machine gunners with their M60's, bloop guys with their M79's, and riflemen with their M16's.

Since M60 gunners also carried the Model 1911 .45 caliber pistol as a personal sidearm; they would fire with those weapons as well. We talked about the range set-up, safety, and ammunition control as well and were ready for the big day. The practice would be outside the wire in the open area at one end of the field that was our landing pad.

The firing went well on the 27th. We stressed taking single, well-aimed shots as well as firing aimed short bursts of three or four rounds. After a couple of hours and burning up a lot of ammo we felt we accomplished the objective, getting the guys to pay more attention to aiming rather than spraying, and ended the training. We cleared all of the weapons and I left. Jimmy stayed behind and did a final "no brass, no ammo" check as the guys came back through the wire. All in all I thought it was a good morning.

While in the TOC, discussing the next day'smission I was told there had been a horrific accident in my area, that one of my soldiers, Will De Long, had been shot while playing "fast draw" with a buddy. The other guy's weapon evidently had a round in the chamber, the trigger was pulled, and Will took a round to the chest.

I don't have a clear memory of time after that; I quickly went down to my area and learned the entire story. I believe Will was still on the ground and he'd already been turned over to the medics who tried to revive him. I do remember being sick to my stomach. What had I done wrong? How could I have fucked up to the point that one of my soldiers had been killed? I evidently hadn't done my job correctly ensuring the weapons had been properly cleared? I was sick in my heart as well; I just couldn't comprehend that this had actually happened to one of my guys.

I honestly don't have any clear detailed memories of events after that. I do know that I wound up at Camp Enari, the Division base camp, shortly thereafter to undergo an Article 32 Investigation. The purpose of the hearing was to determine if there was any dereliction of duty on my part that would warrant a court martial. This process is very similar to a civilian grand jury hearing, I testified in front of a board of officers about what had happened and answered their questions. I believe I had a JAG lawyer and the board was made up of the Staff Judge Advocate and several other combat experienced officers. I think they also called in other witnesses but I don't remember that as a fact.

I don't remember how long I stayed in Enari, I do know I was asked a lot of detailed questions about the conduct of the range, safety provisions in place, and who was responsible for any number of events that occur when conducting a live fire range. The whole event is like a bad dream to me.

I must have satisfied everyone with the answers to their questions and the description of our safety procedures. I remember I was finally told to wait outside of the room while the board discussed the event and my answers, and came to a conclusion about my culpability. I don't know how long I sat there, all I could think of was that no matter what the official determination turned out to be, I was still, and would always be, responsible for the death of one of my soldiers.

I was called back into the hearing room and reported to the President of the Board of Officers. I was left standing at attention while the President prepared to read the Board's finding. I remember being very apprehensive and nervous, my palms were exceedingly sweaty as was my face; my knees were shaking as if I had just finished a long forced ruck march. I tried to prepare myself for the decision that the information presented warranted a court-martial for dereliction of duty. I knew if convicted my short military career would be over and I would probably do some jail time. I just stared at a spot on the wall behind the President's head.

The President addressed me, told me that after careful consideration of all facts presented, that Jimmy and I had been cleared of any wrongdoing. I was told they had determined that the accident could not have been prevented given conditions on a forward firebase, that all reasonable safety measures had been in place for the range firing and the clearing of weapons outside of the wire, and that the death of Will was an unfortunate tragedy. I was free to return to my unit.

I have no memory of returning to St. George or of my first interaction with the Fox guys. I don't even remember the name of the soldier who had pulled the trigger or what happened to him. I'm sure we had him transferred out of the unit as quickly as possible and I hope I recommended he be seen by appropriate medical personnel. I'm sure he must have been a total mental wreck; I can't even imagine what it must be like to kill your buddy because of horseplay. I was to lose a couple more soldiers wounded due to enemy fire but this was during a combat action and thus explainable and a little easier to understand.

I will never reconcile Will's death in my mind, and will carry guilt about that incident with me until the day I die. While Jimmy Harris also carries a huge burden as well, the ultimate responsibility is mine as the unit commander. Even writing about it now is making me uneasy and unsettled.

Around 2006 we had a Fox reunion here at our house in North Carolina. Several of Will's family decided to come because they wanted to get to know the guys he had served with. His Mom, sister, niece and son, among others, came here for about three or four days. When I learned they wanted to come I really became uncomfortable and apprehensive, not because I didn't want them here, but because I didn't know how they would react to meeting me or how I would react to them; how could I face them, how could I comfort a grieving family when I was responsible for Will's death? I was really nervous about meeting Will's mother, how would she react to meeting the one person most responsible for her son's death? I was amazed at what actually happened. The whole family was most gracious, and told us they didn't blame any of us for Will's death, that it had been a horrible accident but that we didn't need to carry any guilt. What incredibly wonderful people. Will's sister, Paula, has become a faithful attendee at all of our functions, whether reunions or funerals, and a dear friend. She's a wonderful woman who has really taken Fox to her heart. I did learn on this occasion that she never received the letter I wrote to her after Will's death. She must have thought no one cared about Will or his family.

Several years after that reunion I made a trip to Enon to spend some time with Will's Mother and family. I will never understand how they could have been so kind to me, so open and loving. Never once have I heard a cross or angry word from any of them. Given my responsibility for Will's death I can't understand this at all. Once again I'm truly blessed to be associated with such incredible people. Amber, Paula's daughter, has also been gracious and loving. This kind of warmth and caring is certainly not what I had expected from Will's family.

I will never reconcile myself to having no responsibility for Will's death. As the commander I was responsible for everything that happened in Fox, good or bad. To this day I cannot look at pictures of Will without a great sadness and guilt enveloping me; I'm sure that I will carry these feelings to my grave. Because of my shortcomings Will would never enjoy his own family and watch his kids grow up. He would not grow old with the rest of us. He never had the joy of reuniting with everyone and enjoying our reunions. He never saw his mother or siblings, to say nothing of his wife and kids again and never met his niece. Had I just done something different he might have lived; had I been at the wire helping to clear weapons as everyone came in he might have lived; had I been in the Fox area I would have been able to stop the horseplay and he would have lived. How do I ever come to terms with this? What kind of commander was I? We remained on St. George after the terrible accident for a couple of days to give everyone a chance to come to grips with what had happened; it was a tough time.

DUTY! HONOR! COUNTRY!

10 – THE SOUND OF MUSIC

On the 28th we conducted some review classes on reconnaissance and scouting techniques.

On the 29th we moved out by vehicle to link up with an RF/PF platoon from Phu Nhon to move into a new AO and conduct a reconnaissance in force to the south, looking for any indications that there were NVA or VC in the area. We continued with the RIF on the 30th and 1st and 2nd of October without any significant findings.

On the 3rd we returned to St George at about 1420 for a 24-hour stand down for maintenance and cleaning of weapons (and bodies). We were deployed again on the 4th by combat assault for a three day operation to find a VC platoon supposedly located in a seven grid square area.

The 5th of October was a busy day for 1-14 Infantry. At about 1000 we found a campsite with three fire sites and an NVA pack that contained a tarp and a small cooking pot. At 1230 we picked up one detainee in a khaki shirt and loincloth. National police with us identified the individual as being on a black list so we evac'ed him to St. George and from there he went to LZ Oasis. Around 1400 we engaged four individuals wearing loin clothes and green fatigue shirts and carrying AK 47s at a distance of about 70 meters. They saw us and ran. That same afternoon an RF platoon working in the same general area engaged a force of four or five individuals while C Company engaged a platoon sized element in a night ambush site at about 1900.

The next day we were to continue a recon in force to the west of St George. Around 1030 on the 6th we found a VC campsite with 20 sleeping positions, some rice and half eaten watermelon. It appeared to have been used in the past two or three days. As we swept the area we found a second site for about 50 VC that had been used in the same general time frame.

A little after 1300 we made contact with a squad sized VC unit at about 50 meters away who fled to the west after we initiated contact, leaving behind one AK-47. They were dressed in black Motangnard loincloths and all carrying AK-47s. I called for artillery and gunships to fire on the direction of escape. After the fire support we swept the area and found two pair of sandals, and two heavy blood trails with drag marks. As we continued to search the area, at about 1530, we found a US pistol belt, a loaded AK magazine, a US grenade and a VC poncho. Given the large amount of blood around the two drag marks we claimed two more enemy KIA's. That night we moved to an area close to a village to conduct a cordon and search the next morning for suspected VC cadre.

The next day we conducted the cordon and searched looking for evidence that the gooks had been in the area. We did pick up three suspicious looking detainees and evac'ed them to the rear, even though everyone in the village claimed that there had been no VC presence in the area for the last 10 days. On the 8th we once again returned to St. George for a 24-hour stand down.

Buck remembered one of our missions:

We were between missions at St. George when Six announced to us late in the afternoon that we had to "saddle up" as we were being helicoptered to help a LRRP (Long Range Reconnaissance Patrol normally consisting of 4 soldiers) *team that was surrounded.*

It was almost dark when we landed about one or two clicks from where we believed the LRRP's to be.
We humped toward them but it was a challenge to find them as they did not want to give their position away with smoke. It was now dark so we could only follow our compass and hope the LRRPs knew their own position accurately.

Finally we linked up without any contact with the NVA and quickly created a larger circle around them. They were the happiest four guys I ever met. We heard movement all night, but the NVA did not attack.

Afterward we surmised that there must have been at most a dozen NVA and when our much larger unit arrived they decided to keep an eye on us but not to risk elimination by attacking us.

We were airlifted out the next morning without incident.

This was just another normal mission for the men of Fox.

From the 10th to the 13th we recon'ed a large area in the Plei Do Lim AO looking for another reported VC platoon. On the morning of the 11th we engaged a squad sized element of VC with small arms fire and gunships. With no other activity or sightings in the area we returned to St. George in the morning of the 13th for another short stand-down.

The 15th found us in the jungles again, leaving St. George about 1400 by combat assault. Almost immediately we found a fresh campsite for a platoon sized element. The next two days we conducted three different village searches picking up a total of 13 detainees while conducting numerous Medical Civil Action Program (MEDCAPs) in all three villages. This program was designed to provide medical assistance and to improve the medical care for the villages. We devoted our organic medics to take care of the local villagers. They did an incredible job taking care of cuts, broken or sprained limbs, and treating all kinds of diseases. I think that at one time they even delivered a baby. Locals with really serious medical problems were airlifted back to one of our hospitals. I'm sure that the helicopter ride must have been a terrifying experience for these primitive people. These operations were done in conjunction with the 38th Intel Platoon out of Phu Nhon. On the 18th we returned to St. George for about four days.

On the 22nd of October we departed to secure a large rice cache. A Ranger team was engaged in a heavy firefight in the afternoon and was finally extracted at about 1500 with their birds taking fire as they left the pickup zone. At 1700 we were airlifted to an area close to the firefight site and were to recon north along a stream the next day. That night, on the 23rd, we heard Vietnamese voices about 200 meters from our night laager. I called in artillery for about 20 minutes on the suspected enemy location and planned to sweep the area in the morning. We completed our sweep at about 0930 with negative results. On the 24th we returned to St. George at about 1630. The next day we remained at St. George and received instruction on route reconnaissance as we prepared to move to An Khe. B, C, and D Companies were also preparing for a move to An Khe which was planned for the 26th.

On the 25th the battalion received word that the move to An Khe had been delayed due to heavy enemy activity in the Plei Me Rong area. The move wouldn't occur until the 28th if at all. At 1600 we left St. George to go back to the Special Forces compound at Plei Do Lim. This time we were to move into the compound to reinforce the US team as they had received Intel that they were to be the target of a large NVA ground assault in the next night or so.

The US team house was in the middle of two defensive rings. The one next to the US team was manned by trusted indigenous personnel, probably Montagnards or Hmong (a Vietnamese minority of Chinese decent), as well as the SF guys. The outer defensive ring was manned by other local troops, many of whom had their families with them. Each defensive ring had its own concertina wire fences around it. The SF team had its own defensive positions surrounding the team house which had been dug in and acted as the tactical command post, bunk house and mess hall as well. There were several other smaller hooches as I remember as well as several conex containers in the central position.

I wasn't real happy about moving my guys into the bull's eye on the compound, but my orders were to reinforce the SF guys so I had no choice. When we got off the birds we were met by one of the team members who guided us through the wire fences into the central American position. There I met the team leader, a captain.

What transpired immediately after we met was unbelievable. We were told that we'd be welcome to stay in the team house for the evening and join them for a meal unless we were attacked. Then the captain issued an order that I found to be incomprehensible, we had to lock all of our weapons in a conex container a ways away from the team house. I couldn't believe the stupidity of this guy; here we were to reinforce him in the event of a ground attack but we were not allowed to keep our weapons . . . unbelievable.

I protested the order as strongly as I possibly could but the captain was adamant; our weapons were to be locked in a conex. We had no choice so I told my guys to secure their weapons as directed by the team chief. We had a meal, and then settled down in the team house to watch the nightly movie, tonight was to be "The Sound of Music". We were getting comfortable and were about half way through the movie when all hell broke loose outside. We could hear the "crump" of incoming mortar rounds and the sound of automatic weapons. We scrambled for our weapons as we hurried outside and then realized we didn't have any. As my guys ran to some bunker positions I looked for some bolt cutters so that we could break into the conex and retrieve our weapons. We grabbed the cutters and Buck, Stag, Jimmy and I low crawled over to the conex, finally gained access, and carried weapons out to the rest of the guys. Fortunately no ground attack materialized but we received 25-30 rounds of 82mm mortars, a couple landing close by. It was an experience to low crawl through incoming mortars!

We employed gunships and had them expend in the area where we suspected the tubes had been set up and prepared to sweep the area the next morning. There were no friendly casualties as a result of this attack. Later that night three VC platoons were observed moving south.

At 0800 the next morning, the 26th, we left Plei Do Lim and moved south. I told the camp commander that we wouldn't enter his position again no matter what happened. If he was attacked we'd support him as best we could from outside the wire; I was not going to have my guys lock up their weapons again. As we swept the area outside of the compound we found two 60mm mortar canisters and at least one mortar position used by the VC the previous night. The battalion ops center had one company on alert to head for the SF compound if required. Buck again recounts:

The next night Six, Stag, Jimmy and I (there may have been a few other volunteers) crawled out after dark and set up about a click from the camp with the goal of finding the mortar team, but they had moved to the other side of the camp.

It was much later that I learned that the weekend we spent with that group of Special Forces, was the weekend of Woodstock back in the States. All things considered, a rock concert would have been more fun to attend rather than a mortar attack.

Our move to An Khe was deferred again due to heavy enemy activity in Pleiku and Kontum Provinces. Battalion was considering moving one of our companies into Weit Davis due to the increased enemy activity.

That afternoon at 1700 B Company made contact with five NVA in green fatigues at a distance of about 25 meters. They employed our 4.2 mortars at Weit Davis. Sweeping the area afterwards they found a rucksack covered with blood, one body, an AK 47 with two magazines and miscellaneous personal equipment. They also found a blood trail heading southeast and followed it for about 200 meters until it got dark. Based on the amount of blood they claimed a second enemy KIA.

We laagered for the night and were ordered to return to Plei Do Lim early the next morning (the 27th) for pick up at 0800 to return to St. George and prepare for the move to An Khe. The rifle companies were making similar preparations as they continued to man their defensive positions. Fox was given a 24-hour stand down and then we were informed we would move back to recon the area around the Plei Me contact. Once again the battalion move to An Khe had been delayed.

Also on this day battalion headquarters received the following warning from brigade:

Increased enemy activity in Pleiku and Kontum area east of Binh Dinh area is directed to a major degree at lands (sic) (lines) of communication. A number of mining incidents can be expected to increase significantly. All units performing Hwy missions to be especially careful and alert in mine sweeps and searches. Potholes in areas of broken pavement will be searched thoroughly. Recon by fire and artillery programs should be programed along routes of approach and security of bridges and culverts will be carefully planned and increased when necessary. Soft skinned vehicles of all types will be sandbagged in accordance with Division SOP. Drivers will be alerted to increased danger to current high point and be advised to stay on pavement to maximum extent.

On the 28th there was a lot of activity in the battalion and reports of sizable enemy forces moving throughout our AO. At 2230 we were forwarded an agent report that there was a VC company at one stated location and two more companies at a separate location. We were to move back to Plei Do Lim the next day to continue a recon to find the mortar teams that had fired on us previously.

At 1500 on the 29th Fox moved into a small village and observed some suspicious individuals. Two guys ran out of the village to the south, both wearing green fatigues. We knocked one down and were shocked at how young he was when we searched the body. A subsequent search found some NVA and US military equipment. On the 30th at about 1745 we reached Highway 14 where we were picked up by the flame platoon of the 2/8th Infantry and given a ride back to St. George! What a treat that was. We remained at St. George for the rest of the month and into early November.

The words in the brigade message above, "Recon by fire…", are a good lead-in to an explanation of our Rules of Engagement. We were free to fire at any time we observed suspicious individuals because of what they were carrying or their actions. There had to be some indication that they were enemy, obviously we couldn't shoot at civilians without one of the indicators above. There were times and places where we had clearance to "recon by fire" which basically meant that you could shoot up any suspicious looking location without waiting to be fired upon. We also had "Free Fire Zones" wherein we could shoot at any living person we saw. These areas had been cleared through US and Vietnamese civilian and military channels to make sure there were no friendlies in the area. Any time we saw definite enemy forces, or were fired upon I could bring to bear any firepower that I could get hold of from Army gunships or aerial rocket artillery birds, to artillery, to US Navy, Marine Corps or Air Force assets. With those I was free to ask for any ordnance that they were carrying to include bombs or napalm in the case of the jets. As a young Army Lieutenant I had access to an incredible amount of fire power if I had need and adequate communications. During our war the lawyers were at Division or higher and had no involvement in tactical decisions that I'm aware of.

In order to protect the lives of my guys I never hesitated to use whatever I thought I needed. Normally I used artillery and Army air assets, but there were a few times when I used the heavier stuff on the fast movers or jets. I think one time I even used a rolling artillery barrage to clear an area ahead of us as we moved because of all of the signs we had seen of a heavy enemy presence. We also recon'ed by fire a couple times with organic assets by firing into tree lines before crossing an open area that had a lot of evidence there were bad guys around. Preservation of US lives was a high priority for most ground commanders.

DUTY! HONOR! COUNTRY!

11 - GOOKS IN THE WIRE!

We remained on St. George from the 1ˢᵗ of November until the 4ᵗʰ. During that period, the battalion's rifle companies found several enemy company-sized bunker complexes in the St. George area. They also received small arms fire in a number of locations. We couldn't know at the time, but all of this activity was a prelude to a major enemy attack soon to come, spearheaded by a unit of NVA Sappres.

North Vietnamese Army Sappers were the most feared of any enemy unit. They were highly trained commandos who could easily breach the fences of triples rows of concertina wire that surrounded all US fortifications. They could slip through wire with ease, and the tangle foot, ground flares, and other obstacles we used were also bypassed, and claymore mines were disarmed or in some cases, turned 180 degrees. The Sappers normally wore only a loin cloth and a shirt, and were armed with AK 47s, B-40s and the dreaded satchel charges that were homemade, extremely powerful explosives wrapped into a bundle and then thrown into bunkers, tents, etc. They moved quietly and quickly. I once witnessed a demonstration by a couple of sappers who had surrendered to US forces. They were able to penetrate the standard US defensive fortification in just a couple of minutes. They cut wire, or elevated it, holding it in place with sticks so that others could crawl underneath. If they cut a path, it was often marked with shaved bamboo slices that glistened in the dark towards their direction. The sappers who hit us were supported by regular NVA, including mortar teams, automatic weapons, and additional ground forces.

During these couple of days, I made a trip back to Camp Enari where I saw one of my guys, Jim "Murf" Murphy, being led around in handcuffs by two guys wearing MP (military police) armbands. When I asked what was going on, I was told that the battalion Chaplain had accused him of threatening to kill the unit executive officer. I refused to believe this and learned later that it had never happened.

Murf had gone back to Enari for some dental work and went to the clinic without going to the battalion area, because he was convinced that the XO put him on guard duty every time he showed up in the rear area out of some type of personal animosity.

When he did return to the battalion area after his dental work, he first checked in at the mailroom, where he picked up some mail, including a "Dear John" letter from his fiancé. That understandably caused him to go into a pretty deep depression, so he went looking for help. He asked the 1st Sergeant if there was a Catholic Chaplain available and was told there was only the battalion's assigned protestant Chaplain, who he then went to see. The Chaplain asked what he could do and Murf asked him to intercede with the XO. Murf explained that he was so upset with the letter that he didn't think that he could concentrate on guard duty requirements. He was told by the Chaplain that he he'd speak to the XO.

After completing more dental work the next day, he walked out of the building to find two MP's waiting for him who then placed him in handcuffs. He was told by the MP's that the handcuffs were required because he'd threatened to kill the XO the night before; a threat that Murf strongly denied. He was taken to the XO's barracks room where the XO came running up to him screaming "You're not gonna kill me!" Murf denied ever making that kind of threat; then saw the Chaplain standing over by the side, the one who said that Murf had made the threat while talking with him the day before. Actions of this Chaplain, or lack of them, were again critical in the near future.

The next day, Murf was escorted to the convoy going out to St. George, but was not given his weapon. Once under way, the handcuffs were removed and Murf started talking with a couple of replacements going to Delta Company as a way to cover the awkwardness of his situation. I think that this was on the 4th. He gave them some advice on whom to listen to in D Company, who might be reliable, and who could teach them the basics of combat survival. He advised the new guys that they should pay attention to what they were told and follow the instructions to a "T."

That night Murf was sent to the LZ communications bunker to sleep under guard. Before coming to Fox, he'd had a commo qualification and had worked in the battalion's Tactical Operations Center. That day, not knowing Murf was back on St. George we received a mission to secure a rice cache and also to recon a village suspected of being a VC logistical base. We were to ambush the village that night and then secure the rice cache the next morning. We left at 1800. We made no contact with the VC squad that night and were directed to return to St. George on the 5th, we got there at 0700. That day we also decided to send Private First Class Gary Kattman and Al Rangus back to the division rear to attend sniper school.

The 6th of November, 1969, is a date that will be burned in my mind forever, even though I don't have an exact memory of a lot of the details or a sequence of events of the mayhem that occurred that night. What I relate here is a compilation of what memories I do have and several discussions with my Fox guys. We had just returned from an overnight mission on the 5th. The firebase security company that day was D Company, and with our arrival we took over our three bunkers from the admin and D Company folks who had manned them in our absence. As was my habit, after cleaning our gear, de-briefing the intelligence (S-2) and operations officers (S-3), and spending some time talking with my guys, I was going to leave them in their perimeter bunkers and go to the BOQ (Bachelor Officers' Quarters) hooch to sleep. This was a general purpose (GP) medium tent with wooden pallet floors and sand-filled 55-gallon drums around the outside as a blast shield. Inside was a line of folding cots down each side, equipped with an Army sleeping bag for padding; a real comfort compared to sleeping on the ground out in the jungle. I always did this after a mission, I felt the guys couldn't really relax and wind down if I stayed too close in one of the bunkers. As our missions were usually more physically and mentally demanding than those of the rifle platoons, and usually involved a lot more contact than the other platoons, I thought that my guys really needed some time without my presence to relax. Besides, the bunkers were crowded enough without adding one more body.

I followed this course on the 5th, and after a couple of beers, I left. In the BOQ hooch I picked an empty cot, the first on the left as I entered, and was really looking forward to a good night's sleep; impossible in the field. And that night, for some unknown reason, I took off my boots – for the first time since I'd arrived in July; maybe that was an omen.

One of the other guys in the hooch had a bottle of bourbon, and after a couple of drinks, a couple more beers and a good BS session with a couple of other guys, I laid down and went to sleep. I enjoyed the feel of the cot and the thick sleeping bag, and thought that I'd really be able to get to sleep soundly for the first time in days as I wadded up my shirt to use as a pillow. I would guess that I was dreaming… and then at midnight what I initially thought was a dream became a scary, hellish reality.

I was awakened from my alcohol-induced sleep by the wailing of the firebase's alert siren, similar in sound to that heard at home at many

107

volunteer fire departments. I think it took me a few seconds to swim out of my mental and alcoholic haze, I remember lying there trying to figure out what was happening and where I was. In addition to the siren, I could hear explosions and could see the stars and bright flashes above where the tent should have been, and there was a strong aroma of cordite. "What in the hell is going on..." Something just wasn't right.

And then it hit – literally. The explosions I was hearing were coming from inside the perimeter, probably from mortars and RPGs. And I was seeing light above me because the tent had been shredded by shrapnel. Another close sounding explosion caused me to roll off of my bunk and hit the wooden pallet floor.

I lay there for a while, probably only for a couple of seconds, trying to comprehend what was happening. The sound of more shrapnel hitting our blast wall, as well as the sound of AK-47s that seemed to be close by, spurred me to action; *"Where the hell are my boots? I can't go outside without my fucking boots!"* This was a critical factor to me in my mindset at that moment, how could I fight in my socks? I remember frantically crawling around my bunk, almost in a state of panic, until I finally found them. I sat on the floor and put them on, tied the laces around my ankles without lacing them up, grabbed my steel pot, knife, weapon and a couple of bandoliers of ammo and ran out into the noise and smoke. *"Holy shit, just what the hell is happening to this place?"*

As I started to sprint down to my section of the bunker line, a distance of maybe a hundred yards or so, I noticed that there were green tracers streaming across my path indicating that we had gooks inside the perimeter, and they were probably shooting at me! Those shitheads! I couldn't fire in the direction of those tracersas I didn't know where our guys were which was really frustrating and a helpless feeling, kinda like being a target at a carnival shooting range. Just after I exited the tent, an incoming mortar round or rocket landed close by, knocking me off of my feet and making me temporarily deaf. I got up and continued my sprint as I checked myself for holes. Fortunately I didn't find any major ones, but my ears were ringing so loudly that the sound almost shut all other sounds out completely – a dangerous situation. As I neared my closest bunker I noticed Redcrouched down beside the entry blast wall to give me covering fire if needed. That was a real relief.

I made it inside safely and stood for a minute to catch my breath, trying to figure out what was happening. My heart was pounding and the sweat pouring down my face practically blinded me; I could hardly breathe. I don't remember feeling any fear beyond being kind of dazed by what I was experiencing; it was all so sudden, violent, and hard to sort out.

The sounds were horrendous; the siren was wailing, mortar and rocket rounds impacting, I could hear other explosions whose source I couldn't identify, and I could clearly hear the sounds of AKs and M16s. The smell of cordite filled the bunker. Guys around me and outside my bunker were quiet as they tried to make sure everyone was safe and organize a defense; it was obvious that we were in real trouble. I had no idea what was happening beside a growing realization that Firebase St. George was in deep shit. I think a lot of my guys had exited our bunkers and were manning the fighting positions along the wall that connected them.

At about the same time fire base Weit Davis received about 20 rounds of 82mm and 60mm mortar fire from the northeast and east of their location. This fire flattened some tires and wounded two engineers, although not seriously. After learning of this after the fact, I guessed this was an effort by the NVA to make our 4.2 mortar crews at Weit Davis unable to support us.

I went over to a firing slit in the front of the bunker to see what was happening. From there I remember clearly that I heard the unmistakable "woomf" of a mortar being fired, and thought that I detected the flash of the tube out to our left front. I yelled "Incoming!" and called over to Red and gave him an azimuth and distance to relay to D company's mortar platoon for counter-mortar fire. He was unsuccessful in raising the mortars, the company CP, or the arty battery.

One thing was becoming more obvious to me—it was impossible to tell from inside that bunker what was happening on the rest of the firebase. Plus, I was worried about what kind of casualties we'd incur if we took a direct hit from a mortar, or if a gook managed to get to our entrance and spray the inside with his AK or throw in a satchel charge. We really needed to man the firing ports, but I needed more guys outside to improve security.

I decided I needed to check on my sector of three bunkers. My first priority was to ensure our area of responsibility was well defended and my guys were all safe, secure, and in good positions to defend themselves. From my entry into the bunker until this point, maybe two or three minutes had passed.

I told a couple of the guys to stay put and man the firing slits in the front of the bunker, and told the others to follow me outside. I crouched and moved slowly to the entrance and out to the blast wall so I could look around. The siren was still screaming, there were loud explosions and a lot of small arms fire. There were flames to my left and a blanket of smoke hovering pretty close to the ground caused by weapons, explosions, and what I later found to be burning bunkers; it was an incredible and horrible sight.

With Red and a couple guys, we quickly made our way to my other bunkers. Fox had already reacted well; guys were manning fighting positions between the bunkers and were oriented 360 degrees to counter the bad guys running all over the base. At that point I had no casualties and my sector of the perimeter appeared to be well secured. There didn't seem to be any enemy in the wire in front of our bunkers or around our positions.

My third and last bunker was located on the west side of the road that led in and out of St George. The perimeter on the other side of the road belonged to D Company and the first three bunkers were my responsibility as Apache 6 in Charlie Company. What I saw there was horrifying; smoke coming out of the first few bunkers and flames from others that appeared to be severely damaged.

Silhouetted against the flames, I could see people moving around but couldn't determine if they were enemy or friendlies. I couldn't even imagine what I was seeing was real. What was obvious was that part of the D company bunker line was empty because of the destruction and the fact that I saw no outgoing red tracers, inviting more attackers to enter St. George through that gap.

I remember wondering what I should do; should I orient some of my guys to cover the road and those destroyed bunkers; should I send some guys to check the area? It was obvious my right flank was exposed, with no one to tie-in with.

I decided, as the senior officer on that part of the base, (as far as I could tell), it was my responsibility to figure out what was happening. I needed to go check out my former area to determine its status; I was more familiar with it than anyone else. I had not been able to talk to the D company CP or battalion TOC. I didn't want to weaken my platoon defenses or put any of my guys at needless risk, so I figured I'd go make the initial recon myself.

Years later, at our first Fox Force reunion in the year 2000, Charlie "Red" Siner, bitched at me and asked me why I had not allowed him to come with me that night; he'd been carrying that issue for more than 30 years. He had felt that night that his mission was to cover me as always, and was really pissed when I told him to stay put. I had totally forgotten I had forbidden him to come with me as well. I was about to go into that burning hell, and for the first time that I can remember since arriving in

Vietnam, I was convinced that I was probably going to die. I simply told him to stay put because I didn't want him to die as well. He was needed on our bunker line. I found out later Charlie didn't do what I ordered but went around to the other side of the perimeter to check on that part of the bunker line which was mostly manned by the admin sections of the forward deployed battalion headquarters and some former Recon guys. He spent a lot of the night there as well as moving about St. George while sending SITREPs back to the TOC to keep them informed of what was happening. He was evidently their only "outside" link.

At the request of the TOC, Charlie moved around a lot that night, always at risk of running into an NVA or being hit by a rocket or mortar round, to report on the overall condition and status of the firebase. Charlie was one hell of a soldier and just couldn't stay in our area and not help out someplace else as needed, particularly with his radio. I also found out later Diz DesJardins was also up in that area of the bunker line, having gone to visit some friends at the 106mm recoilless rifle bunker. He ran into Charlie while up there and was told to return to the Fox bunker line. So at least a couple of my guys were augmenting a pretty soft part of our battalion defenses.

I checked to make sure I had enough ammo and was sorry I hadn't grabbed any frags. I made sure I had a round in the chamber and my CAR-15 was off "safe" and that I had my knife in my boot. Those memories of the preparations and seconds before I started across the road are still very clear, they seemed to pass in slow motion. The air was filled with smoke, the siren was still wailing, and there was the sound of sometimes intense gunfire and occasional explosions. My heart was beating like a bass drum and my hands were slippery with sweat as I ran in a deep crouch across the road toward the first D Company bunker after telling a couple of my guys to keep watch in that direction. I don't remember being scared, but I was really pissed at what was happening to our firebase.

While I don't remember talking with Jimmy Harris before I left our sector, I knew I didn't have to worry about the guys in our area; I knew Jimmy would have them squared away and would take care of any command and control issues that arose. That was one of the great things about working with someone like Staff Sergeant Jimmy Harris, I had complete faith in him and his leadership abilities.

As I was moving towards the bunkers, I also scanned the nearest artillery pit to see if the guns were being readied for direct fire, but saw no activity. The barrel of at least one of the howitzers was pointing skyward. I could see past that pit but there didn't appear to be any movement inside the arty positions and no fire coming from their guns. When I reached the first bunker, I hit the ground and began to low crawl, I had no idea how many of the enemy might be around. As I was getting close to the bunker, I crawled up to a couple of bodies, not sure who they were. They were GIs, and with a quick check I found no sign of life. I made a note of their location and continued.

The next few minutes, which seemed like hours, were filled with events that are difficult to think about. I crawled into the first bunker which was still in pretty good shape, but I could find no one alive inside, I think there were a couple of bodies. I do know being in that place was scary; it smelled of blood and smoke. I didn't want to get trapped, so I backed out as quickly as possible.

I crawled carefully over to the second bunker, which was nearly destroyed and was still in flames; this one had been my CP while in Charlie Company. The air inside was as hot as a blast furnace, filled with thick, acrid smoke, and the sweet smell of burning flesh; something I've never forgotten. The roof had collapsed and there were timbers blocking easy access. As I crawled in, I felt a boot and what I thought was a leg which seemed to move as I grabbed it; maybe this guy was alive. I backed out pulling him behind me but saw as I got outside that all I had was a boot and what appeared to be part of a leg. To this day I'm not sure of what I had, or what I saw. In any event, I quickly let go, feeling the bile rising in the back of my throat. As I paused for a moment to get my stomach under control, I scanned the area around me and up the bunker line for any movement, and listened closely for any human sounds; it could be that there were some wounded grunts nearby that needed help, or maybe more sappers moving into the area.

The entire bunker line, as far as I could see, probably four or five down the line, appeared to be deserted; there were no grunts in view, no outgoing tracers, which would have indicated an active defense. There was absolutely no sign of any action from the artillery gun pits behind the bunkers either. At that point I heard noises coming from the right side of the remnants of my old CP. As I slowly crawled to the edge and peered carefully around it, I couldn't see anyone on the inside of the fighting wall that connected my former CP with the next bunker, which was also in flames and obviously destroyed. I still heard some muffled voices and now they seemed to come from the other side of the wall. I slowly, quietly and carefully crawled up to the wall and realized the voices I heard were speaking Vietnamese in a low, hushed conversation. I reached to grab a grenade off of my harness and then remembered; I had none.

112

What the hell was I going to do? Since I hadn't yet fired my weapon, I thought I'd just pop up to my knees and empty the magazine into whoever was on the other side; anyone there and speaking Vietnamese couldn't be a friend. I had 19 rounds; we never loaded our mags to their capacity of 20 in order to prevent jams. I normally carried two mags taped together so I could do a quick reload, and was carrying 14 others in two bandoleers.

As I lay there, I began to worry that the guys on the other side of the wall might want to come over it to join their buddies who were running around inside of our perimeter raising hell. Should that happen I was dead for sure. *What was I going to do?* I could just crawl back to the road and call to some of my guys to come join me, but who knew what the enemy were planning, I might never make it to the road, or possibly be ambushed on the way back and no one would know of the dire circumstances of D company. So I decided to pop up, spray whoever was there with one magazine, and then try to make it back to my bunkers as quickly as possible in the resulting confusion. . . These thoughts flashed through my mind in a millisecond. It's amazing how in that situation events and thoughts seem to move in slow motion but the actual time frame can actually be milliseconds.

I couldn't think about this plan too long so I gathered my legs under me as quietly as possible and sprang up to my knees to see and shoot whoever was on the other side. HO-LEE SHIT, there appeared to be at least seven or eight, or more, enemy sappers on the ground in front of me, a couple staring up with a startled look on their faces that I've never forgotten. I pulled the trigger and attempted to spray the whole bunch of them, then dropped down on my back on my side of the wall and quickly flipped to the other magazine preparing to make them pay dearly if they came over the wall to get me. The next morning a couple of these guys were found wearing bandages so I must have hit some of them.

When the enemy didn't immediately appeared over the wall, I turned and started to crawl backwards towards my part of the bunker line; there was more here than I could deal with by myself. When I was halfway between my old CP and the last D Company bunker next to the street, suddenly a body landed on my back. Hands reached around my head, knocking off my steel pot, and pawed at my throat, I had no idea what was happening. I don't remember what happened in detail except that I lost the grip on my weapon; I must have reached my knife as we rolled on the ground. I had the impression he was small but hard as iron and a lot stronger than I would have expected. He had on a shirt and loincloth and really smelled; his breath was particularly rotten. I shook the body off and checked out my surroundings to see if there were any more around. I have no idea why he just hadn't shot me; he certainly had the advantage of surprise. Maybe he had lost his weapon or was out of ammo. In any event, I was one lucky SOB! With my adrenaline pumping, I grabbed my steel pot and weapon, got to my feet and ran in a low crouch toward my flank position. At that point, I saw three guys moving quietly and carefully toward my bunkers. At first I thought they were Americans, but then in the light of a parachute flare, I saw they were NVA. As I had reloaded after firing at the wall, I knocked all three down, they had no idea that I was behind them.

I moved on slowly, just as afraid I could get shot by my own guys as the bad guys. There were a couple of our guys on the ground that appeared to be either dead or seriously wounded, maybe the same guys I'd seen earlier. As I checked on them I saw what appeared to be three more enemy soldiers firing into the backs of my bunkers, one from under a disabled engineer 5-ton truck. As I maneuvered into a better firing position, they saw me and quickly turned their weapons on me, fortunately they weren't good shots. I dropped two but couldn't get a good bead on the other one under the truck. I noticed one of my guys from the back of one of my bunkers was also firing at that guy. Somehow I wound up on the other side of that truck to where the medics' hooch was and where the battalion surgeon was normally stationed. I have no memory of how that happened. It didn't appear to be damaged but there was no visible activity, maybe everyone inside that bunker was dead... Our ammo bunker was located next to the medic hooch. I got into a good position and tried again to take out the gook under the truck; he was lying behind the four rear wheels closest to me. The guy firing from one of my bunkers was Jimmie Harris, and I yelled to him that we'd take the SOB under the truck, who was still firing at us, under crossfire. I thought I could see where he was. I emptied a couple of magazines but the fire didn't slacken. Jimmy was also putting a lot of rounds into the area. I saw movement to my right and swung around to protect myself when I saw something so comical that I laughed out loud. Running up the street toward the rear of the truck, was an American officer who I recognized as the Support Platoon Leader, in his boxer shorts, flip-flops, T-shirt, and flak jacket with a .45 in his hand that he was firing furiously at the source of AK fire.

He and I had attended the Infantry Officers Basic Course together at Fort Benning the previous summer. He reloaded as he approached the vehicle and fired as fast as he could at his target, then turned and ran back from where he'd come. As I reloaded and looked to see green tracers still coming from under the truck, the apparition appeared again, dressed as before and firing furiously once again. Again he ran right up to the back, squatted down, and fired a whole magazine towards his target. "Hey," I yelled over, "what the fuck are you doing?" He yelled at me as he ran back up the street, "The son of a bitch wouldn't die!" That hit me as so funny that I had to stop firing for afew seconds, hard to believe that I was laughing so hard in such a horrendous situation.

The next morning we found a couple of sappers there under the truck just full of holes. He was one lucky son of a bitch; there is no explanation for why the guys under the truck hadn't taken him out while he was running down the road other than that they were too preoccupied in their duel with Jimmy and me.

As the firing from under the truck had ceased, I very cautiously moved up to check the area. While all of the gooks around there appeared to be dead, I also saw an American GI laying there who also appeared dead with several bleeding wounds. I was horrified as he appeared to be in the same location I had been firing at; I had killed him! I was stunned, I'd killed one of our own guys, I just couldn't believe it, I was horrified. (Years later I ran into a soldier at Ft. Benning who commented on my 4th ID combat patch. As we talked we found that we were in Vietnam at the same time; he mentioned the 1st of the 14th and that November night at St. George. He went on to tell me that he was an engineer truck driver and was wounded while trying to hide under his truck where he had been sleeping and that he'd left his weapon in the cab. When the gooks moved in he had to play dead so that they wouldn't shoot him. He was the guy I thought I'd killed, my feeling of relief was incredible, and I was able to unload one of my personal demons! I apologized to him over and over for probably being the guy who had shot him in the legs a couple of times, he held no rancor and shook my hand in thanks for what my guys had done that night to save his life. I think his last name was Pruitt.

At this time a resupply bird was coming in to drop off more ammo. He was inbound to the parking area behind my CP, which contained the damaged 5-ton engineer vehicle we'd just been shooting at; they must have been navigating by the light provided by the fires. As it got closer to the ground, I saw the battalion CSM, Jasper Wiggins, cursing and yelling, holding on to the frame of the cargo door with one hand, firing a .45 with the other, while kicking boxes of ammo out the door. I also saw a B40 rocket go in one door and out the other side without hitting anything or anybody. What a soldier he was, risking death to help his men.

Everything still appeared to be OK in the Fox sector, a quick check showed no apparent casualties and my guys were defending their area. It was obvious to me that I needed to somehow plug the gap in the perimeter where the D company platoons had been to make sure that no more NVA came through the wire. So I gathered several of my guys, to include Danny Stagner, a machine gunner, Gary Nelson, one of my best point men, Jim Murphy, as a rifleman, Alan Buckelew, my other RTO, and Beasley, and briefed them on what I knew about the rest of the firebase. I couldn't find Charlie. I also informed them of the concentration of gooks I had seen outside the perimeter wall on the other side of my old CP; and that I wasn't sure if they were all dead. I told them we were going to plug the gap to prevent any more NVA from getting inside our wire.

My plan was to put Stag and the other guys on top of my old first squad bunker to fire down on the large group and any other gooks they spotted trying to get through the wire. I thought with that area under control, I needed to check the rest of the perimeter. I also wanted to check out the artillery battery area for additional help, but it was ringed by its own concertina fence and hard to get to.

I gathered my four or five guys together and started for the D Company area. We crouched down on the friendly side of the first bunker and I had Danny spray the area in front of the next couple of bunkers. As we approached my old CP, I realized there was not much of the top remaining, so I had Danny and Gary Nelson climb to the top of the first bunker while the other guys and I provided cover from the ground. Once up there, they immediately opened fire with no shortage of targets. The battalion artillery liaison officer suddenly appeared and started handing me more ammo from the artillery pits for the M60, which I passed up to Stag.

Buck's memory of this event is as follows:

I slept in 1ˢᵗ squad's bunker. I had finished my watch a couple of hours earlier and was fast asleep when the sound of satchel charges going off woke me. I put on my boots, grabbed my M16 and rushed out of our bunker.

It was pitch dark but soon someone launched a flare and I could see that the two bunkers adjacent to the Fox bunkers had been blown to pieces.

About this time, Six arrived and instructed Stag and myself to follow him to where the bunkers had been destroyed. We discovered that three bunkers had been bombed, but one was still partially standing – it was just across the entrance road to the firebase from the Fox bunkers. Six instructed us to stay there and prevent any more sappers from entering the firebase and of course kill any trying to escape.

116

Stag, who was carrying the first squad's M60 (machine gun), and I fired whenever we heard movement in front of us. Unfortunately we had only the half-blown up bunker for protection, otherwise we were completely exposed. Stag and I held our position all night. We could hear fire from within the firebase and voices yelling for support and flares. I left Stag for a couple of minutes to get my radio as helicopter gunships had now arrived on scene. I was able to contact them and directed their fire in our section of the perimeter. Six came back a couple of times to check on us, but as we were fine he would move on to check other areas of the firebase. I never embraced firefights with anything but dread, but as the night wore on I felt concerned but not afraid – I was getting accustomed to war I thought to myself.

At sunrise we were all exhausted having been up much of the night and drained from adrenaline highs. The sun's rays were like daggers in our eyes, but it was good to see all that was around us. To my and Stag's horror, seven, eight, or nine dead NVA lay a few feet in front of us – their bodies were a mess so it was difficult to count accurately. We or others who had preceded us had killed nearly a third of the total that would be discovered that day. At that point, looking down on their swollen bodies, I saw my hand shaking.

Oddly, now that the battle was over I was feeling somewhat afraid.

I think that after this, and knowing that my guys were in a pretty good position, I checked most of the rest of the D Company perimeter and don't remember finding any of our guys there, just a lot of quiet bunkers and some bodies, whose I couldn't tell. I had a scare when a sapper appeared around the edge of a bunker up the line and ran at me, firing and screaming as he did. I dropped to a knee and took aim with single shots, watching my rounds impact his torso. Still, he ran at me but had emptied his magazine. I must have hit him five or six times before he went down about five feet from me, I thought the guy must have been high on some kind of dope; he sure scared the crap out of me! At this time I think I also went to the battalion TOC since it was nearby, and updated the S3 and others on what I knew and the danger of a largely undefended perimeter in the area I'd checked which was probably a third of the entire bunker line.

I was on my way back to my guys, to check on their status again, when I ran into LTC Vic Robertson, Dragon 6, alone and carrying an M16. I was shocked and asked him what the hell he was doing roaming around by himself while we had bad guys running around inside the perimeter. His response was one that I'll never forget; "I have to check on my men." I was still upset with the belief that I'd killed one of our own and told Dragon how bad I felt. He told me not to worry about it and we could check it all out once everything quieted down. When he didn't relieve me on the spot as I expected, I felt reassured. I stayed with him until we got to my recon bunkers and then moved back to where I'd left my other guys to check on the arty positions. I had also remembered that we had two tracks from the 2/8 Mechanized Infantry Battalion in the general vicinity of my segment of the perimeter, I thought they were flame tracks (fired napalm out of a turret) and asked about getting at least one of them to come over to the D company area for reinforcement and to cover the large avenues of approach through our wire. I was later told that one couldn't move and the other couldn't fire.

I don't remember seeing anyone in the artillery area but the liaison officer who handed me more ammo for the M60 on top of the bunker; I remember seeing that barrel glowing white, all of the guys up there were OK. Stagner was really working out with that machine gun. Somehow I wound up in one of the gun pits when I saw several sappers trying to get through its protective wire to get to the guns to disable them. I dropped down behind the pit's sandbag wall and took them under fire as well as a couple of other guys I saw running toward our hasty position on the bunker top, there were probably five or six sappers making this attack. I don't know if I hit any of them, but their efforts ceased. We found when the sun came up that they were coming from the major NVA infiltration route into our perimeter.

Sometime during this period I had an experience that will always be with me; I felt something pulling on my legs and whirled around ready to shoot whoever it was. To my surprise it was one of the battalion cooks who was crawling around with a couple of mermite inserts, one full of hot coffee and the other with hot soup; "What would you like, sir?" Holy shit, this was just unbelievable; I had a couple of swallows of the best coffee I had ever tasted. I've often kicked myself in the ass for not taking the time to find out the guy's name so I could recommend him for a medal. I don't even know if he survived the night.

Soon after the cook's visit, my Company Commandershowed up with a PRC-25 on his back so he could talk with the TOC as well as the inbound air support. It was a very cloudy night with low ceilings, so the birds were having trouble getting into us until a flare ship arrived. We were unable to get any flare support from our artillery battery or the D Company 81mm mortars. We had our battalion 4.2-inch mortar platoon firing in support from Weit Davis, using HE (high explosive) instead of providing illumination. My CO and I took up a position inside the gun pit closest to my guys on the bunker, so we could both protect them and direct the birds as well as our own mortars. Somehow I now had a radio, I guess I had called Al Buckelew over, and got on the horn and directed mortar fire into our perimeter because there were so many bad guys around. I wanted to close their access route into St. George with a wall of HE, my CO directed the gunships and fast movers at potential assembly areas and avenues of approach. A lot of the fire I was controlling from the mortars was pretty close and we had shrapnel coming into our location.

While researching this battle, I came across a story of a life sacrificed to save us that none of us had ever heard before. This story came from the Vietnam Helicopter Pilots Association website and concerns a story of helicopter UH-IH, tail number 66-16454. The crew on the night of 6 November was First Lieutenant Timothy La Tour, Aircraft commander, Chief Warrant Officer-2 James Snyder, Pilot, Specialist-4 Edward Skaggs, Crew chief and Sergeant Gregory Rugenstein, Gunner. I will describe the events by quoting from parts of the account of Lieutenant La Tour.

"Camp Enari near Pleiku, II Corps, November 6, 1969, 4th Aviation had the primary stand-by flare mission. My unit (D/1/10 Cav) had the secondary stand-by flare mission. We were scrambled in the wee hours of Nov 6, 1969 to help Fourth Aviation drop flares for LZ St. George, south of Pleiku. Just before dark we had pre-flighted the ship and loaded the flares. Although the wind was high, the tail rotor was not tied down at that time. But someone (perhaps 328's regular crew chief) had gone back out after dark and tied down the rotor."

"Not knowing the tail rotor had been tied down, I tried cranking. And when it popped, I shut down. We quickly moved to the slick in the adjacent revetment (454) and moved the flares over. Then we took off for LZ St. George to relieve the 4th Aviation ship on station. After arriving we dropped a couple of flares for Dustoff who came in for some wounded. While preparing for the next drop, the flare exploded in Greg's face and blew his helmet out the door. He dropped to the floor in a pool of blood, and the crew chief, Ed Skaggs, was knocked out temporarily. The flare fully deployed and ignited inside the ship. Ed came to in time to toss the burning flare out of the ship, but the parachute caught on the M60 gun mount. He cut the lines and the flare fell away. I had to abandon the mission, but St. George had just requested darkness anyway. They had called for Spooky, and they didn't want any more flares until Spooky arrived. So with the lull in flare requests, the accident didn't affect the situation on the ground."

"We took Greg to the 71st Evac in Pleiku where the hospital personnel were waiting on the pad. They tried to save his life, but apparently they couldn't stop the bleeding and he died a few days later. I have also corresponded via email with one of the EM who was on duty in the 71st Evac ER that night we brought Greg in. He told me about the nature of Greg's injury and of the many units of blood (70+) they used trying to save his life."

119

Note: Both of the birds involved that night, the first with the tied down tail rotor and the one flown in the incident, were destroyed in a sapper attack on Camp Radcliff on April 4th, 1970.

Finding a story like this is a sobering event, another life lost by a man doing his best to save us on the ground by volunteering to fly a very dangerous night mission and providing some much needed illumination; very humbling. The accident investigation concluded a faulty round caused the flare ignition, not any mistake on the part of Sergeant Rugenstein.

My company commander and I stayed in the gun pit for what seemed like quite a while, directing support as best we could while watching for more sappers; the skies began to lighten and we began to see the devastation around us. Because we were on what was evidently the enemy's primary access route to the interior of St. George, there had been a lot of action. We had the gunships and fast movers working on the outer perimeter and what we figured would be their escape routes. My guys on top of the bunker were finding a lot more targets as the surviving sappers began to try to escape from the firebase. They had evidently killed everyone in the large group past the second bunker, which we later deduced to be the NVA command group. I saw Stag catch a couple of guys in the wire and make short work of them, cutting one in half. His gun barrel was glowing white and smoking. There were several destroyed and burning bunkers to our front.

As the sun came up, the surviving NVA tried to make their way out of the perimeter, providing some easy targets as they got hung up in our wire. we stayed where we were for a while longer, controlling the fire support, until it appeared that things were quieting down. Then it became a lot quieter, I noticed the siren had stopped, and the firing had died down to a sporadic burst once in a while. The silence was almost deafening. When I tried to stand up I found I could barely move, the adrenaline was quickly draining from my body, my knees almost buckled and I suddenly felt completely exhausted. It was probably about 0800, we'd been fighting since midnight.

I surveyed the area for a couple of minutes, verified that there didn't appear to be any NVA left alive in our area, and then shook hands as he left to go to the TOC while I started off to return to my bunkers. We'd had had quite an adventure. I checked with my guys on top of the bunker and they were OK, but also exhausted. I asked them to stay where they were, keep a watch as far up the bunker line as they could see until we could reorganize a better defense and started moving back to my CP. When I got there, my guys were slowly beginning to move around but were silent with a tired, vacant look in their eyes. The ground was littered with the refuse of combat: shells and casings, weapons, discarded bandoleers, paper, first aid field dressings and whole and parts of bodies; all that I saw were NVA.

Sometime during that fight, Private First Class Gary Nelson, my "free spirit" point man, exhibited some incredible heroics. During the initial enemy assault, Gary ran across an open area to provide covering fire for a couple of medics who were treating wounded soldiers. A sapper suddenly appeared between two bunkers, moving in their direction. Without hesitation, Gary moved to an exposed position and killed the enemy soldier. Gary then moved to another location to assist other wounded soldiers when he saw a squad of the enemy in front of his bunker. Again exposing himself in an open area, Gary engaged this group, killed three, and caused the others to flee. For these actions, among others, Gary received the Silver Star, the third highest award for valor.

As soon as I reached my CP a commander's worst nightmare occurred. I had recently received as a replacement, an "old" guy named Allen. He was a Korean War veteran and had been an E-7 or E-8. Somehow he got into trouble and came to me as a Sergeant, an E-5. He had been a 60-millimeter mortar man in the past and so became my gunner with the mortar tube I had traded for in an SF camp. He was evidently running around the corner of one of my bunkers, yelling "Friendly" when he was shot by another of my guys who fired at the movement; Allen was hit in the armpit. I got to the site immediately thereafter.

When I saw Allen on the ground I told Red to call the TOC and tell them that we still had gooks running around the area. In a low voice he told me that it wasn't a gook, Allen had been shot by one of our own guys… Goddamn that was hard to accept. But as we stood there, with first aid being administered to Allen, the shooter owned up, he admitted he'd fired the shot. He was understandably extremely upset, saying over and over again that he couldn't believe what he'd done; I think he'd only been in the unit for a few days. I'm told this soldier then went into a kind of shock and trauma so we had him medevac'ed with my wounded. I don't think I ever reported this incident; it was one of those things that occur in this type of combat action, hell I'd done the same thing earlier that night. Plus there just wasn't time to make out a formal report; we were kept too busy on the following days.

121

I thought I had also lost one of the guys I'd taken to the D company area, Jim "Murf" Murphy. I don't remember his getting hit, nor do I know how he made it to the medics. I remember him propped up against one of the "D" company bunkers, I don't know if I stopped to check on him or give him any first aid. That guy haunted me for years. I couldn't track him through the medical system; every time I inquired about him I was told, "He's gone." Since nobody could tell me what that meant, I assumed he'd died. Because we left the firebase on another mission two days later to chase the gooks that had attacked us, and then shortly thereafter moved to the Ban Me Thout area, I couldn't get back to the evac hospital to personally search for him. I couldn't find out anything about Sergeant Allen and I couldn't track the kid who'd shot him. I think I also lost a black kid that night whose name I can't remember. A commander is supposed to go to the hospital to check on his casualties but I just didn't have the opportunity. I carry this guilt over their loss and not checking on them in the hospital to this day.

I learned Murf's story years later and I'll relate most of it in his own words. While confined to the commo bunker he had conned his guard into getting him a soda. As soon as he left Murf left the bunker and started moving to the Fox bunkers to see some of his buddies. He went to a couple of bunkers before he found who he was looking for. They were playing cards and he started to explain his situation.

In his words he "...heard BOOM BOOM BOOM BOOM! We all looked at each other; someone said what the fuck was that? BOOM, BOOM BOOM again. We all headed out grabbing weapons and ammo as we went. I had no idea whose weapon I had, but nobody was without a weapon."

"We hit the firing position beside the bunker and opened fire immediately. The explosions kept going off. Then small arms fire from behind us. Sappers had made it through the wire and were active at what they did best; destruction and chaos. Some of the sappers had crawled under the convoy trucks that were parked behind the bunker lines and were firing at us from underneath the trucks."

After a short while I looked up and there was Six, LT. Hedley. He said I need some guys to go with me; they've knocked out Delta Co bunkers and have a free lane in. The next thing I know there were several of us heading across an open area towards the Delta bunkers. The first three to the right of the gate are LEVELED. There's some fire and some screaming coming from each one."

"Somebody says check out the bunker. I walked to where the entrance used to be, looked down and there were several of our brothers laying there dead. One of them was the kid I spoke with on the ride out to St. George. I just remember my insides were going to come up and out of me. I felt like I was going to start screaming. That kid had *just arrived at St. George the day before. Then someone said there's a gook on the sandbag to your right, he's still moving. I turned went toward him to finish him off, just light him up. As I aimed my 16 I saw 12 to 15 sappers bunched up against the sand bag walls we had around the entire firebase.*" (I believe these were the in the same group that I'd engaged earlier.)

I remember thinking what the hell are you doing out here. I emptied the magazine into the pile of sappers. I dove over the sandbag wall, my first thought was to get into a firing position. Instead I went on the other side of it. Loaded a new mag. As I lifted my 16 in the direction of the sappers, I saw an arm raised up with a satchel charge in hand. I pulled the trigger and emptied the mag into the arm.

The satchel charge and hand fell into the firing position, then came the explosion. A white flash followed by dirt, grime and a shock wave." (Years later Murf told me that his initial thought had been to jump into that fighting hole for protection but he had decided against it at the last minute. Had he followed his initial impulse there is no doubt that he would have been killed by the explosion.)

"When I opened my eyes I was on my back, looking up at the sky. It was kind of pretty, stars, flares. When I sat up I could see the muzzle flashes and tracer rounds back and forth. I remember saying to myself, OH SHIT, I'M NOT DEAD."

"I got myself situated again and began to return fire. Another Fox guy, Gary Nelson, was on top of the sandbags firing away. Then I saw him signaling he was out of ammo. When I was on my way out of the bunker I thought, you might need extra ammo for this one, so I grabbed extra bandoleers. I tossed one of the bandoleers to Gary, I never found out it was Gary until we went on the Alaska cruise for my first time attending our reunions."

"Then someone slapped my leg, I looked and was told to move back, they were gonna bring one of the APC's (armored personnel carriers) down. Between the guns on the APC's and Stag lighting up the area I had to move. I don't remember a lot after moving, just the pain in my head, neck and back."

"All of a sudden it was daylight. I know Six and Red were getting everyone together to make a sweep. I couldn't hear anything, my ears were bleeding. Both eardrums were ruptured. Somebody took me to the medic's tent. Then I got medevac'd out later, I spent several days in the hospital. I was returned to the 1st-14th but because of my injuries could no longer be in the field. I was placed with a civil affairs team in a Montagnard village outside of Camp Enari. I was reissued my weapon, sent to the village, and never heard anything about the incident."

(In 2005 we had a large Fox Force reunion aboard a cruise ship headed to Alaska. I was sitting in the hotel bar with a couple of the guys the night before sailing when another guy of mine came running into the bar and told me that I needed to get to the front desk ASAP; he wouldn't tell my why. I got out there quickly to see a man who didn't look even vaguely familiar, standing there with his family waiting to check in. He called my name and told me he was Murf. I can't describe the emotions I felt; Murf was back! Relief flooded over me and the tears began to flow. I hadn't lost Murf; here he was with his wife and two beautiful daughters. I will never ever forget the feeling of relief and joy that swept over me.)

I quickly surveyed my recon area and all seemed to be in as good an order as I could expect. We all seemed to be moving and talking in slow motion. The night had been unreal. I went back to the D Company area to look at the group of NVA that I had fired on the night before near my old CP bunker. When I got there, I found six or seven enemy soldiers who had been killed during the night, maybe by me, maybe by Murf, maybe by Stag's gun. Several were bandaged, which led me to believe I had hit them and they had subsequently been administered first aid before Stag and Murf finished them off. I remember one of the guys was huge by Vietnamese standards. He was tall, broad shouldered and well muscled. His feet were large, so I took his Ho Chi Minh sandals as a trophy of that night and wore them once in a while during the rest of my tour. I know they came home with me but I have no idea what finally happened to them. I also looked for the guy that I had tussled with but couldn't find him; he may have survived and escaped, or his body may have been dragged away by his buddies.

As I've looked back on that night since we started Fox reunions in the year 2000, I've tried to examine my actions and motivations. One major factor that influenced my action of going into the D company perimeter by myself was a strong desire to protect my guys; to not risk their lives needlessly until I knew for sure what was happening and clearly understood the situation. I know at times I was really scared, felt vulnerable and kind of like I was just hanging out in the wind. For a while I was really concerned we might lose the firebase. D company was largely ineffective from what I could see; the company CP and 81mm mortar platoon never got into the fight that I know of. A couple of years ago I did run across, on the web, a recording made that night of actions in the D Company CP. From that source it would appear there was a lot going on but I never witnessed any action on the part of D company. The artillery guys were invisible to me except for the LNO who passed me ammunition for Danny Stagner's gun. I don't remember seeing any live or active American in the whole sector as I checked it out, there didn't appear to be any effective force to stop any major assault.

I also heard a story about the Battalion Chaplain, the man who had been Murf's problem. I hadn't seen him at any time that night administering to the wounded or dead. I'm told that he was found the next morning in his bunker rolled into a tight ball, he hadn't reacted at all. This was the same man who listened to radios in the TOC, particularly if there had been a fight, and would then come find me and critique me on my actions, or lack thereof. I don't remember ever having seen him again in the battalion area after that night.

As it turned out, I found later that there was a sizeable NVA infantry force on the other side of the perimeter that was apparently waiting to be told that the artillery's guns were out of commission so they wouldn't be subjected to direct fire from the dreaded "Beehive" round. This was essentially a 105 mm shotgun shell; the round was packed with little winged flechettes, maybe 1 ½ inch long, that could nail a body to a tree. We were lucky that we interfered with the NVA command group and internal communications, as the infantry force evidently never learned the guns were unmanned. Had they been on our side of the perimeter, and had they come through the same gaps the sapper command group used, they might have overwhelmed us and the end result could have been very different. On the other hand, had they penetrated the bunker line in their area, which was manned, I believe, with soldiers from the battalion headquarters, I believe they might have successfully penetrated in that area and then who knows what the final outcome might have been?

The battalion duty log for 6 November lists the following facts about the attack: After the fight we policed up 11 AK47s with ammo, 10 B40 launchers, 61 satchel charges, 15 B-40 rounds and one 9mm pistol with ammo. Casualties were reported as nine US KIA, eight infantry and one artillery, and 42 enemies KIA. I have no doubt that we had killed a lot more of them, but the gooks had dragged bodies and wounded off of the battlefield; they were masters of that action. I believe this was borne out by the fact we found no surviving wounded enemy inside our wire.

All of the 31 US wounded were infantry, 23 by shrapnel, five by small arms and three by satchel charges. The US KIA were two from a B-40, four by shrapnel and three by small arms. 30 % of the US casualties were in bunkers when they were hit, 70 % were in fighting positions, trenches or outside bunkers. Additionally, our perimeter wire had been cut to the southwest and west.

I've always thought the report of our casualties was a little light based on what I'd encountered that night. I've also read in places that the total US wounded was 41, I'm not sure about what time these figures were tallied and if all of the destroyed bunkers and other structures had been completely cleared.

When I was sure we had reorganized and the battalion staff was as up to date on the security situation as possible, I found a place to sit so I could take stock of myself and prepare for whatever might happen next. I tried to light a cigarette but couldn't because my hands were shaking, but I did drain the water from a canteen that I'd found lying on the ground.

I checked with Jimmy Harris to make sure my guys had ammo, water, and could take time to eat a bite if they wanted. At that time, someone came up and told me that I was wanted in the TOC. The Assistant Division Commander was coming to St George later in the morning. I was told to make sure that our section of the perimeter was cleaned up and manned with everyone wearing flak jackets and steel pots. In the meantime, we did a sweep around the perimeter to make sure there were no live bad guys still hanging around.

Years later while living in Boston after I went to work for Raytheon, a friend asked us to take a cruise on a large sailboat that another friend had recently purchased so he could start a dinner cruise business. While sitting in the cockpit with the owner, we talked to get acquainted. We had both served, and were in Vietnam at about the same time in the 4th Division. He was in another brigade as a mechanic. When I told him I had served in the 1st-14th he asked if I'd been involved in the St. George battle. When I told him I had, and that I was Fox 6, he had an incredible reaction, telling me that he knew all about that night and the actions of Fox! He offered me a free meal after he got his business started but we never followed up. Small world!

Vietnam was a vicious war and I'm sure there are many other heroic stories like that of the flare ship that no one has ever heard or will ever know about. I'm really glad that I'm able to relate the heroism of that entire crew, and the sacrifice of Greg Rugenstein. Undoubtedly there are men alive today because of their efforts that night. I hope that my story has helped her daughter realize what a hero he really was.

DUTY! HONOR! COUNTRY!

12 – POW

After making sure that all was squared away with my guys I made my way to the TOC. The air was still filled with the acrid smells of the night's fight, smoke from the burning bunkers, and the smell of cordite. The ground was littered with the refuse of war; shell casings, empty magazines, and pieces of paper and in some cases parts of bodies. I remember clearly looking down at part of a hand.

When I got to the TOC I found the S3, Major Ray Sales, and Dragon. They had been planning the consolidation of our positions in the remnants of the bunker line while trying to reconstruct the events of the evening. Being early in the morning it was really difficult to determine exactly what had happened. I went over with them what I had seen and witnessed, and where I thought the breach in our defenses had occurred. I also reported that I didn't believe that the company CP or their mortar platoon, or the artillery battery had ever gotten into the fight. Everyone was pretty exhausted and trying hard to figure out what to do next

Since Fox was the only fully operational unit on the firebase that morning I was told we needed to make a sweep around St. George outside the wire. I was to look for enemy bodies, anything that might be of intelligence value, and to look for any wounded NVA that could be brought in as POWs so we could more clearly determine what happened. I was given strict orders to not shoot any wounded, but to have my medic's patch them up and carry them into our first aid station. I was also told to be careful as we had no idea where the remnants of the attacking force had gone, they could still be in the wood lines surrounding the base; we would be out in the open as we made our search. To help us with security we were assigned a dog tracker team that had just arrived at the firebase at 0755.

I left the TOC and returned to my bunkers and got everyone together. I told the guys of the importance of this next mission, and the rules of engagement. I also told everyone to be on high alert (not really necessary) and to keep an eye on the wood lines. We would move through the south gate and spread out in a single line oriented to the west so we could make a clockwise sweep around the entire perimeter. I reinforced my order to not shoot any wounded. We'd carefully check them for hidden weapons or booby traps, patch them up, and get them inside the wire.

After a few minutes for everyone to get their gear and ammo, drink some water and smoke a cigarette we slowly filed out of the wire at 0830 and started to cross the open area to start our sweep.

When we were basically on line and dispersed as much as made sense, we began to move. We couldn't cover the entire area to the wood lines because it was so wide. Red, Buck and I were in the middle of the line. We walked slowly, trying to keep on line, and to watch the area all around us in case there were any live munitions or bad guys still alive. There were bodies of NVA lying around, plus some weapons and other gear. None of the NVA we passed appeared to still be alive; we jostled each one with a weapon as we passed by after checking for booby traps to ensure they were dead. In most cases there was no doubt.

A couple of shots rang out to my right; everyone immediately hit the ground. I moved down to where the shots had come from to learn that my Kit Carson Scout had just killed a wounded NVA claiming that the guy had a hidden weapon. The Kit Carson Scouts were former Viet Cong or NVA who switched sides and were trained and employed as intelligence scouts for the US. When we checked the body we found that the sapper had a satchel charge attached to his stomach and also two plastic bags, one with some documents and the other with a lighter. We policed those up to turn in to the S2. I was really pissed that the guy had been killed; I knew that the Scout understood enough English to have understood my orders.

We got everyone up and continued the sweep without any more incidents. As we finished we filed back into the wire to return to our bunkers and hopefully get some sleep. We stayed locked and loaded as we weren't sure all the enemy had left the base. One of my guys shouted out that he saw a gook,

"Hey Six, there's a gook hiding here under the bed of this five ton truck on top of the frame!"

My guy had walked passed the rear of the truck and looked in the opening under the bed and saw an enemy soldier hiding there. All right, here was our POW if in fact there was a guy there. We surrounded the truck from covered positions, weapons ready, and thought about how to get that guy out as he was out of sight and we couldn't fire at him.

Someone told me that we had a case of tear gas grenades in one of our bunkers and I thought that might work; I doubted the sapper had a gas mask. A couple of us grabbed a grenade and ran up to the truck, pulled the pins, and ran back to cover since we didn't have gas masks either. The gas billowed up under the truck but there was no resultant sound of coughing or hacking. That was hard to believe as CS (tear gas) is really nasty stuff, it burns your eyes and any open wounds, gets into your lungs causing hacking coughs, makes your nose run and generally disables you for a while. We grabbed some more grenades and tossed them under the truck, still nothing; I think we used the whole case!

This was puzzling and frustrating; my guy swore he'd seen someone hiding under the bed of that truck. Someone looked over and saw an engineer bulldozer sitting a little way away. He said he could drive it and suggested that he go climb on, see if it would start, and then drive it over behind the truck. If he could hook the blade under the bed he could raise the truck via the blade, hoping to dislodge the sapper and have him fall to the ground where we could secure him.

This sounded like a reasonable approach so I told one of the other guys to go with him to sit up top and provide security. They ran off, climbed on board, started the dozer and drove it slowly toward the back of the truck with the blade raised as a shield. When they were right behind it they slowly lowered and then raised the blade, hooked the 5-ton bed, and lifted the truck a foot or so. They then lowered the blade suddenly causing the truck to come down hard and bounce on its flat tires; nothing!

He went through the process again, this time raising the truck up higher before he let it crash down; this time we had some success, an AK-47 fell to the ground under the truck. One of the guys ran up and retrieved the weapon. The process of raising the truck higher was repeated and this time a medic stretcher fell out when the vehicle bounced. The sapper was pretty resourceful having pulled up the stretcher to lie on to provide some comfort; but still there was absolutely no noise from the enemy soldier; hard to believe after all of the CS and bouncing around.

The dozer once more hooked the truck and raised it even higher before letting it go. This time there was success, a tall, skinny NVA sapper in a loin cloth and shirt dropped out from under the truck! Fortunately my guys were alert and aware of the importance of taking the guy alive so no shots were fired. We had our POW. We called the TOC and told him what we had and escorted the new prisoner over to that location. This was a successful and rewarding end to what had been a harrowing 12 hours or so.

About this time I was told that the Assistant Division Commander (ADC) was coming out to St. George to survey the results of the night's fight. At least we had some good news for him soon. The preliminary casualty reports were nine dead and more than 40 wounded, some seriously. This was almost 50% of the total force on St George. There had been more than 40 bodies of dead NVA collected from both inside and outside the wire. They were collected and thrown into the back of an operational deuce and a half and taken outside the wire and buried in a mass grave. Given the enemy's normal procedure of removing as many dead and wounded as possible from the battlefield, and the fact that I'd not been able to find the guy that I had tussled with, I suspect that the actual enemy dead and wounded total was a lot higher.

We were told to put on flak jackets and man the perimeter to provide security for the ADC. I heard the bird land on the pad we normally used and checked my area to make sure all was secure. When the ADC came to my area I discovered that his aide was a classmate. The general and his aide looked a little out of place on that battlefield in their starched jungle fatigues; spit shined .45 cal holsters and Army soft caps. It was hard for me to believe that they had come out dressed as they were without steel pots, flack jackets and better security as there could still have been bad guys in the area. As I remember I spoke with my classmate briefly and then accompanied a couple of my soldiers over to the TOC to be presented impact valor awards. Those were for recognition of bravery that could be presented immediately without having to first do the paperwork. Shortly thereafter the VIPs left, we were allowed to remove our flak jackets and steel pots, and set about trying to clean up the area and get back to some semblance of normalcy.

My guys had acquitted themselves in a professional and heroic manner over the past night and day. I'm convinced now that those I took over to the destroyed D company bunkers saved the firebase. I believe their valiant fight from the ruins kept the sappers from accomplishing their major objective of neutralizing the artillery battery. While those guns were never fired they also were not destroyed. I also believe their defense of the otherwise abandoned D Company perimeter had kept any NVA reinforcements from coming through the wire. Basically they blunted the attack and saved St. George from being overrun that night.

The interrogation of the POW we had secured revealed some pretty interesting details. First off, that guy was not a sapper, but an NVA engineer who had come along on the attack to see for himself how Americans fought. He had been led to believe capturing St. George would be relatively easy. He also revealed there were several mortar and automatic weapons positions around St. George to support the planned attack of an NVA infantry battalion that was to attack on the opposite side of the base from the sapper breach to completely overrun us. This attack was to occur after being informed the artillery had been neutralized so they wouldn't be subjected to direct fire and the dreaded beehive rounds. Needless to say, they never had the opportunity to execute their plan. Had they been successful the outcome of the night's fight could have been very different. Their planned access point was in the area of the bunker line manned by headquarters and admin troops and in an area where it would have been impossible for the artillery to use direct fire because the guns were on the opposite side of the perimeter with too many structures and Americans in the direction of fire.

He also revealed there had been a Chinese Communist advisor with the sapper CP, an engineer Major. I believe he was the big guy I noticed in the NVA command group we destroyed and whose Ho Chi Minh sandals I had appropriated.

I don't remember much about the afternoon of November 6th, I think that I must have fallen asleep somewhere. The battalion log reflects we were deployed again outside of the perimeter from 1400 to 1600 but I don't remember that at all. That night we were hit again with mortars, rockets and automatic weapons fire but no ground attack. I'm not aware of any casualties from those incidents. The XO was fired on at about 1600 while 600-800 meters to the southwest of St George. That night D Company saw lights and engaged enemy units about 100 to 200 meters to the northwest who were engaged with M-79's and 81 mm mortars. We remained at St. George to augment the security of the firebase due to heavy casualties in a couple of D company's platoons. The battalion also repaired the damage as much as we could and continued to improve fields of fire.

On the 7th St. George was reinforced with a flame platoon of the 2nd Battalion, 8th Infantry. The tracks were placed in key positions on the perimeter. All of the battalion's companies were moved into positions around St George several clicks out to look for survivors of the NVA attacking force. Even D company was to deploy to the south on the 8th to sweep to the north to try to locate enemy that had evaded in that direction based on Intel provided by a CIA element that had arrived at St. George. B Company was to return to the firebase on the 8th to take over the security mission. We remained at St. George on a 15-minute alert status while continuing to repair the damage from the night of the 6th. That night, we were again hit by B-40's and mortars resulting in three WIA, one

131

from the artillery and two infantry. Later that night we were hit again resulting in two more US WIA. Needless to say we didn't get much sleep.

In the morning of the 8th, around 0800 Fox departed from St George to sweep to the northeast to track suspected enemy formations. While sweeping the east side of the perimeter we found a fighting position about 150 meters out from the perimeter. There were fresh footprints leading to the east and southeast as well as two homemade hand grenades made from banana leaves. We returned to St. George at about 0950 and B Company returned at 1430.

All of the other companies were deployed in various directions from St George sweeping to find any elements from the units that had attacked us. That day A Company picked up 6 young Montagnard detainees because they were found with a lot of military equipment. Because they had both US and enemy equipment they were brought to St. George; one died en route. They had been found with one GI helmet, three US canteen covers, one US pistol belt, one NVA jacket, three VC canteens, two NVA khaki shorts, four NVA ponchos, two 100 foot coils of rope, one pair of tennis shoes, one pair of GI low quarters, two VC cone hats, three old pair of black pajamas and a lot of blood stained clothing.

B Company, while making a sweep, found two fighting positions about 300 meters from the wire made of logs and sand bags. There were three satchel charges found as well. These could have been the NVA automatic weapons positions that supported the sapper attack and would have supported the advance of their regular troops. That night we were also alerted to the possibility of another attack.

The previous couple of days had been trying for all of us. Once subjected to the ferocity of a sapper attack it's difficult to return to a sense of normalcy; our mental security bubble had been vilontly popped. We were all on edge and didn't get much sleep because of the continuing attacks. Each time we received fire we suspected that a major ground attack might be coming. Fox was run ragged during this time with the myriad of patrol and ambush missions we were given. All of the destroyed bunkers were searched to ensure that there were no more casualties. I have a distinct memory of lifting off in some birds from the VIP pad and seeing the rotor wash blow the poncho liners off of stretchers holding some of our dead.

It had been a tough couple of days.

DUTY! HONOR! COUNTRY!

13 – SURROUNDED

On November 9, 1969, just three days after the sappers penetrated St George, Recon was directed by the Division CG to make a late day combat assault into an area to the northwest of St. George to track NVA who were possibly retreating from the attack on us. The order was received at the TOC at 1726; we left St George at 1822 hours and hit the LZ at 1834. Because of the urgency of the mission and the short reaction time, it was impossible to do an aerial recon to select an appropriate LZ. The best that could be done was that we, the S-2, S-3 and I, selected what appeared to be an appropriate location from looking at the map. We wanted to be in the area of the suspected NVA location. There was also a LRRP team in the area that had requested a unit to help them secure a rice cache, and we were to assist them as well after we got set up.

I was concerned about the availability of support in the designated area for the LZ as it appeared that I'd be beyond the range of the 105mm battery on St. George. After some lengthy discussion the S3 promised that he'd put two guns in a better place the next morning on a hip shoot. A hip shoot was a temporary displacement of artillery pieces to cover a long-range contingency mission. He was reluctant to do this, dispatching two guns would seriously degrade the fire power available on the firebase. The battery was already short one gun. We also talked about air support and I was promised a couple of gunships on stand-by the next morning. There were no assets available to support my combat assault however.

After we had selected what appeared to be an acceptable LZ, I returned to my CP and gathered my platoon sergeant and squad leaders and RTOs. I informed them of the mission. We had an opportunity to track the bastards who had killed so many at St George a couple of nights earlier and maybe exact some revenge. We also discussed how best to operate once we had landed because it would be so close to dusk. Once we had agreed on a course of action my NCO's went back to their squads to get everyone ready to saddle up. The division would supply enough birds, reportedly four, so we could go in as an entire unit, something that didn't always happen.

We assembled on our pad outside the wire in front of our bunkers and waited for the birds to arrive as the NCOs checked to make sure everyone had all of their equipment. There was a palpable sense of nervousness as it was getting close to dark, which made the operation potentially very dangerous, again, the night belonged to Charlie. But at the same time there was also a strong sense of resolve and determination, maybe we could find and kill the sons of bitches that almost took our firebase and killed and wounded about 50% of the total GI's there to include several from Fox who had been medevac'ed. When the birds arrived, everyone quickly boarded and took their positions inside or in the doors.

The birds lifted off and we started to our LZ. I looked down as we left and again saw several stretchers near one of the bunkers with something covered by ponchos. I thought at that time those may be our casualties from the attack but rethinking it now it makes no sense that they would have remained on St. George so long after the attack. When the pilot told me we were three minutes out I motioned to everyone to lock and load; I could hear bolts being released to ram rounds into the weapons' chambers and could also hear the clicks as safeties were moved to the "safe" position where they would be until we exited the aircraft, unless the LZ was hot. We were as ready as we could be and ready for whatever we would find.

When we landed it was close to dark, it was critical that we find a safe and concealed place to hunker down for the night. We formed a hasty perimeter in the wood line next to the LZ and waited until almost dark when we moved to the top of a nearby knoll that had been selected during my briefing at St George. It would give us good visibility of the surrounding area when the sun came up. The terrain was mostly gently rolling hills with some rice paddies interspersed with small areas of what appeared to be thick jungle vegetation. There were some taller ridgelines a couple of klicks (kilometers) away.

The hill that we selected had a good amount of trees and secondary underbrush, which provided us some cover and concealment while also ensuring that anyone coming up the hill would probably be noisy, the elevation was probably about 200 - 300 meters above the LZ. It also appeared to be the best place for a chance at establishing communications; we learned when we landed that we were beyond the limit of our radio range. In reality, we were in a very precarious situation as we were also outside the range of artillery support. I prayed the S3 would follow through with the hip shoot, getting a couple of guns closer to us for fire support. That night we were completely on our own.

We had initially formed a perimeter a couple of hundred yards from our desired location to not let any watching VC or NVA know where we were setting up. As dark fell we moved as quietly and quickly as we could up the hill and established a 360-degree perimeter around the military crest. I don't remember exactly how high that hill was but it seemed to take a while to get to the top. We were below our usual field strength of 25 or so guys because of the casualties from the sapper attack, so there would have been nine or ten two-man positions with my CP, my two RTOs and me, somewhere in the center below the crest. Jimmy Harris manned one of the perimeter positions with one other guy. Usually there is a military advantage to the high ground; it's easier and generally more accurate to shoot down than up. We always set up on the military crest of the hill, an imaginary line around the top that marked the limit of being able to stand without showing yourself above the top of the terrain feature so as to not silhouette ourselves against the sun or moon and become a good target. Fortunately for us the top of this hill was pretty small so we were able to extend our line of positions all the way around it. There is also, however, a major disadvantage to defending a hill. If the bad guys find you, there may be no place to go. We had seen some signs of the enemy as we left the birds and moved toward our position, but the area did not appear to be highly trafficked, and the signs did not appear to be recent.

I remember being somewhat uneasy as we settled in; we still had no commo and if discovered, no fire support and no escape. This is the time the responsibility for men's lives really hits hard. We were where we were because of my decision. If we were compromised anything that happened would be my fault. I then focused on an excellent tool I had come to rely on by this time in my tour to assure the best chance of success of any task at hand. I mentally war-gamed all steps in whatever mission we had been given, factoring in both friendly and possible enemy actions, reactions and counteractions. This process had proven itself useful several times, allowing us to maintain the all-important tactical initiative leading to mission success, and keeping my guys alive. Good leaders constantly worry about mission accomplishment and taking care of their men. I used my war-gaming process to try to assure the accomplishment of both goals.

As night fell, I had seen no other viable night defensive position close to the LZ through either a map recon or checking the surrounding area once we arrived. I hadn't called in artillery registration rounds, I hadn't been informed that the hip shoot was in place. If I was right in regards to location, the defensive registration would have pretty much pin-pointed my location for anyone else. I did study my map and mark some registration points around where I thought we were so that I could call in target coordinates quickly if required, and if we could establish communications.

I directed my squad leaders to put out two-man listening posts on the most likely enemy avenues of approach. It was their task to lie quietly some 20 to 50 meters in front of our positions and listen for any suspicious sounds, and to report them to my CP if heard. LP duty was lonely, often very scary, and not much liked by the troops even though they knew how critical the mission was to everyone's survival. This was particularly important that night as we were all still exhausted and shaken from the events of the past two days.

After all of this was taken care of, I remember looking out over the valley a couple of hundred meters below us bordered on the other side by some rolling hills as the sun was setting,. It was dusk, the colors of the vegetation in the waning light and shadows were beautiful, and everything was quiet and peaceful. It was really a pretty place; a nice place to vacation I thought again, if there was no war going on with people shooting at you.

There are some tough decisions required of a small unit leader in a combat environment. At times like this it was generally impossible for me to sleep soundly, which was probably a good thing. There is an old saying that it is "lonely at the top", and command at times was a very lonely mental experience. Even if others agreed with you, the actual final decision was yours and yours alone. I think that this was particularly tough when you commanded a small, specialized, independent unit like Fox Force. Even though I tried initially to maintain the separation of command, I quickly found it was impossible not to become emotionally close to the guys in the unit. We were too few in numbers, and too totally dependent on each other's skills for our survival to maintain any type of real separation. We had been through a lot together. My decisions would influence the life or death of "my guys"; soldiers who were becoming as close as family members.

The hardest tactical decisions were those that carried with them the high probability of loss of lives. This could be difficult enough to handle and justify if the decisions were correct, the actions proper, but the result was the loss of life or limb. In that case, a commander was supposed to be able to deal with the losses and continue the mission without any burden of guilt. If, on the other hand, the decisions were

136

wrong and poorly thought out, then the loss of life of even one of your soldiers could create a burden and pressure that many small unit leaders couldn't cope with, and that would probably haunt you for the rest of your life. Commanders at all levels share these responsibilities, but it is those commanders at the lowest levels, those who are the closest to the troops, who I believe find the burden the heaviest.

Thus the small unit commander was ultimately and completely responsible for all successes or failures resulting from his decisions. If men died, were badly wounded or captured, then the burden of command could become unbearable for those who were not well trained in leadership principles. A leader learned in his earliest education that mission accomplishment was the highest priority, higher even than safeguarding the lives of his soldiers. That was an incredibly tough situation to be placed in and a very heavy burden for a young combat commander. And Vietnam was truly a small unit commander's war, with most actions being taken at company level or below.

To add to these thoughts was the knowledge that just three days earlier we had literally fought for our lives all night long as the NVA tried to overrun LZ St. George and had almost succeeded. My guys were still numb and tired from that experience, deep in their own thoughts and reflections of that terrible experience.

There were a lot of thoughts and influences that were subconsciously running through my mind that night on that hill. Were we in the proper place? Would we have been better off somewhere on the low ground? Could I have selected a better and more defensible position? Should we have continued to move away from the area under cover of darkness? We were far from help and all on our own. If I had made the wrong decision, then the morning could find us in an absolutely terrible situation, if we lived that long. Where else could we have gone? Were there other areas that could have afforded us adequate cover and concealment? Given enough time I might have been able to find one, but I was convinced that the position I had selected was the best available given the planning time, and the circumstances and time of our landing. Besides, being on high ground gave us the best opportunity to establish communications.

All sounds are magnified at night and the eyes convince you all of the bushes are moving toward you. We had been trained to never stare directly at an object at night, as your eyes could play tricks on you. Rather we were to scan an area and examine desired specific points out of the corner of our eyes. That night was clear and the moon and stars were beautiful and bright overhead. Because there was absolutely no ambient light in the Vietnamese countryside the heavens were incredible; you could actually see the Milky Way. It was just so gorgeous there couldn't possibly be any danger. After we settled in we opened C-ration cans and ate the cold contents, not daring to warm them and give ourselves away by the light or the smell.

After eating and quietly disposing of the empty containers, everyone made themselves comfortable in their selected positions and the night became quiet, totally so, no insects or any of the other usual night noises. The back of my neck began to twitch. In a combat environment your body develops signs and signals when danger is close. It's that combat 6th sense that has saved many a life in every war ever fought. In my case, I could feel danger through the hairs on the back of my neck and head; they would become very sensitive. Yet there was nothing else to indicate danger except for the total absence of normal nighttime jungle noises, maybe I was just plain scared, it sure wouldn't be the first time. There were a myriad of thoughts running through my head as I tried to visualize where we were and what type of contingency actions might be required if we were discovered. The fact we were beyond the limit of effective communications further complicated the situation. Red had not yet been able to contact anyone on the battalion frequency.

A couple of hours passed, I think I may have dozed off a little despite my best efforts to stay alert. At about 2100 Buck moved, he was getting a transmission from one of the squad LP's on the eastern side of the perimeter,

"Fox 6, Fox 2 alpha, we have movement to our front, over."

Oh, Goddamn it, was this movement being caused by humans or animals? If human, they sure as shit weren't going to be friendly. I whispered to Red who was on the battalion freq and told him to try to raise higher again.

"2 alpha, 6, how close are they, how many?"

"6, 2 alpha, I think they're close and it sounds like a lot."

A few minutes later another call came from one of the other squads on the northern part of the perimeter; they too had movement. In both cases it appeared to be the sound of men or animals trying to move slowly and quietly through the jungle at night. A little later a similar report came from the south side of our position. One suspected enemy soldier was supposedly sighted but it was difficult to be sure in the dark. The report was that the gooks were close enough that my guys could hear what sounded like rifle slings being dragged on the ground.

Aw fuck me; I'm in deep shit now. What if these really are gooks and not wild pigs as we sometimes heard at night? What could I do, where could we move to in

the dark? I was now getting amped up; we appeared to be in an extremely tough situation. I had my guys on a hilltop that was now possibly surrounded by VC or NVA. I realized I could not give in to my growing sense of apprehension. I just had to grab hold of myself and figure a way out of this mess. Suddenly, another call came in an urgent whisper,

"6, 2 alpha, I hear metal on metal, these are fucking gooks out here!"

"Red, have you raised battalion?"

"Negative."

"Keep trying; they've got to hear us."

Now the real dilemma… I didn't want anyone to fire their weapons as the gooks could pinpoint location by muzzle flashes. I could have the guys roll hand grenades down the hill, but they could get caught in the underbrush and go off too close, and besides, any action would just confirm to the bad guys that we were there. My fervent wish was that if we just stayed quiet they'd give up and go away – big fucking chance that would happen!

At times like this I always tried to crawl into my adversary's head to try to figure out what he was doing. My analysis at this point wasn't real good. It was pretty obvious we had been spotted when we landed, and my opponent probably had a pretty good idea of how many guys I had. I figured he must have been a lot stronger than Fox or he wouldn't be sending his guys out to find me. He had me practically surrounded, the only area not reporting movement was to the west at this time… *and why was that? What lay in wait for us in that direction?* The situation as I saw it was not real promising. *How should I react to this? What could I do to ensure we survived whatever was coming our way?*

There were several options to be considered. If we didn't do anything until the last possible minute and they were on us we were probably all going to die or be captured. That wasn't an option, what would happen to any wounded? If we waited until we could actually see them before we opened fire, we would probably be forced into hand-to-hand combat and it might be impossible to disengage without trying to kill every one of them. And we weren't carrying bayonets, even though everyone packed a pretty wicked knife of some sort, so close quarters combat would be really ugly. What the hell, maybe we should just do a "mad minute," which involved everyone firing their weapons on fully automatic using one or two magazines at a specific time. The idea was to create a wall of lead, which no one could survive. There may not be a lot of them, we would probably kill some, and maybe the rest would run away. At least we could go down with a fight if there were a lot of them.

139

And still no communication with higher, we were totally on our own on that little hill top.

As I considered that option I got another idea; why not use a mad minute to cover a withdrawal from the hill; a nighttime "Break Contact" and E&E (escape and evasion) plan? It didn't make a lot of sense to me to stay where we were no matter what course of action we took. I checked my map under the cover of Red's poncho liner using a red flashlight filter, and selected an azimuth to the west that would lead down the hill to what appeared to be another small jungled rise about 300 meters away. I could only pray the enemy commander hadn't planned for this reaction and was actually lying in wait for us to try to escape in that direction. There didn't seem to be any other viable option.

Because of the situation and late insertion I had not been able to recon and disseminate a rally point for us in case we had to abandon the hill. I hadn't expected to be observed; with bad luck our LZ must have been close to the NVA positions. I decided I'd pass the word to the team leaders to move their guys out, under the leadership of Jimmy Harris, my Ranger qualified platoon sergeant, who had been trained in this type of maneuver, on that azimuth for 300 meters immediately on the conclusion of the mad minute. Once moving they were initially to move quietly, but then if discovered to keep up a constant high volume of fire to their front and flanks as they ran down the hill in the dark. Boy that scenario was just a fertile ground for all kinds of problems, but there was really no other recourse other than to fight and die in place, the Fox Force Little Big Horn, and that wasn't much of an option.

I'd tell Jimmy that he would be in command; it was his job to make sure everyone got the word and got started in the right direction. I decided I'd play rear guard to cover our withdrawal, and then hopefully link up with them later. I just couldn't sit in place and wait for the inevitable; I needed to get as many of the guys out of that situation as possible. Since I was completely responsible for us being in this untenable position, then it was unquestionably my responsibility to do whatever was needed to make sure we left no one behind in the dark, and to get as many out alive as possible. If that meant lagging behind to slow down any pursuit, then that's what I'd do. This could sound kind of hokey and overly dramatic in today's environment, and especially to anyone who has never been in my boots, but it was my thought at that moment.

By this time we had movement pretty much all around us so it was obvious we were going to have a real fight on our hands. I sent word for the LP's to come back to the perimeter and take up good defensive positions. After waiting for them to close with us I was just about to talk with Harris and get the plan spread around and order the mad minute when Red grabbed my shoulder,

"Six, I have Puff."

Puff was short for Puff the Magic Dragon, a name taken from a Peter, Paul and Mary song that we gave to armed U.S. Air Force AC-47 two engine gunships. The big bird was armed with three 7.62mm General Electric Miniguns, which fired at an unbelievable speed, either 50 or 100 rounds per second and with incredible accuracy. Even though only every 5th round was a tracer, the rate of fire of the minigun was so fast it appeared to be a solid stream of red coming from the sky when they opened up; hence the name. The electrically powered gun in that airplane was a direct descendent of the Gatling Gun of Civil War fame. The Gatling gun was the forerunner of the machine gun, it had a very high rate of fire fed by huge magazines of ammo.

The original Gatling had multiple barrels that were rotated by the gunner via a hand crank. Each barrel was rotated in front of a firing pin which contacted the round in the chamber. As the crank was rotated a fired barrel was moved away from the pin, the empty cartridge was ejected, and a new one loaded. The rate of fire was controlled by the speed of cranking. The modern minigun operated under the same concept but was electrically fired and had a rate of fire of thousands of rounds per minute that could cover the area of a football field, placing at least one round in every square yard, in a 3 second time period. It was an awesome sight from far away; it would prove to be indescribable when you were in the center of a cone of that kind of firepower.

Evidently this gunship had been requested by battalion and had picked up my RTO's efforts to contact battalion for help. We later found out that our radio was being monitored from the Division rear in Pleiku and was being relayed to our battalion TOC even though their transmission didn't reach us. So he answered and asked if he could be of help. Puff was not only a dragon but at this time was also the US cavalry galloping over the ridge coming to the rescue. I got on the horn and identified my call sign,

"Puff, this is Fox 6, over."

"Fox 6, this is Puff, what's going on down there?"

I quickly filled him in, telling him that we were a small unit on a hilltop with the sounds of potential enemy pretty much all around us moving up the hill; and asked how I could get some fire support. He asked if I had a strobe light, which I did. He then suggested that we abandon everything but weapons and ammo, that I have all of my guys pull back and put their feet in my lap. I was then to put the strobe light in my upturned steel pot (helmet) held in my lap next to everyone's feet and turn it on. The thought was that being inside the helmet the light would be directed upwards and hopefully not too visible to the bad guys. He then wanted a distance from the light, which was occupied by us, everything outside of that was his! With the light in my helmet we hoped that it wouldn't be visible to the bad guys and give them an aiming point!

This would be a heck of a maneuver. If I followed his suggestion then the whole platoon would be in a circle of about an eight-foot radius, an extremely easy target for the NVA. Hell, one well-thrown grenade would probably take out half of us. But the only other alternative was equally as dicey, trying to fight our way off of that hill in the dark. If one guy stumbled on a rock and fell he could be left behind, to say nothing of injuring some of his buddies in the process.

There was really no other solution. Doing what the Puff pilot suggested sure seemed better than a fight to the last among the trees and rocks, and also better than just picking an azimuth, getting everyone headed in that direction firing on rock and roll, and hoping that some would make it to safety somewhere in the pitch black of night, while I hoped to slow down or stop the pursuit by the NVA. I briefed my RTO's and the three of us passed the word by whispering to the nearest guys, and instructed them to pass the instructions to the other positions; telling the guys to count to 10, then move back to me with only weapons and ammo as quickly and quietly as possible. We soon had all of us together with 20+ pairs of boots in or near my lap. I called Puff and told him that everything 15 feet out from the light was his. His response was that I was to get everyone's head down when he alerted that he was about to open up.

As soon as everyone was accounted for I put the strobe light in my helmet and turned it on. I hadn't used it in a while and wasn't positive that the batteries were still good. Fortunately for us they were, and the light began to work, emitting a periodic light so bright that I was sure that the whole world could see it. My guardian angel hadn't abandoned me; I hoped it wouldn't take Puff too long to locate us and begin to fire. If you believe in God and His protection, then He had sent us an Angel in the form of Puff.

"Fox 6, this is Puff. I have your light. Tell your guys to get their heads down, I'm about to open up. Everything from the 15-foot line out from your light is mine. Get ready, it's coming in about 5 seconds."

We passed the word for everyone to scrunch down as deeply as possible into the earth, make sure their helmets were secure, and to put their hands over their ears with their mouths open to equalize pressure.

Quickly the Puff guns opened up. Holy shit, it was like being in the middle of a tornado-like cone of fire. That red breath of the Magic Dragon completely encircled us, the noise was deafening. All of a sudden we were in the middle of some type of hail-like storm as pieces of hot metal began to come down by the hundreds. We quickly realized that these were the metal links that belted the rounds together and the hot shell casings discharged through a hole in the aircraft's belly.

Anyone caught in that firestorm of bullets would be shredded. I'm sure there must have been screams although we couldn't hear much over the loud buzzing sound of the guns, we did hear some secondary explosions caused probably by enemy grenades getting hit, but we couldn't hear anything else. I don't know how long the fire lasted, probably no more than 15 to 30 seconds, but it seemed like an awfully long time. When it ceased I thought I was deaf, there was absolutely no noise. Then gradually I could hear my breath again and my heart beating in my ears, and then some low noises from my guys as they were shaking themselves to clear their ears. We strained in the deafening quiet, not sure if the silence was due to damaged ears or the situation. Everyone was alert for anything but there was no more sound or other indication of movement.

Puff called down and asked for a status report; I replied that we couldn't detect any more movement but we had heard what sounded like secondary explosions from enemy grenades. He asked if there was anything else that I needed, and I asked him to come back in an hour or two just to check up on us. I'll never forget his answer,

"No sweat, Fox 6, I'll be up here the rest of the night. Why don't you try to get some sleep?"

Holy shit, this guy was willing to fly cover for us until the sun came up; he was concerned about my sleep! Unbelievable!! God Bless the United States Air Force! He then told me they were picking up some other movement that they wanted to check out, but he'd be in the general area and constantly monitoring our frequency. As he flew off we could see what looked like a column of flashlights coming down a distant ridgeline in our direction, maybe reinforcements for the original NVA unit. I knew US forces never used flashlights for night movement, so they probably belonged to an enemy force that had no concern for security as they were in their own country. Puff breathed some more fire and the lights went out; we didn't see them again that night. I moved the guys back out to their original positions for improved security about 20 minutes later when we heard no more movement. I never did go to sleep, but we all sure breathed a little easier.

143

The rest of the night was tense but quiet. As the sun came up we surveyed the terrain and then moved quietly and slowly out of our positions to sweep the general area around us. The underbrush had been shredded, and there were numerous indications of blood, but no bodies. Evidently the NVA had returned sometime during the night and carried off all of their casualties, par for the course. Our hill was surrounded by low ground including a small blue line and rice paddies; there was scattered thick jungle all around. There were a couple of ridges off in the distance where we had seen the flashlights the night before. After some hot coffee and a quick breakfast we saddled up and left that hill a little after 0900. We didn't want to go there again.

We moved carefully on a northern azimuth towards where we had seen the lights to try and track the guys who had been spotted by Puff. Maybe the guys who had moved against us the previous night were the same unit that had attacked us on St. George. A couple of klicks from the night position we found what appeared to be a fresh large grave. As I remember there were a couple of hands or feet pointing up from the ground. We didn't dig the area up but suspected it was full of NVA casualties from the night before. I could only hope this was part of the element that had attacked St. George. Later that afternoon we were ordered to stand by for pick-up and were flown back to the remnants of our home and firebase. We never linked up with the LRRP team.

I was proud of but not surprised at the courage and discipline of my Fox guys. They were almost all draftees, all about 20 years old, but they had reacted the night before with incredible professionalism. There had been no panic, no discussion. When they backed into my CP to put their feet in my lap they were all in good firing positions with ammo and grenades handy. Had Spooky not been able to stop the NVA advance there is no doubt that we would have given a good account of ourselves, even though we were in a very tight and vulnerable group. Everyone moved quickly in the morning and when we left that hill we were a highly lethal and professional fighting force.

I had learned more about myself and more real-life lessons in the profession of being a small unit leader in combat. Responsibility for men's lives was awesomely heavy. The leader alone was responsible for decisions and actions. A good part of that responsibility, at least for me, was to consider recourse if your decision was bad. Being responsible was just that, not only in easy situations, but also in the most difficult. I had learned something about myself that night, that I loved my guys more than I had realized, and that I would willingly do whatever was required to safeguard their lives. I could not just abandon my job and just let nature take its course; I couldn't have just ordered the mad minute and then dealt with whatever occurred, thereby abandoning the responsibility for lives; I had to have a plan and be willing to do whatever was required to ensure the survival of as many of my guys as possible.

Some forty years later I met an AC-47 crewman for the first time. I described the incident to him and told him that guys like him were responsible for a lot of my guys, and probably me, still being alive. It was a very emotional time; we were both in tears as we parted. When I got in the car where Margie was waiting for me I couldn't drive. I needed someone who would understand my emotions and called Red to tell him what had happened. The meeting had brought back a rush of memories, ones that I had put away and not thought about for at all for 40 years. It took a while before I was able to get control of myself and drive home. Thank God for Margie being there.

DUTY! HONOR! COUNTRY!

14 - CHANGE OF COMMAND

On November 11, 1969, the Golden Dragons left FSB St. George for the last time after about five months, headed for a new AO near Ban Me Thout and a new firebase. It had been an eventful five months at St. George, probably too long a time to keep an infantry battalion in the same area. However, the firebase location allowed the battalion to successfully interdict NVA movement into South Vietnam from the Ho Chi Minh Trail. It was tough to leave after the fight of the 6th; some said that the NVA had kicked us out of the AO. I don't believe that; we inflicted a pretty serious defeat on that sapper unit and its supporting units in the days since the attack. The ARVN were vacating the Ban Me Thout area to move south to Bu Prang where there was a major fight with the NVA brewing. I-14 Infantry was sent to the area to provide security when the ARVN left. St. George and the events surrounding the attack and its aftermath was a name that would remain in our memories until the day we die.

Ban Me Thout had already played a role in American history as President Teddy Roosevelt had a tiger-hunting lodge built there. We were to learn firsthand all about those big cats. We flew down to the Ban Me Thout airfield on Chinooks on the 10th, spent the night there, and moved by truck to LZ Lois, our new home, in the morning of the 11th in advance of the rest of the battalion. No one knew the significance of the name of the new place; we found out years later that it was Dragon's wife's name. We spent the night in our new home prepared to conduct patrols around the area the next day. The truck convoys carrying the rest of the Battalion arrived at the new area in the afternoon of the 11th and throughout the 12th.

Our primary functions in our new area were improving our positions and fields of fire, and to conduct daily patrols around the area to get an idea of the enemy's presence and routes of advance into the new zone around FSB Lois. Lois was located north of Ban Me Thout near the Mewal rubber plantation. When not in the field, we served as the battalion's ready reaction force maintaining a 15-minute alert status. We were also subjected to frequent visits by officers from both the brigade and division headquarters. On one such visit on the 13th the CG had observed soldiers involved in commerce with some locals at the wire and the battalion was directed to stop such interaction immediately!

On the 14th Fox did a recon in force to the north of Lois, and on the 15th to the southeast. On the 16th the battalion was warned about a suspected increase in enemy activity from Ban Me Thout to An Khe. We also had a trip flare go off in the perimeter and went to 50% alert, but had no subsequent activity.

On the 17th we were once again on a recon in force when we linked up with a local RF/PF platoon who had observed nine VC that morning. We scoured the area but found nothing. That day both the division CG and Brigade Commander again came out to Lois. That evening D Company at nearby LZ Purtle was probed a couple of times and responded with small arms and 81mm mortars. From the 18th to the 21st we continued our daily patrols and position improvement at LZ Lois. On the 20th A Company had a couple of contacts resulting in one friendly KIA and three WIA with three confirmed enemy KIAs.

On the 21st we left Lois again on another recon patrol about 1430. We were to interdict known enemy trails and set up ambushes at night. On the 22nd we met with locals from the Mewal Rubber Plantation who told us about a village the VC move into every night and then left again in the early morning. This same day C Company was told of the location of an NVA company that had been in place for about two weeks. Another report received at battalion concerned sizable VC presence in three different locations. All of this activity demonstrated a sizable enemy presence in our immediate area, both VC and NVA.

In the early morning hours of the 24th C Company took incoming B40 and small arms fire resulting in seven US WIA. At 0730 we received a warning to prepare for an immediate combat assault into the A company area to search and clear trails and streambeds. That order was subsequently canceled and we returned to Lois at about 1430.

On the 25th we stood down in the morning to rehearse a change of command ceremony for Dragon. At 1130 we left again to patrol the area around Lois to protect both the CG and brigade commanders who arrived at Lois at 1415. We returned to the firebase at 1600.

The 26th was a sad day for the guys in Fox, for on that day the battalion changed command and our Dragon, LTC Vic Robertson Jr., turned the battalion over to a new Dragon 6. LTC Robertson was a pivotal man in my life, as well as a great supporter of the men in Fox

Force. The color guard for the change of command was my Fox guys in their red scarves, an honor I had requested of the battalion S3. After the ceremony we presented Dragon with a steel pot with a dud 60mm mortar shell attached and I tied a red scarf around his neck in honor of all he had done for us. From then on he would be an honorary member of Fox Force, Recon Platoon, 1st Battalion, 14th Infantry, 4th Infantry Division. On that same day C Company suffered five WIA in a sharp firefight.

On the 26th of November we sent Coleman, Diz, Kenny and Al Rangus back to the rear for Sniper Training. It was a 10-day course and when they returned they were equipped with match grade M-14's that fired match grade ammunition. The only cleaning that was allowed by anyone other than an armorer was to oil the outside and run a patch down the barrel. That night we left Lois to conduct ambush patrols on a trail network south of the firebase.

Years later we would reconnect with Dragon and meet Lois, and they would become an integral part of our reunions until Lois passed away in 2011. Dragon continued to participate and we were all the richer for his presence. As he lives in Columbia, SC, less than two hours from our home, Margie and I are fortunate to spend a lot of time with him. I feel that over the past few years we two old soldiers have formed an almost father-son relationship. I was in awe of Dragon in the old days; I treasure him now. There is a special bond that occurs between men who have shared combat; it is indeed a special one when that bond is between a senior and a junior officer. These days I'm not the least bit ashamed to say that I love the man almost as if he were my Dad, Vic does in fact remind me a lot of my own Father.

DUTY! HONOR! COUNTRY!

15 - LZ LOIS

The day after the battalion change of command, the 27th of November, was Thanksgiving. The battalion mess team worked incredibly hard to prepare turkey for everyone in the battalion. We were still on the firebase when the meal was served and I managed to talk the mess sergeant out of a real turkey leg, my traditional piece of the bird for as long as I could remember. We ate first as we were scheduled to leave that afternoon on another mission to find several VC units reported close by. Lois also received a couple of mortar rounds during the meal, C Company also had several sightings of enemy units that day.

We remained out until the 29th, patrolling and ambushing. Several times during this period we left stay-behind units to try to catch the enemy trailing us and checking for useful garbage at our rest stops. I believe it was at this time we had an incident, another of several that have stayed with me to this day. We had stopped for a rest and then moved out, leaving a squad stay-behind. We moved several hundred meters when we heard the sound of small arms from the stay-behind location and I received a radio transmission that they were under attack. At that time we were in triple canopy with extremely thick secondary vegetation of wait-a-minute vines and bamboo.

At the sound of the firing we moved as quickly as we could through all of that crap to get back to our guys. We threw caution to the wind, hacking with machetes and throwing ourselves on the vegetation to try to make a trail. I remember almost a sense of panic on my part, I'd left guys behind and they might all be dead by the time we could get back. That was a horrible feeling; we just couldn't move quickly enough; the firing stopped and I remember thinking that we hadn't been able to get back in time. We redoubled our efforts, our guys were back there, and they needed us. We finally broke into the clearing near where we had left them to find everyone OK; they had driven off a couple of VC. We were absolutely exhausted both physically and emotionally. I learned then to be more careful about where we went if we were to leave another stay-behind, we had to be able to get back quickly in the event of an emergency. Another lesson learned in the art of small unit warfare, and another example of how heavy the weight of command can be, thinking that I had done something stupid by leaving those guys where I couldn't get to them.

I went on R & R during the end of November and the first week of December on the recommendation of the battalion S3. Fox had experienced a pretty rough November and he thought I needed a break. I spent that time in Hawaii with my first wife, Suzanne, and had a great time. We stayed at the Hilton Hawaiian Village in the Rainbow Tower right on the beach with a beautiful view down to Diamond Head. We even went to a Don Ho show where he honored all of us there on R & R.

On the 4th of December, I returned to LZ Lois and Fox, the firebase was on a stand down. On that day, the battalion S3 received some "Hot Intel" from brigade headquarters. In our area of operation there were four Montagnard villages that were suspected of hiding a platoon of VC. There were another four villages that housed a company-sized unit of VC. There was also word that an "agent" would finger a VC Major or Lieutenant Colonel who had been on temporary duty in Cambodia for six months who was also staying in one of the villages. The orders from brigade were to establish an ambush screen around the named villages and also to consider an early morning search as well.

Due to this intelligence, Fox left Lois at 0900 with a scout dog team on the 5th to conduct a reconnaissance in force and screening of the trail networks in the vicinity of the villages. At 1450 we picked up one detainee who was evac'ed to Lois. That night lights and enemy movement were detected around Lois; use of a starlight scope revealed at least two individuals.

The action picked up again on the 6th of December (my Mother's birthday). On that morning we had movement in front of us at about 0945 but didn't find anything. At 1020 we found a heavily used trail that intersected with a couple of others and ran into a village. The dog was picking up a lot of scents, which was not unexpected as it looked as though 20-30 people had used the trail. The battalion ready reaction force was alerted and standing by at 1030. We remained in the jungle that night conducting several ambushes. The battalion's line companies had a lot of sightings of enemy troops and fire fights that day as well. There appeared to be sizable numbers of VC and NVA moving around in our entire AO.

The next day was a busy one for all of the battalion elements in the field. B & C companies were preparing a cordon and search of a couple of villages. At about noon C Company engaged a small force of apparent NVA, killing one while suffering two WIA who needed to be medevac'ed. The enemy soldiers were wearing green fatigues.

At around 1400 it was our turn. We were securing a pickup zone to be transported to an area close to B & C Companies to support their cordon and search the next day. I remember resting under a small hooch we had found off to the side of the PZ with Jimmy, Red and Buck. It had a thatched roof and might have been used for shade or rice storage. There was another open area that came together at its southeast corner and the northwest corner of our PZ. I had put a squad-sized element on a trail close to the junction to provide security.

There was the sharp sound of gunfire as our security element employed small arms fire at seven enemy soldiers about 50 meters to their front. This was my first combat operation after returning from R & R in Hawaii, and I remember I was so shocked at the sound of gunfire and the cry of "Medic!" that it took me a while to react. I had been dreaming of white sandy beaches, swaying palm trees, and time with Suzanne and the sound of gunfire was a rude interruption that took me a few seconds to process. Red and I jumped up and fired in the direction of the bad guys as he called battalion to report the contact. Return fire wounded one of our guys, Frenchie, in the leg. The wound was serious enough to require a medevac. Contact was quickly broken and I took a few guys in pursuit of the enemy in the direction they had disappeared. Fortunately I quickly came to my senses and returned to the rest of the guys to organize a controlled pursuit.

The battalion CO arrived in his command and control helicopter (Loach) and performed a medevac. Our guys had observed one carbine, one M79, one M16 and AK 47's. One of the enemy was wearing a bush hat and GI boots, the rest were dressed in Montagnard clothing. After employing artillery and gun ships in the direction the enemy had disappeared, we moved out to follow them. We moved in the direction the bad guys had taken and found a well-used trail heading due east that led to a platoon size base camp with trails running from it in all directions. We found documents and a loaded M16 magazine but nothing more. We were airlifted at about 1800 to a firebase named Marianne to be co-located with B Company. C company had contact with the enemy and killed one, suffering two WIA.

We had an unpleasant experience being located with the B Company guys. They were noisy and not too concerned with security, at least not to the level that we usually followed. My guys were really uncomfortable with this situation so we packed up and moved a couple hundred meters away to ensure our security and safety.

On the 8th we were to conduct a cordon of a village named Buon with a platoon of B Company, 2/35th Infantry attached. After the cordon was complete we were to clear the area to the immediate west of the Mewal Rubber Plantation and be prepared for extraction and return to Lois. On the 10th we returned to Lois. On the 11th of December we recon'ed a sizable bunker complex and stirred up a hornet's nest.

DUTY! HONOR! COUNTRY!

16 - THE BUNKER COMPLEX

On Dec 10th, 1969, I was called to the S2's hooch to meet with him and the S3. Recent intelligence gathering had indicated there were sizable formations of the North Vietnamese Army coming across the border from Cambodia into our area of operations. No one was sure if this was true, or where they were headed, or what their mission was. It was suspected and feared the NVA might be planning a sizable attack on US installations around Ban Me Thuot, particularly the airfield at Phuong Duc. We were given the mission of reconing their suspected avenues of approach to see what we could find about their locations and size.

After some discussion it was decided that Fox would conduct a series of Eagle Flights, the name for a tactic of making single, or possibly multiple, insertions into different LZ's on the same day in order to quickly assess if there was enemy activity in that specific area. Eagle flights were conducted as a one-day operation, starting early in the morning and usually ending with the final extraction before dark. If we spotted any enemy units, there was supposedly a company-sized reaction force prepared to come to our assistance and exploit the opportunity.

As a part of this concept we also planned some phony insertions where we would hit an LZ but not get off of the birds. The birds would remain on the ground for the 30 or so seconds it normally took for us to get out, and would then take off to get us to the next LZ. By doing this we hoped that we could confuse any enemy that might be within hearing range of the helicopters. Because we thought we might encounter sizable NVA formations, I was more than anxious to keep them guessing if possible.

Since there was no plan to spend the night in the field, and to ensure that we could move quickly and quietly once we left the birds, we traveled light. We carried no rucksacks or other gear like claymores and trip flares that we would use around a night laager. We took only rations for a day, extra water and extra ammunition. Our first insertion on this particular day was to be far from Lois, toward the east, and if we didn't find anything, we would work our way back checking closer areas as we returned to the firebase.

Our first LZ was near a suspected newly constructed bunker complex area straddling a stream that B Company found a week earlier. During that operation they had killed three NVA in the vicinity of the complex. Because it was so large, electronic motion sensors had been dispersed in the complex area, either by airdrop or a LRRP team. The S2 reported those sensors had been activated the night before, indicating that someone had moved into or through the complex. Our mission was to check out the area to determine if the complex had been re-used by the NVA.

Due to the high probability of enemy contact we were assigned a scout dog team to accompany us. Scout dogs were specially trained to alert their handlers at any sound or smell of enemy forces. They were trained to alert silently and to remain motionless until released from that pose by their handler. On this particular day, I was assigned a dog named Red, a Golden Lab type of dog that had a slight reddish tint to his coat. I guess it's symbolic of the importance of the man versus dog role, but I unfortunately have no memory of the handler's name!

We loaded up early in the morning of the 11th to hit our first LZ. My new company commander showed up with the battalion CSM at the pad, informing me they would be going with us so my CO could see how we operated. The captain told me they would just be additional riflemen should we get into contact, and I shouldn't be concerned about them accompanying us. This captain had yet to spend any time in a combat command or any time humping in the boonies.

Because of the importance of this mission, I was given enough birds to take the whole platoon in one lift, in this case five slicks and two gunships. This was unusual, but necessary because of the nature of the mission. I had at times made a platoon sized combat assault with only one bird. When that occurred, those of us on the first bird, normally five to seven guys, would have to go to ground and secure the entire LZ until the bird could return to the fire base or PZ, pick up the next load, and then return to our LZ. The number of guys the bird could carry was dependent to a large degree on the weather, temperature and the altitude in which we were working. The hotter the day, the less weight the helicopter could carry. While times like this seemed to require hours for the turn around, I think it was usually about 30 to 45 minutes between insertions. Those of us on the first lift endured a tension-filled time. If there were bad guys in the area, the sound of the helicopter would alert them to our presence and general location. Given the nature of the operation, had we been

154

discovered during this time it would have been impossible to get reinforcements any quicker than the already pre-determined turn-around time. In this situation there was never a sweeter sound than the "wop wop wop" of Huey helicopter blades, as the next bird load was inbound. We would usually face the same situation when extracted, departing the PZ one bird load at a time, leaving a smaller and smaller force behind on the ground with the departure of each load. Since I was always on the first bird into an LZ, and on the last bird out when we were moving, I spent a lot of time suffering from constipation.

We were lifted out of LZ Lois at around 0900 on the 11th to begin our series of checks. Each man carried rations, water and extra ammo. It was a gorgeous day and the scenery en route was beautiful. As we neared our LZ, everyone locked and loaded, muscles tensed, breathing quickened and heartbeats got louder. Would this be a hot LZ with green tracers zipping our way, or cold with no visible enemy presence?

As we neared the ground there was no indication of the enemy. We un-assed the birds quickly and secured the LZ as the birds took off. After they were gone the silence was incredible; not a bird or animal sound could be heard. After a few minutes we formed up in our normal wedge formation with a wider spread between guys because we were in a pretty open area, and moved toward a tree line at the edge of a jungled area that reportedly concealed the bunker complex. The dog team was in my CP group, with the leading team between the flank teams. A map recon conducted in the TOC the day before indicated that this jungled area could conceal one of the main NVA routes into our area. Because of security considerations, I was not able to make an aerial recon of all of the planned LZs the day before.

As we moved cautiously toward the tree line, it became obvious there was incredibly thick underbrush under the canopy. It would be exceedingly difficult, if not impossible, for us to break our way into that obstacle without making a lot of noise. Since the sensors had been tripped the night before, I thought it was very likely we would find enemy forces in the area. As we got nearer to the trees, a gap appeared that could be a trail leading into the jungle, or at least a less densely vegetated area. So I did something that we very seldom ever did, I directed my point team to head for the open area. But in this case it appeared we didn't have much choice. We would just have to be incredibly vigilant.

As we entered the cleared area we saw that it was in fact a well-traveled trail, forcing us to move from our wedge formation into a basic file. There were numerous boot prints that appeared to be fresh. I moved the dog team up with the point element for extra security and early warning. My CP group came next, followed by the rest of the point team and then my other two teams. As we entered the jungle my sixth sense began to work.

My sense of foreboding was clearly shared by everyone, there was an almost detectable increase in awareness, and everyone started moving even more slowly, carefully and quietly. It was as though each man was carefully considering where to place each boot before he took a step. There was an eerie feeling about this place. I became so uneasy that I detached a security element from my trailing team to secure the entry point into the jungle, as the further we penetrated into the vegetation the more it became obvious the only way out was the way we had come in. I normally wouldn't have done this since we were a small unit to begin with, and leaving people behind severely reduced available firepower.

As we moved deeper into the jungle, the air was scented with the aroma of roasted corn, a sure indication there were some bad guys in the vicinity, or at least that they had been there recently. This was verified by evidence we began to see as a bunker complex became visible off to our left. As we cautiously moved in to check it out, we discovered the site was huge; we found one area that had probably been occupied the evening before by what appeared to be a company sized unit. I normally sent a team to check a bunker while others maintained an over-watch position. There was a lot of disturbed earth and vegetation, remnants of cooking fires, etc. The bunkers looked like they had been occupied for at least a day or two. In one area we found what appeared to be relatively fresh blood stained bandages. Although we hadn't heard of any contact in the area in the past few days, maybe Bravo Company had wounded a couple guys in their firefight the week before. I had a thought that if we could pick up their trail, maybe we should follow them to see where they were headed. This was only a fleeting thought, quickly quashed by what happened in the next few minutes.

Seeing all of this caused our sense of alertness to increase even more. We moved very quietly, as spread out as the vegetation would allow, with guys scanning all around us. Each foot was placed very carefully in an area of the ground that didn't have anything that could make a noise, like sticks. The trail went downhill, crossed the small blue line, and then hooked left while going up the hill on the opposite side. There appeared to be additional bunkers over there as well.

Then the dog stopped dead in its tracks alerting to our front. At about the same time one enemy soldier appeared to our right front. He was wearing green fatigues, web gear and a soft cap; and had an AK. He might have been a rear security guy who thought he had heard something and was coming to check. He was immediately dropped by Red, and CSM Wiggins. We all quickly hit the dirt and scanned the trees and vegetation around us while I got on the horn to try to report the sighting and enemy KIA, we had little to no communication with Battalion. Had the dog not alerted us to the enemy presence this guy might have gotten the drop on us and it might have been one or two of my guys that had gone down instead of him.

Given the dead man's uniform I thought that he was probably NVA. And since we never encountered individual NVA troops I felt pretty sure there were more in the area. My senses sharpened even more as I scanned the terrain. I moved my weapon around so I could fire it as I was talking on the radio if necessary. Given our almost linear formation I had my own field of fire to cover.

I was becoming more and more concerned. We had seen evidence of a large enemy force in the area, suspected they had been in the complex the night before, and we had no idea where they were now, or in what number. If that suspected company sized unit was still nearby I was in deep trouble. We were relatively exposed, being in light ground vegetation in this area with minimal cover or concealment and I had little or no commo with battalion HQ. The guy we had just killed had not been wearing a rucksack, which indicated he was probably living somewhere in this huge bunkered area. I had no idea of just exactly how big this complex was; it could contain a lot more NVA troops further up the trail.

When no more NVA showed up after a couple of minutes I sent a couple of guys up to strip the dead NVA of his weapon and web gear and to check him for any documentation, maps or other items of military interest while the rest of us provided security. Suddenly there was more firing, three or four more NVA, equipped in the same manner as the first, had been spotted about 25 meters to our right flank. We quickly killed at least two. At this point, as I wondered whether to go out that far to retrieve their weapons and equipment we began to take scattered fire from several different locations across our front and down the right flank. Jimmy Harris quickly ran to the bodies and stripped them of anything of military value.

My immediate reaction was to go to ground, form a hasty perimeter, and take these guys on, but I became concerned that we could be flanked or at least cut off from our initial entry point. Were that to happen, particularly with a company or larger sized NVA force moving against us, we'd be in serious trouble as there were only 20 or so of us including my company commander, CSM Wiggins and two medics. I had split my force by leaving the team at the entry point, which also reduced my machine gun assets by a third. We had no defensive weapons with us, no claymores, trip flares or even grenades, just primary weapons and ammo. While the underbrush was relatively light where we were, there was a solid jungle canopy overhead, which would have made it impossible to get arty, air support, medevacs or resupply.

At this point one of my M60's malfunctioned, the gunner tried frantically to correct the problem but with no luck. I now had one M60 that was essentially a large, single shot weapon, leaving me only two that were operational, one was with the security element at our entry point so I only had one with me that worked. (I was told at this year's reunion – 2017 - that in fact I had only one operational M60 that day as a second had malfunctioned as well. Even though those events were almost 50 years ago I'll admit to a feeling of relief that I'd made the correct dedcision that day to get out of the complex and the area. Only one of three machine guns operating correctly would have put us at a severe disadvantage.) That wasn't a whole heck of a lot of firepower. I had never before turned away from the enemy, but to not do so now might be foolish. We had penetrated fairly deeply into the bunker complex. There was nowhere in the immediate vicinity where I could form a strong, concealed perimeter. It now seemed possible my small unit could be surrounded and cut off from our original entry point, which in turn would have separated us from the security element. They weren't strong enough to stand on their own, making them very vulnerable. As a last consideration, it would have been impossible to get extracted due to the overhead jungle canopy and the close proximity of a sizable enemy force. These kinds of thoughts just flew through my mind. They weren't clear, or even separate entities; they were all jumbled and kind of rolled around themselves as they flashed by. With all of these thoughts racing through my mind, I gave the word and we began to move backwards down the trail, moving as quickly as possible while still maintaining security and scanning the areas from which we had been fired on. There was nothing to be gained by staying where we were. Fortunately we had not sustained any casualties. While on the move we had really poor commo with our battalion HQ, although Red had been able to contact an Air Force FAC (Forward Air Controller) flying overhead. A FAC is an Air Force fighter pilot flying in an OV-10 propeller driven light aircraft as a Forward Air Controller. OV-10's were unique in that they had two propellers, one in front of the cockpit and one behind between twin booms that were connected at the tail by a cross member. These aircraft had two vertical stabilizers and rudders. He was responsible for coordinating with the ground element and then directing any air support assets in how to make their runs to expend their ordinance in a way that would make sure that the jets didn't drop on a friendly position.

FACs carried white phosphorous rockets under their wings to be used to mark targets for the jets or "fast movers". WP, or "Willy Pete" to the troops, burned with a large amount of white smoke. It was also a very effective anti-personnel weapon and would serve to keep the bad guys distracted or under cover while the jets made their runs. It was insidious stuff; because it generated its own oxygen when it burned it was impossible to put out. If some landed on your arm it was possible that it would burn a hole clean through and keep burning whatever it landed on when it fell through.

It took what seemed to me to be an awfully long time, but we finally hit the original tree line and linked up with my stay-behind security element. We paused briefly as I surveyed the area and then moved toward a sizable vegetated area containing a lot of bamboo; it was maybe a couple of hundred meters on the other side of the clear area that we had used as an LZ. It was the closest area that provided enough cover and concealment. We moved quickly across the open area, constantly scanning our rear and flanks. We moved into the cover provided by the bamboo and formed a hasty perimeter with all of us on the line. I placed my CP on the firing line on the side that had direct vision of the area we had just left, the most likely enemy avenue of approach. We all went to ground and quickly burrowed down into the bamboo as far as we could get, trying to find fallen logs or other items that they could place in front of themselves as some kind of shield. As the guys settled down things got eerily quiet and everyone was intently watching to their front. I looked at Red, he had not yet made contact with battalion, although he was still talking with the FAC whose call sign was Panther 531. At the time that we entered our defensive position there was no Army armed helicopter air support and we were near the limit of friendly artillery. During this time we were also having commo troubles with battalion and the FAC was relaying information for us.

Suddenly a couple of shots rang out within the perimeter. I immediately thought the NVA were sneaking up on us from behind and had engaged one of my guys. I was relieved when the word got to me that one of my medics had a Bamboo Viper crawl over his arm, and the snake had been summarily dispatched. (Bamboo Vipers were highly feared because they were so venomous. If bitten there was almost no chance of survival, rumor had it that you would be dead within two steps. Hence they were known as "Ol' Two Step" by some of the grunts. The snakes were of a luminescent green color that made them hard to see in the bamboo. They had long fangs and highly toxic venom. Most of us were extremely wary of, and scared by, these snakes. I think that I saw two three of them during my tour, one crawled over my arm one night).

After being reassured the shots were not due to enemy presence, we continued to scan the tree line for signs of NVA. Scattered fire started coming our way and some of the guys reported seeing movement. Red then reported that the FAC had seen sizable enemy forces deploying to attack us. I talked briefly with him and he reported seeing what he thought were a couple of NVA rifle companies as well as a heavy weapons company in the general vicinity of the complex we had just pulled out of. Holy shit, if this was true then we were probably facing an entire reinforced NVA infantry battalion, which could number more than 500 soldiers. They had probably moved out in the morning headed for their next objective but, hearing gunfire, were returning to defend their bunker complex. And I still didn't have communications that would allow me to call for fire support.

This information did, however, verify that I had made the correct decision to back out of the complex and try to find a more defensible location. Had I gone to ground when first fired upon we could have been quickly surrounded by an NVA battalion with the end result probably being the same as that of an illustrious West Pointer, who commanded the 7th Cav at the Little Big Horn, General George Custer. Yeah, I had made the right choice.

Now I began to feel better about my decision to get out of that bunker complex, we had relatively open fields of fire all around us and some appreciable cover and concealment from the bamboo and other large vegetation. To get to us, the enemy would have to come out into the open, giving us better targets as well as an easy target for air or artillery support. And at least I had a FAC overhead.

We passed the word around about what the FAC was seeing, and everyone hunkered down even more in preparation for what might be coming our way. Then things began to happen quickly. The FAC sent us a couple of Army gunships who came in to support us. I know that they came in low and fast and their mini-guns and rockets raked the area in front of us.

About the time that the FAC called down to let us know that he had two Marine F-4's inbound for our support, NVA troops began to appear in the tree line as if to advance on us, probably a company sized element of around a hundred strong. Facing them on our perimeter I had probably 10 guys in position to fire, including me and one of my still working machine guns (as I thought then). The others were all oriented to our flanks and rear. As we prepared as best we could to take on this new threat, the FAC radioed the jets were beginning a run to take out the approaching NVA. In most situations, the FAC would ensure that any weapons runs by fast movers were made parallel to the friendly unit's front line. This would prevent any short rounds from landing on the friendly position. These planes were loaded with 500-pound bombs and napalm. I looked up to find the incoming fighters and to my surprise it sounded to us like the two jets were approaching from our rear. That could put us in danger in the event of a short drop, as well as minimize damage on the approaching enemy formation. Red and I turned around to verify the situation and as he began to call the FAC to alert him, we saw the lead jet release what appeared to be a 500-pound hi-drag dumb bomb. A hi-drag bomb deployed fins after release from the aircraft to shorten its glide path to the target. To our horror they deployed behind us! Oh my God, I could just visualize it impacting in the middle of my position. Red and I yelled for everyone to get down as we had potential friendly incoming. Red got on the horn and started screaming, "Abort!" "Abort!" to stop the second jet from releasing its ordnance in the same place.

We watched the bomb slowly approach, kinda weaving from side to side because of the drag of the fins. It then thankfully passed over us. It detonated a short distance in front of us a few seconds later with such force that the blast lifted Diz, Red and me from the ground and then slammed us down. The concussion temporarily deafened us, sucked the air out of our lungs, and impacted our minds such that everything appeared to be silently moving in slow motion. I saw some of my guys looking our way with their mouths moving but could hear nothing for a few seconds. There was an incredible amount of smoke and all kinds of debris rained down around us. It was truly a scary moment. I knew I had to get my shit together as quickly as possible and maintain control of the situation.

Then my hearing returned, I checked my own body quickly and found no sign of blood, and we began a quick check to see if we had received any casualties from that near miss. Fortunately nobody was seriously injured, although I think a couple reported some shrapnel hitting their backs. I got hold of the FAC and told him what had just happened. He must have already realized his mistake as the second plane had passed over us without dropping any ordnance.

We raised our heads to check out the area as the two fighters began new runs, this time in the proper direction, and flying parallel to our position. There were no enemy soldiers visible anymore. The two jets dropped their remaining bombs and napalm and then came in low and fast on gun runs. At this time we could see what appeared to be NVA rounds hitting the aircraft as they seemed so low that the pilots were almost at eye level with us. I could hear what sounded like at least one NVA .51 caliber machine gun firing at the aircraft. The noise was deafening, accompanied by clouds of smoke, dust and debris and massive shock waves as the bombs and nape detonated. It was impossible to see far to our front.

As they finished their runs Red was talking with them and suddenly a look close to rage passed across his face.

"Here Six, you better talk with them."

I got on the horn and asked what was going on. The reply was that they had expended all of their ammunition and had to hurry back to their base to make Happy Hour! I'm sure they were just trying to give me a little comic relief; there really wasn't anything else that they could do for us. But I have to admit that it was a little difficult to see the humor in their comment given our situation on the ground; it really pissed me off.

In reality, had it not been for those two fighters, we would have been in serious trouble. The FAC had detected a battalion sized force moving against us. We had not been successful in getting commo back to our battalion and our direct support artillery. We might not have been able to hold off such a large sized force until help or extraction birds arrived. The suspected .51 caliber machine gun that had fired at the F4's would have decimated us, to say nothing of the thin skinned helicopters we depended on to get us out of harm's way.

We were finally successful in contacting artillery support and getting a couple of batteries lined up to fire for us when my battalion commander appeared overhead to try to get involved in the fight. Flying overhead in his C&C ship, the commander was in fact flying on my gun-target line (The projected flight route of the artillery rounds after they left the tube en route to the target) so the red legs (artillerymen) couldn't fire. I talked with him on the radio and let him know he was interfering with my fire support. He didn't seem too concerned, he was more interested in trying to tell me how to fight my battle. There were some more words exchanged until he finally relented and flew off into a different orbit. When that happened, we could finally get the support we needed and I eventually had five artillery batteries firing in my support. During this time the NVA had reappeared in the open, we got supporting fires just in time.

Now approaching late afternoon, the CO had a new plan, he wanted me to stay where I was all night to "develop" the situation. Deployed on an eagle flight we had no rucksacks, no claymores or trip flares, and not a lot of ammunition, food or water. All of this weighed against staying where we were, plus my guys were pretty exhausted from the events of the day and my firepower was seriously degraded because of the inoperable machine gun. Couple that with the information that there was probably an NVA battalion in our area, that they knew exactly where we were, and the order to remain in place could have been the end of us. I had no idea of the casualties inflicted on the NVA by the jets or artillery, or if they had moved from the area or had just gone to ground. If they were still in the area they'd be really pissed! I explained all of this to Dragon over the radio but he didn't agree with my analysis, he still wanted me to stay in place. There was just no way I felt I could do that, I didn't want this to be the Fox Force Little Big Horn that I had already successfully escaped once that day. The discussions with Dragon 6 were becoming more and more heated.

During this time he frequently flew across my gun-target line again as he directed his pilot to get lower so he could see more clearly, interfering again with my fire support. He became even more adamant I stay the night, yelling so loudly on the radio that my guys who were close by could hear his words. I repeated my previous responses, asking that he call the birds and get us out of there; at one point one of my guys pointed his M-16 up at the bird as if to shoot it down himself. Almost 40 years later I learned that the battalion artillery LNO had also been in the bird, and he was scared to death that we WOULD shoot him down.

Finally the CO relented and agreed that he'd call the birds to take us back to LZ Lois. With that he flew off and disappeared. When the birds came in we were extracted without incident. The air strikes and artillery pounding must have caused the NVA to hunker down somewhere deep in their bunker complex. I must admit it was a huge relief when I was told all of my guys were on the birds and to give the pilot the signal to get us out of there.

I don't remember much of the ride "home". After intense combat I usually went through an adrenaline drain as I began to relax a little and try to smoke a cigarette. I also reviewed the events of the day as completely as possible, and kind of double checked my decisions to see if I had done the right thing, could I have followed other options, did I accomplish my mission and take care of my guys? On this ride I was pretty convinced that had I agreed to stay on the ground, where we were, I would have possibly been signing the death warrants of a lot of my guys. There was nothing of a military nature to be gained by staying on the ground at night, and a lot to lose. I figured I might be in trouble but I also thought whatever happened I had made the correct decision.

As Buck remembered; *The Phantoms were out of ordinance and so they headed home. We called for immediate extraction, but our new battalion commander denied our request and ordered us to hold our position until the next day when he could send a line company to assist us.*

Knowing that we would likely all be killed, we called in our extraction without his approval and within an hour were headed back to Lois. (Actually in a separate conversation I had received a reluctant approval from the CO.)

LZ Lois finally came in to view and after we landed, an exhausted Fox Force moved toward the gate and their bunkers. As we entered the firebase the battalion commander was standing on top of the TOC and yelling at me to report to him. I moved in his direction as did a couple of the guys directly behind me. I don't remember what the Colonel was saying to me but I know it wasn't nice, I think I heard words like "insubordinate" and "coward".

Suddenly I heard the unmistakable sound of a bolt going forward and turned around to look behind me. One of my guys had a look of murderous rage on his face, had locked and loaded, and was glaring at the Dragon. I quickly stood him down and directed him and the others to go to our bunkers; I'd join them soon. I turned around to continue my ass chewing. The colonel finally quieted down, told me if I wasn't careful he'd court-martial me for insubordination and cowardice in the face of the enemy, and told me he'd talk with me again later in the evening. I walked to my CP bunker pretty well convinced that my military career might have come to an abrupt end. The one bright spot was a visit to my CP by the artillery LNO, the same guy who was at St. George. He asked if I'd *like to transfer to the Field Artillery and become an FO (forward observer).* Artillery FO's moved with infantry units and coordinated all supporting artillery fires. He told me that I had been coordinating the firing of four 105mm batteries and one 155mm battery!

Later that night the colonel, the S3, and the CSM called me to the TOC bunker to talk about plans for the next day. The CO was really hot on developing the situation we had stirred up that day, he didn't want that NVA battalion to get away. No problem there, I totally agreed. We had probably inflicted some large casualties on them and should take advantage of their damaged state, if they had stayed in the area and not retreated back across the Cambodian border to regroup. We had an almost certain opportunity to make a sizable NVA formation virtually combat ineffective. Then he floored me with his directive; I was to go into the same LZ tomorrow and take the same path into the same part of the bunker complex in the hopes I would get into another fight. He would then have one or two of our rifle companies come in to support me from different directions and hopefully trap the NVA among us all. I had no problem with taking on the NVA again, but I was absolutely floored at his plan. Every infantry commander knew from his first days in the jungle that you never took the same route twice; that was an invitation to disaster. The bad guys would invariably be waiting for you with a nice, well-planned ambush.

I guess my shock at his proposal must have been obvious; I looked at the S3 and he just kind of looked away. This was a replay of the afternoon; the CO was asking me to do something that could be suicidal. A lot of thoughts and images flashed through my mind; getting trapped in that complex by an over-whelming NVA force and watching my guys die around me... what should I do? I was faced with that age old dilemma of a commander in combat; mission accomplishment or safe guarding the lives of soldiers, or how to combine both in the best way possible..

Rather than confronting the colonel directly I looked at the map and found another close-by LZ that could also afford entry into the bunker complex from a different direction. It looked as though we could accomplish the mission without taking undue chances with my men's lives. It would still be easy to bring in the supporting companies to develop the situation and trap the NVA if they were still in the AO. Without even thinking about my proposal, the colonel refused my idea and demanded that I follow his plan. I got really upset and don't remember many of the details of what happened next, but I know that I ultimately agreed, but argued to go into another LZ and take on the NVA in a situation other than a pre-planned ambush. I think the situation got really tense and the S3 and CSM finally weighed in on my side and suggested to the CO that he might be better off to select an alternate LZ of his choosing and a new route into the complex. The colonel finally relented but threatened me once again with a court-martial for cowardice. I asked if that meant that I was relieved from command of Fox and he said "No." A strange decision if he thought I was a coward.

As things turned out, we didn't go anywhere the next day, or the day after that. At one point I was directed to go see the battalion commander in his hooch. He told me he was bringing me up on court martial charges for "Cowardice in the Face of the Enemy" and "Disobeying a Direct Verbal Order in Combat... Twice". But, even with that, I was not immediately relieved of command of Fox.

A couple of weeks later, after Christmas, the 1st - 14th was told to abandon LZ Lois and move back to Camp Enari, the division rear, for a New Year's stand down. That was welcome news to us all, November and

165

December had been a couple of tough months for the BN, and for Fox. During that stand down I was asked to recommend a replacement for command of Fox. Well, this is it; I was being relieved of command pending court martial for cowardice. This was the end of my career, even though I believed in my heart I had done the right thing and no board of combat officers would ever find me guilty. However, strangely enough, I was given another command, this time of the battalion HQs Company, with the mission of overseeing the battalion's role in the move of the division rear from Pleiku and Camp Enari, to An Khe and Camp Radcliffe. This was a strange turn of events if I was in fact going to be court martialed. I made the move to HQ's Company and got involved in my tasks. As I left Fox, I was able to take care of some of my guys and get them out of the field. One of my prime accomplishments was to have my "hippy grunt" assigned to the commanding general's mess as a steward. This same guy had been awarded a Silver Star for his actions during the Battle of St. George.

In early April, the helicopter carrying the CO was shot down and unfortunately he was killed. Shortly thereafter, while I was on a firebase, the S3 came to me with a sheat of paper, which he tore up in front of me. This was the formal paperwork recommending my court-martial; evidently it had been prepared but never submitted for action. I was saved. Despite our differences I was saddened by Dragon's death. He was extremely aggressive in his desire to fight the NVA, and I'm sure he didn't realize the effects of some of his actions. The death of someone of his rank was rare in Vietnam, and his loss was a sad event. Years later, when I took the guys and our families to The Wall in Washington, D.C, I placed a wreath at the bottom of his panel to honor him.

DUTY! HONOR! COUNTRY!

Battalion Headquarters at Camp Enari

Camp Enari, Pleiku

VIP entrance to LZ St George

Camp Radcliffe, An Khe - Battalion Rear

First Operation with Charlie Company; my Command Post

LZ St. George in the monsoon

Fox Bunker on St. George with Harris and Stagner

Fox bunker on LZ St George

Apache 6

Command SGM Jasper Wiggins

Robin Sneeden

Al Buckelew

Fox 6

Jim Murphy

Bob Beasely

Danny Stagner

Robin Sneeden & Bill Strate

Gene Charny

Greg Kriha

Gary Felten

Gary Nelson

Harris and Hedley

The Author - Thanksgiving '69   Will De Long & Sue

Buck Buckelew and Danny Williams studying communications

Heroes of St. George - (Kneeling) Bob Beasely, Alan Buckelew, Ron
Shewell; (Back Row L to R); - First Sergeant Carter, Dan Stagner,
Jimmy Harris, Johnny Hingson

Ron Shewell being decorated with a Bronze Star for Valor

Fox Guys, Strate, Harris, Stagner, Beasely, Shewell, Classen with Author before my Departure for The World

Sneeden, Author, Harris

Fox 6 cooking for the troops

Ken McLacklan and Bob Beasely

Donut Dolly with the Fox guys

Preparation for Combat Assault
Combat Assault!

Charlie Model Gunship

Cobra gunship

Bring in the bird!

Resupply

Ready for liftoff to the Bunker Complex – Danny Williams & CSM
Wiggins

Central Highlands from a Helicopter

Sapper destroyed slick on the golf course at An Khe

Fox and Villagers prepare for a toast!

Montagnard Family

Fox in a Montagnard Village II

Water Buffalo at Montagnard Village

The River Leading to the waterfall

Greg Kriha with Montagnard children

On the way to the bunker complex

Bath Time

Convoy to New Plei Jerang for Cambodia Invasion

Into The Ming Yang Pass

Apache working with villagers on self-defense

Author, ADC, Dragon & Red

Santa & Helpers CPT Threadgil, B Co

Christmas '69 at LZ Lois

Division Band members at LZ Lois at Christmas

CS Gas used day after fight at St. George

Harris, Sasser & Author's 5 Ton Truck

Destroyed Bunker - my Apache CP

Battle of St. George – The Morning after at a Fox Bunker

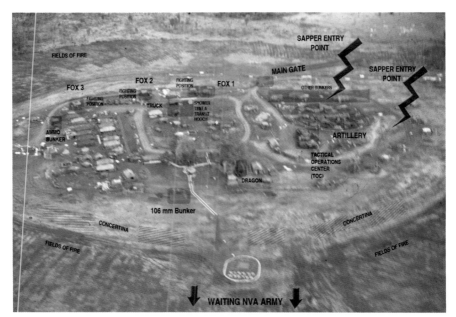

Sapper Attack Routes

Sapper Command Group

Charlie Red Siner

Danny Williams

Kenny McLacklan

Author

Jim Murf Murphy

Danny Stagner

Al Buckelew

Gary Felten

Gene Charny

Ron Classen

Larry Diz Des Jardins

Bob Beasely

Bill Strate

Vic Robertson
"The Dragon"

Roscoe Worley

Jimmy Harris

Robin Sneeden

Greg Kriha

Rockie Lynne and Gary Nelson

Fox Force Pheasant Hunt, Nebraska. Proud Diz and Charlie with birds

Fox Memorial at Norfolk, NE

The Whole Family

John with 1-14 Scouts at Guidon Presentation

Author with new Fox, Schofield Barracks 2014

Fox guys on parade field in Hawaii for Scarf Ceremony

Old and New Fox Force

17 - KING COBRA

LZ Lois under the new Dragon was a different experience. One of the first things he had done was to ring the perimeter of Lois with floodlights facing into the wire. By doing this he effectively made Lois an illuminated bull's eye for any enemy that wanted to take a shot at us. When the lights were put up I went to the S3, my old C Company commander, and asked what the hell was going on. He said he understood my concerns and that he was sorry, but it's what the commander wanted. I vowed then to spend as many nights in the jungle as we could; we'd be safer.

It soon became obvious the VC were taking advantage of the situation and moving mortar teams through the Mewal on a regular basis. The incoming mortar rounds became an almost nightly occurance. This issue lasted over a period of several days and we began to suspect the mortar crews were moving through the plantation to set up, fire and then escape. With just a few rounds fired it was difficult to get a good location on the tube for counter battery fire and the situation made for a difficult night's sleep.

The CO decided he wanted to go out to the Mewal and have a talk with the owner, Mr. Santelli, as it was suspected that Santelli was paying protection money to the VC who transited his plantation, as he never seemed to be messed with. If this was the case he could then certainly provide us with pretty good information on NVA movement through his area. Dragon was going to have a discussion to convince Santelli he should either stop the enemy from using his land, or at the very least he should give us some advance warning of NVA movements so we could prepare to ambush them or at least be able to fire back more effectively. Dragon proposed that Fox escort him, which kind of surprised me after the events of a few days earlier. Santelli was coordinated with, probably by the battalion S5 team, and arrangements for the meeting were made.

On December 14th, Fox formed up to escort Dragon to Santelli's on the ground rather than by air. I'm not sure of the rationale but maybe Dragon just wanted to get out with some grunts for a while. I remember

Dragon looked sharp with pressed jungle fatigues and spit-shined jungle boots. Since the battalion CO was "dressed up" we took a relatively easy route to the plantation house, knowing that he wanted to present a professional image to Mr. Santelli.

It was a beautiful day and it took us maybe a little more than an hour to get to the house. Since we knew the bad guys were probably making good use of the area we were very careful and alert to not walk into an ambush and get Dragon killed or wounded. When we arrived Santelli greeted us on the porch and asked the CO, Jimmy Harris and I to join him for a meal inside while Fox provided security. I put the rest of Fox into a security perimeter around the house just in case we had been observed. When inside we were seated at Santelli's dining room table and served a good lunch with wine, by his Vietnamese wife and another young Vietnamese woman. When I saw the food I asked his kitchen to also provide my guys outside with some lunch; Santelli assured me they would be taken care of. I learned later I had committed a grave error by not checking to see what they were offered. They had been served plates of plantains, which were like little bananas.

Jimmy and I, with Dragon, had a great meal and an interesting discussion with Mr. Santelli. He admitted he knew the VC were moving mortars and other military equipment, as well as troops, through his plantation, but he had to give them permission to do so in order to protect his assets and his family. After some more discussion he agreed to provide us as much information as he could about VC and NVA movements in his area. Santelli was in a tough position with the local enemy units. I'm sure he paid them monthly to leave his house and operation alone and also agreed to let them transit his property. But I believe he and the battalion commander had reached some kind of an agreement.

When lunch was over and an agreement of sorts had been reached, we prepared to return to Lois. Santelli accompanied us out to the porch. As Jimmy was getting Fox ready to move he came to me and pulled me aside. He quietly told me that the guys were pissed because they'd had nothing to eat but some little "frigging bananas". To say they were upset would be to put it mildly. And I would hear of this issue for more than the next 40 years!

Gary Nelson, the designated point man for the return, asked if we could have some fun and mess with the colonel a little and return over a different and much more difficult route. Since there was no way I was going to return over the same route we'd used to get to the plantation house, and since the guys needed to burn off a little steam over the lousy way they'd been treated with regards to the food, I agreed.

"You betcha, Saddle Up and let's go."

The route back was much more challenging than the route in. The trip took a lot longer and was over much more difficult terrain to include a marshy area and a couple of streams to ford. It was hot and humid and we had soon all built up a pretty good sweat. After what seemed like an eternity we finally saw the wire of LZ Lois in the distance. Once we made it through the wire, a hot, sweaty and no longer spit shined Dragon angrily asked me just what the hell we were doing making him walk through such a difficult area, and why didn't we use the easier route that had taken us out to the house. I replied that we never took the same route twice for fear of ambush, and that if we'd been spotted by the bad guys earlier in the day, and had they seen that Dragon was with us, they would certainly have been watching our original path and devising ways to interdict us on the way home. Therefore we had taken the most challenging route possible where hopefully, they wouldn't expect us. I told him since I was responsible for such a high value target I wasn't going to take any chances. In sum, we had taken that difficult path primarily to protect him. He looked like he didn't believe me but there wasn't much he could say. He went off to his hooch and I didn't see him for the rest of the day.

We remained on Lois on the 15th and 16th. We performed a security patrol around Lois on the 16th and found 10-15 freshly dug foxholes close to the firebase. On the 17th we provided security for a mine sweep operation on the road leading out of Lois.

Sometime during the month of December, we had an encounter in the jungle of an entirely different kind than a meeting with the enemy. We were moving down a trail and my point element disappeared around a bend; suddenly the column stopped and everyone got down facing alternately left and right in accordance with our standard immediate reaction drill. Guys up ahead were motioning me to come up to the front, but very quietly. As I got close to the bend I noticed that the point element guys that I could see were standing as still as if they were carved from stone. I slowly peered around the bend and saw a sight that could make any man's heart stop. In the middle of the open area was an enormous snake, elevated high enough to have his eyes on the same level as my point man's. And then I saw his hood expand and recognized that this guy was a KING Cobra! I don't know exactly who killed that monster but a couple of us fired at the same instant knocking that guy over backwards. He writhed and thrashed for a few seconds and then became still. One of the guys walked up and put a couple of rounds into the monster's head just to be sure. Once sure he was dead, we moved down the body to try to determine just how long this guy was, seemed like he went on forever. We called back to the TOC to tell them what had happened and a few minutes later received a call back; they wanted us to skin that guy and evac the skin back to Lois. When I questioned why I was told that from my description they thought that we might have a record of some kind and they wanted to check out the possibility. I wasn't real excited about the directive but was told I had no choice. So we set about skinning the body, wrapped it around a small tree we cut down, and carried it with us until we got to a clear area so we could call in a bird to extract it. We threw the head into a sand bag to go along so that its length could be added to the total. I never found out if we had killed a record Cobra but assume we didn't since I never heard anything more about it.

On the 18th we left the firebase to conduct a RIF and ambushing of trails in the vicinity of the villages suspected of harboring VC or NVA units. The next day we found a US grenade in a tree configured as a booby trap, and shortly thereafter we found three fresh foxholes. We continued our patrolling mission on the 20th with no significant events or findings. That night there was reported enemy movement around Lois at about 2100.

On the 21st we set up a couple of ambushes during the late afternoon because C and D companies found several large and intricate bunker complexes big enough to shelter three companies. Later, while moving to a brigade designated ambush area, we found three new bunkers still under construction. That evening at about 2100 one of our LP's spotted three or four individuals about 50 meters from their position and moving towards them; they may have been the guys who had been building the bunkers. The LP blew one of their claymores and returned to the night defensive position. Red got the artillery on the horn and we fired several fire missions for a total of one smoke, 11 illumination and 55 high explosive rounds. Movement continued all around our position until about 0030 hrs. For those who have never experienced it, the sound of bad guys moving around at night close to where you are can be a really scary thing. You know they're there, but you can't see them and have no idea what they're up to. Will they attack? Will they try to infiltrate? I guess this night they just pulled back and went about their business. Lois also reported more movement that night.

That morning we left our NDP and set out for the Ea Tuk River to the south to set up more ambushes and interdict enemy suspected of moving in and out of the village of Buon Ea Poc. When we did our initial sweep of the NDP area we found that three of our claymores had been turned face down on the ground! I guess we were lucky; it sure appeared some enemy unit was preparing an attack on our position. We moved out at about 1000. Shortly after we started we found one US claymore trigger, "clacker" and a plastic B-40 cover. That evening on the 22nd we set up a couple more ambushes. That same day the line companies found several more very large bunker complexes. That night we did a cordon and search of the village and continued our mission on the 23rd. On the 24th we were directed to RIF towards Lois in preparation for the Christmas stand down.

During this mission I was called by the TOC and instructed to move to a nearby stream. Once there I was to call in and then prepare to receive some soap, shaving cream and razors! When I asked why I was told the CG was going to fly out and visit us, and we needed to look sharp. I told the guy on the other end, I believe it was the S3, that there was no frigging way I was going to have my guys shave in the field. The enemy would be able to smell the soap and shaving cream from a mile away. And to have a bird come in and give away our position, boy was I pissed but I was told I had no choice, the commanding general was coming.

Soon a bird came by and dropped off the shaving materials and we all dutifully shaved, washed up and tried to clean our uniforms as much as possible. Shortly thereafter the CG's bird called and asked us to pop smoke, which we did. He landed and got out of the bird and came over to me; the bird never shut down. I reported to him and briefed him on our mission. I also introduced him to some of the other guys. As I remember the general had no real words of wisdom for us, just small talk and a short "keep up the good work" speech. He then got back in his bird and left, I think he was on the ground for maybe 10 minutes, a dangerous move for us and a real waste of time as far as I was concerned. We'd had our position compromised and now carried a scent with us that would take a while to dissipate. While we certainly smelled better than we normally did in the boonies, it was definitely not a good thing.

On the 25th, Christmas Day, we stood down on Lois with B Company. The day was as festive as possible, small Christmas trees sprouted up around the firebase, and in the late morning we had a special visitor. Santa Claus arrived on a Huey with several "Santa's Helpers", Donut Dollies dressed in very short red dresses, smiling and bearing gifts. About five or six musicians from the division band were also on hand to play Christmas Carols, which we all sang with tears in our eyes and lumps in our throats. Some of the guys had received Christmas packages from home so there were a few decorated trees and other holiday decorations scattered around. As usual the cooks worked hard to prepare a good Christmas dinner for everyone on Lois as well as for those troops in the field, a turkey dinner with all of the trimmings. We were observing a Christmas-New Year's cease fire so things were quiet as far as enemy activity was concerned. I remember that one of my guys, Greg Kriha, shared a bottle of Royal Salute with me over a couple of evenings even though the battalion commander had directed that there would be no booze on FB Lois. There was just no way we could waste a whole bottle of Royal Salute! I took a chance with my future but it was sure worth it! Christmas is a very special holiday for most folks, and the most difficult to spend away from family and friends. The battalion mess team also airlifted Christmas dinner to the companies in the field. The day was long, but for us it was quiet and restful.

On the 26th we went back into the jungle, this time attached to B Company to search the large bunker complex they had found and to conduct ambushes towards the northeast. That day the battalion S5 team (Civil Affairs) had a horrible day. The team's mission was to visit villages in the area, perform medical assistance and to pass out candies and other goodies to the inhabitants. There were also a couple of Vietnamese attached to the team to act as interpreters and representatives of the government. This was our attempt to "win the hearts and minds of the people." That morning the S5 team was traveling down a road in their ¾ ton truck to reach a local village when they were ambushed by 15 to 20 enemy troops set up on both sides of the road. Three Americans were immediately wounded and fled to a local village where they commandeered a Lambretta scouter and high-tailed it back to Lois, leaving their comrades behind. One of the Vietnamese was killed, the other severely wounded. One remaining wounded American called in a dust off and was evacuated about 1130 along with the wounded Vietnamese. The enemy was reportedly wearing South Vietnamese tiger fatigues, and the US support team that arrived shortly after the firing ceased reported that it appeared that the enemy left on bicycles because of the trails that were used. Final casualty count was four US WIA, one Vietnamese KIA, and one Vietnamese WIA. I have always wondered what happened to the American members of that team, I wonder if any of them were ever prosecuted for leaving the scene of the action and leaving wounded behind. At the very least they should have been charged with cowardice and abandoning their fellow team members.

On the 27th and 28th we remained in the field, this time with A Company as they searched a huge bunker complex. We were told to be prepared to return to Ban Me Thout East for movement back to Camp Enari for a New Year's stand down. We were picked up on the 29th at 0945 for transport to the airfield and at 1000 hours Vietnamese troops arrived to take control of LZ Lois. By the 30th the entire battalion had returned to Enari and had started a five-day stand down. New Year's Eve was a real show when the entire division bunker line erupted at midnight in streams of tracers, flares and anything else that could be shot off to mark the end of the Year 1969. I know I attended a show put on by an Australian band that night, which featured a gorgeous blond round eyed lead singer dressed in a very sexy black negligee. Sometime that evening she had a red scarf put around her neck. I don't remember how that happened but we have pictures to prove it.

This was a really bittersweet time for me as I knew I would soon have to give up command of my special Fox Force, guys I had come to admire and respect as we survived all that was thrown at us during the past five months. I had learned a lot about small unit warfare and about myself. Time in the field was hard on everyone, but it was especially hard on a small, specialized unit that operated on its own, many times beyond the range of supporting artillery and sometimes communication.

We could never let our guard down; we were always alert and ready for action, we had no one to depend on if we got in trouble but ourselves. We were always careful to move as quietly as possible, for the threat of ambush was always present. Life was constant tension, even on those days without contact, there was no way to know the enemy wasn't near, but just out of sight.

We'd been fortunate, we didn't incur many casualties, which was primarily because my guys were skilled in their craft. We were never ambushed but managed to get the drop on the enemy several times. That fact alone speaks volumes. We had all learned a lot about teamwork, and that each of us had to perform our job as well as possible as the lives of all of the others depended on it. Guys walking point couldn't afford to daydream or be distracted. Those on flank security had to be especially vigilant, it was from the flanks that an ambush was most likely to occur. At night there could be no excuse for falling asleep while on guard, or making needless noise when out on an LP. Noise security was our most important asset.

I never knew of any drug use in the field, I don't doubt that there was some weed smoked on the firebase. But even then, I knew it wasn't done before or during pulling guard duty. One of the facts learned after the attack on St. George was that the NVA had recon'ed us for a long time. That should have been obvious as we often found footprints inside

211

our outer wire barrier. I suspect they even watched as the line companies rotated in for firebase security and knew which ones had weak points. I was told the primary access through our wire and bunker line was in front of a bunker where the inhabitants often smoked while on guard duty.

I only had one disciplinary problem in all of those months. We had one guy assigned after I took command who just didn't want to be there at all. He complained all of the time he couldn't deal with the rucksack load and other physical requirements (he was a little guy), and was always noisy when in the field. Finally Jimmy and I had just had our fill of his bitching and bellyaching. We had several guys carrying extra weight as we'd removed most of this soldier's gear and distributed it among the others so we could continue to move. Even with all of that, at one point this particular soldier just sat down and refused to move any more. There was no doubt he'd be a serious liability were we to get into a firefight. Jimmy and I were out of patience. We decided we'd make one more effort to get him to pull his weight. Since he refused to move, we agreed with him and told him we'd just leave him. I don't think he believed me. We took all of his gear except for his rifle and one magazine and proceeded to move back into the jungle. We had the platoon move a couple hundred meters and set up in a defensive position while Jimmy and I immediately circled back to a point where we could observe our problem child; we certainly didn't want to get him into trouble. He just sat there and cried. After about five minutes we called out to him to let him know we were nearby, and moved into the clearing to police him up. We rejoined the rest of the unit and continued with our mission. When the next resupply bird came in I sent the young man back to the firebase with a note to the Sergeant Major telling him the guy just wasn't cut out for Fox.

New Year's Eve was a sad time for me. There was no way I wanted to leave Fox, even for the unexplained command I'd been assigned. That move made no sense to me as I'd been told I could expect a court martial in the near future due to my actions during the Bunker Complex fight. So I figured 1970 would be my last year on active duty, at some point I'd either be dismissed from the service, or at the worst, find myself in prison somewhere. While I thought I'd made a great choice in Bill Norton who I'd recommended to replace me, there was a large part of me that didn't want to trust my guys with anyone else. There just wasn't anyone who would look after them as I had. Fortunately Bill proved me wrong.

It had been one hell of a year, one filled with dread, fear but immense satisfaction. There is a certain "rush" that comes from armed combat, all senses are highly tuned and the mind works at warp speed while sometimes the action appears to be in slow motion. I had really enjoyed my time in the field and had gained a lot of confidence in my ability to deal with hairy situations. I'd "seen the elephant" and survived, so there wasn't much else that life could throw at me that could frighten me.

I didn't know what the next part of my combat tour would bring, but I did know that nothing could ever compare with my time commanding Fox Force.

So ended the Year of our Lord 1969, and within a few days, unfortunately, my time as Fox 6, because a couple of days later, I had to say good bye to those guys who I had grown to love, admire and respect, and move to my new position as HQ Commandant as I awaited a sure courts martial at the hands of Dragon. It had been quite a year.

DUTY! HONOR! COUNTRY!

18 - THE LONLINESS OF COMMAND

The bunker complex operation had really been a test of that old combat dilemma for me, mission accomplishment versus preservation of life. Vietnam as a war was a real transition period in American military thinking. There was still some holdover from WW II wherein civilian and military casualties were OK if they were sacrificed for the greater good; think D-Day or the bombings of Dresden or the fire bombing of Japanese cities. On the other hand, after the atrocity of My Lai and the poor performance of Lt. Calley, we were more aware of preventing needless civilian deaths and tried to minimize even military casualties, particularly as the war was running down to its inevitable end and there was questionable value in the loss of any more American lives.

My toughest test came at the end of the day when the battalion commander told me he wanted us to stay in place for the night. That was a no-brainer for me; there was absolutely no value to be gained by staying put, and a whole lot to potentially lose. If pulled out we could live to fight another day. Plus, had we stayed, with the NVA knowing exactly where we were, and probably really pissed by the casualties we had inflicted, they would probably have stopped at nothing to exact revenge.

The plans for the next day, with the benefit of hindsight, were maybe not as cut-and-dry an issue. But, still, it was a Vietnam War axiom among grunts that you never went the same way, or used the same trail, twice. We'll never know if the NVA were in fact waiting for us to come back, and then retreated. But, there is no doubt, at the time, I was convinced there was no value to going back into the same LZ, and a whole lot of risk to the lives of my unit if we did. This was especially true after I found another LZ that would accomplish the same mission with a whole lot less risk.

This is a good example of the loneliness of command, especially at the small unit level. Soldiers don't want to die needlessly, and are capable of incredible heroism if put into a risky but understandable situation. The ultimate decision, and responsibility, rests on the shoulders of the unit commander. In both cases I think that I accomplished my mission without needless risk of the loss of soldier's lives. I think that I could have beaten any courts-martial on the cowardice charge; but the disobedience issue might have been problematic. Depending on the make-up of the court martial board, I could have been convicted on the disobedience charges. At the very least that would have terminated my career; in all probability I could have gone to jail.

I am particularly convinced during Fox Force reunions these days when I see my guys and their families; there is no doubt I did the right thing. Even after all of these years, especially with a lot of thought as I've relived that day while writing this book, I firmly believe I made the right decision to pull out, that the sacrifice of my guys, soldiers who just a month ago had fought bravely all night, and put themselves into harm's way to defend LZ St. George, and then, a couple of nights later prepared to go down fighting if needed on that hilltop, didn't deserve to pay the ultimate price when it would have gained nothing but their deaths.

Had the Dragon offered to put a line company or two on the ground with us that night, and have my guys' rucks been flown out to us with their claymores, trip flares, and additional water and ammo, then there might have been a reason to stay to further damage the NVA unit if they tried to come against us. This would have been an easier decision if he'd promised to have the artillery fires on a priority for us and ordered flare ships and air support as well. The potential sacrifice of American lives without all of this just made no sense, and in my mind would have completely compromised my sacred duty to protect my guys against such ill-advised action. I believe that I followed the request in the Cadet Prayer, "Help me to choose the harder right instead of the easier wrong".

Again, from Buck; *I learned later that our platoon leader had been written up for cowardice for his actions. As I now watch specials on Vietnam or other wars it's often easy, in hindsight, to see where commanders make serious blunders.*

While it may have seemed reasonable to ask his Recon platoon to keep the NVA prey under surveillance; it was clear to us that the NVA knew someone orchestrated the jets bombing runs and they would be looking for revenge. Outnumbered 10 to 1 we stood little chance of living through the night unless we started running away, which would also have violated our orders. Our deaths would have served no benefit and hence in my mind the order was illegal or at the very least immoral.

Note: Some 40 years later I learned who these helicopter gunship guys were. After moving to NC it was recommended that I visit a coffee shop in nearby Mooresville that was run by a Vietnam Veteran, Richard Warren, who had a real soft spot in his heart for vets, especially Vietnam guys. Richard had been a gunship pilot in Vietnam about the same time that I was there.

Pat's Gourmet Coffee shop had become a real vet's hang out place with lots of memorabilia hanging on the walls and Vietnam era music playing from a tape deck. In 2006 I sponsored a Fox reunion at my new house on Lake Norman and I wanted to take my guys up to see Richard and to experience the coffee shop. We were wearing our red scarves and all loaded up early on Saturday morning to get up there before the regular opening hour.

When we got to the shop Richard had the door open and we entered to the sounds coming from two tape recorders; one played Vietnam era music, the other a recording of the Wop! Wop! Wop! Of Huey helicopter blades, a sound near and dear to the hearts of Vietnam War grunts. Richard had all the guys sign in to his Book of Honor and everyone was presented with an appropriate key chain, unique to Richard's, with an emotional "Welcome home, thanks for your service." by Richard and a big hug and kiss on the cheek by his "Girl Friday" Cheryl Ann. Everyone was affected by the atmosphere and sincerity of Richard and Cheryl Ann, I saw some of my hard-core combat infantrymen standing or sitting with tears streaming down their faces. We spent about an hour and then loaded up to return home; it had been quite a visit.

I couldn't believe it! After more than 35 years I was face to face with someone who had probably saved the lives of some of my soldiers and maybe my own! Unbelievable! A couple of years later I was fortunate to go to Iowa to a small air museum where his bird was dedicated to be the center piece of the Vietnam part of the display. At that time I had the opportunity to meet his other crewmembers and even to sit in the door of that bird; what an emotional experience that weekend was.

DUTY! HONOR! COUNTRY!

19 - HHC COMMAND

I started my new command time near Pleiku at Camp Enari, the base camp for the 4th Infantry Division since 1966. Because the political decision had been made to reduce US forces in Vietnam, with eyes on an eventual total withdrawal, there were some major troop movements under way. The First Cavalry Division vacated its division base camp at Camp Radcliff outside of the city of An Khe as it moved closer to the coast to return home. In line with this movement, the 4th Infantry Division was ordered to move closer to the coast, vacating Camp Enari to occupy Camp Radcliff. This was to be a major undertaking. Not only did all of our equipment and personnel have to be moved, but Camp Enari was to be left in pristine condition for the ARVN forces that were to occupy it after our departure. As the Headquarters and Headquarters Company Commander or Commandant, 1st – 14th Infantry, it was my responsibility to move the entire battalion rear area from Pleiku to An Khe, a monumental task involving a 95 Kilometer move east on QL 19 through the Ming Yang Pass. The move was to begin in March and end in April. During this time the 3rd Brigade, 4th Infantry Division returned to the US in April and was deactivated.

Preparation for this move was non-stop, and necessitated my making many trips by road between the two base camps, which required passage through the infamous Ming Yang Pass where the famous French Mobile Group 100 was virtually wiped out in a massive ambush in June of 1954. MG 100 was one of the most famous and battle hardened units of the French Army in Vietnam, several battalions had covered themselves with glory fighting with the US Second Infantry Division in Korea, and wore the US Division patch on their uniforms. After the defeat at Dien Ben Phu, the French attempted to consolidate their positions in Vietnam in preparation for withdrawal. MG 100 was directed to evacuate An Khe and move to Pleiku, linking up with other French units en route. On the southeast side of the camp, between it and the highway, was a C-130 capable airstrip originally built by the French. I believe this airfield was the marshaling area and starting point for the French MG 100 when they abandoned the area

The unit moved out at 0300 on the 24th of June in an attempt to beat major Vietminh (precursors to the Viet Cong of our day) units that were racing to QL 19 to cut them off. They didn't make it. In five days of fighting MG 100 virtually ceased to exist. They started with about 2500 troops, by the time they reached Pleiku on the 29th they had suffered 500 KIA, 600 WIA and 800 captured and had lost 85% of their vehicles, 100% of their artillery, 68% of their communications gear and 50% of their weapons. It's said that hundreds of the French dead were buried on the surrounding mountaintops, standing up and facing toward Paris. Also the area was heavily limed to prevent anything from growing on the graves. Originally each grave had a marker but the Vietminh subsequently removed them. The remnants of MG 100 were to face another devastating ambush days later on the road from Pleiku to Ban Me Thout.

Traveling through the pass was agonizing with trucks laden with heavy equipment; particularly full fuel trucks. The big guys had to slow to about 5 MPH to make the grade and get to the crest. We were sniped at a few times but never subjected to a major ambush. The trip up to the pass sometimes seemed to take forever and was always accompanied by a lot of tension and apprehension. There were a couple of small firebases along the route manned by Cav Units and artillery batteries, which helped to keep the NVA or VC away from the highway. In addition, the Cav conducted periodic aerial recons of the highway keeping a watch on things and to provide early warning if there was an enemy unit found in the area. I did fly to An Khe and back a couple of times and we generally followed the route of QL 19. Flying over the pass once, someone did point out the French Cemetery to me but it was hard to see because of cloud cover.

Radcliff was a huge place. There was an enormous open space in the middle that had been the airfield for all of the First Cav's helicopters and was known as the Golf Course. It got the name because the general responsible for overseeing its construction directed that all ground cover such as grass and other plants would be kept and encouraged to spread. Had this not been the case the area would have become hard packed dirt and the dust raised by all of the birds who took off and landed every day would be dangerous to man and machine alike. During the monsoon period it would have been virtually unusable. On my first tour of the base camp I was impressed by a beautiful stone chapel. A short distance away was another very attractive stone building, which I learned was an Officer's Club. Hot shit, I went there for lunch and had a steak, fries and

218

a beer; I knew I was going to like this place! It turned out to be my only visit, the building was commandeered by the division staff for their use.

On the next trip I was taken by a guide and shown where my new area would be. Again I was really impressed, the buildings were in great shape and well laid out. There was a large mess hall with what looked like almost brand new kitchen equipment, store rooms, arms rooms, a motor pool, barracks for those assigned to the area as well as several extras that could be used by units when they came back on stand down. There was also an officer's hooch with individual rooms. It looked like I was going to live well.

There was a mountain within Camp Radcliff's perimeter called Hong Kon Mountain; probably several hundred meters high. I thought that was really strange. On one side there was a huge painted area with the yellow First Cav patch. There was also a 173rd Airborne Brigade patch on another area; I believe they were the unit securing the camp during the transition from the First Cav to us. Hong Kon Mountain was actually connected by a saddle with another hill not quite as high, which was outside of the perimeter. I wasn't sure how that made any sense at all. We controlled the bottom with our base camp, and the top with a communications relay station. However, it was said the middle was controlled by the NVA and VC – hard to believe. Some old timers said the mountain was pock marked with caves and the interior was filled with a lot of tunnels. It was hard to believe that if this was true; that this kind of situation had been allowed to exist. If there were enemy on that mountain it would not have been too difficult to eliminate them. During my time at Radcliff I heard a couple of reports of enemy activity on the mountain and in the vicinity of the relay station but there was a never a major incident to my knowledge.

Finally the day arrived for the final convoy from Enari to Radcliff. It seemed like there were a couple hundred trucks assembled on the major roads with MP escort vehicles and gun trucks. It looked like the whole remaining rear area was going to move at once. Before we could leave, however, my area was inspected by the brigade S4. I was required to leave the place inspection clean with good screens on all window areas and an operational light bulb in every socket. The floors had been mopped and the mess hall cleaned so all of the kitchen equipment shone like it was brand new. We were required to do this for our Vietnamese allies who would come in to occupy the place after we left. My guys had really worked hard. I subsequently heard from a friend who had to return there that the place was trashed about two days after the Vietnamese arrived;

buildings were stripped of anything useful to include every damned light bulb!

The convoy finally departed in smaller units called "serials;" the trip was uneventful and we arrived at our destination at nightfall. We got everyone into billets and secured the area for the night.

My time as HHC Commander at Camp Enari and then particularly at Camp Radcliff was really kind of dull after the excitement of chasing bad guys through the jungles. The move had been challenging but after that was completed life was pretty boring. I did have to deal with the usual problems associated with REMFS (holy crap, I was now one!) and other administrative issues. My boss was the battalion XO whose primary concern was how we would pass an unannounced division inspection, CMMI or Command Maintenance Management Inspection. The team would arrive unannounced in the middle of the night and check all our property books and vehicle maintenance records. To fail that inspection would be a major black mark for the battalion XO and I'm sure for me as well. When asked that same question for about the third or fourth time I jokingly responded that if they were stupid enough to come into my AO I'd shoot them all. Needless to say that response did not endear me to the XO. This was the same officer who had caused problems for Murf at Camp Enari. We did undergo a CMMI while I was in command, I remember a huge effort to get the books right and make sure we had all of the vehicles on our records. As many of them were forward deployed in the field, and the inspection team was not about to go out to check them, all emphasis was on what I had in my motor pool. I had an outstanding Maintenance Warrant Officer who somehow made sure that everything in the motor pool was squared away. We passed the inspection.

In the division base camp I had some pretty serious morale and "motivation" problems as well as some that were race related. In the US there had been enormous race riots in the preceding years, resulting in the burning down of large sections of some cities, maybe the most famous occurring in the Watts section of LA. In Vietnam I never personally witnessed any racial problems among white, black or other ethnic groups in the field where everyone's life depended on the action of everyone else.

In the rear areas, however, there was often a different situation. Here it was easier for the troops to segregate themselves. In those days black soldiers developed a ritual called "dapping" whereby any number would form two lines and go through a ritualistic hand shaking and hand bumping to a specific cadence. When they did this on the walkway outside the mess hall at the end of chow it could be very intimidating to other soldiers trying to leave. After receiving several complaints I had my First Sergeant accompany me to the mess hall one night after dinner, both of us armed with our .45's. I approached the senior black soldier there, an E6 as I remember, and told him that we would no longer tolerate this kind of activity outside of the mess hall. I had no particular problem if they wanted to "dap", but they would have to move away from the building to a place where they wouldn't interfere with entry or exit. When I detected the beginnings of belligerent refusal, I ordered my First Sergeant to prepare to unlock the cover of his .45 holster while I moved my hand down to mine. I think the guys got the message even though we didn't open our holsters. I didn't sleep much at night for a couple of weeks thereafter; I stayed awake in my hooch with my .45 in my lap waiting for a "frag" attempt. Fortunately that never occurred.

This type of sensitive atmosphere of racial tensions and the natural conflicts between field soldiers and REMF's, to say nothing about issues between commanders and soldiers, made for a very ripe atmosphere for drug and alcohol abuse. These issues in Vietnam were bad enough and most of us were tagged with the "druggie" label when we returned home. But when those issues are considered in the context that we were in a war that the country had no intention of winning, and so therefore death or injury could be considered without purpose, moral and discipline were tough areas to address.

During this time, I decided that my rear echelon soldiers were bored, with not much meaningful "soldiering" to do, and that could lead to issues. I decided to put them to work building a firebase-type defense around our battalion area on the edge of the Camp Radcliffe perimeter. The Golf Course area in the middle of Radcliffe had been assaulted a couple of times by NVA sappers who made it through the wire obstacles, through the battalion rear areas and other administrative facilities, and up to the Golf Course where they destroyed numerous helicopters and usually killed some soldiers as well. They had come close to us a couple of times. Once we found holes in the perimeter wire opposite our battalion rear, and one night enemy were sighted as they came through our area. We seemed to be on a primary avenue of approach into the base camp and up to the airfield. That prompted me to harden our area; I didn't want any of my guys injured or killed.

Between us and the outside perimeter was a motor pool area and the perimeter road. I ringed my battalion area with a triple strand concertina fence and had bunkers and fighting positions dug and prepared. To top it off, I called alerts periodically in the middle of the night requiring everyone to man their assigned defensive positions. This proved to be very unpopular until one night in April or May when we had to man the positions for real. We repulsed an NVA force trying to make it to the airfield; killing a couple and forcing them to go around us through an adjacent undefended battalion area. After that, my rear area soldiers no longer considered themselves as REMFs but rather as real combat soldiers; my disciplinary problems were greatly reduced and morale sky rocketed for most of the troops. I was also finally able to get a good night's sleep when we weren't being mortared, which seemed to occur on a regular basis.

Several months later, Sergeant First Class Bob "Smitty" Smith, Jimmy Harris's successor as Fox 5, had a similar type of experience.

After almost nine months in the field with Fox Force, I was accepted in graduate school and took advantage of the early out program to start school. As I made my way to the rear to catch the freedom bird, I had to spend a few days at the Fire Base. The First Sergeant told me that he had a special opportunity for me.

Resupply and food quality had reached an all-time low, and the battalion commander was determined to get this straightened out. The hot food delivered to the firebase was terrible and usually the troops preferred LRPs. Resupply in the field often included worn out socks, camos, and other poor quality materials. Loose ammo was delivered in the ammo boxes and different caliber ammo was all mixed together and most of the ammo had to be cleaned before it could be used. Our battalion commander thought he had an answer to improving quality for the troops, and he required all supply staff and all cooks to come forward from Division to the firebase.

I was assigned to train them as three man sniper teams. I tried to teach them the correct side of the claymore, use of the clicker, and some basic rifle training and other survival skills. After an intense "three hour" retraining period, we divided these "well trained" men in to three man sniper teams and then escorted them outside of the wire into observation posts, where they spent the day, one night, and one following day about a click outside of the fire base perimeter.

The supply and mess staff avoided contact and made it through their time in the field, and returned to Division safely. From that day forward, we had the best hot food, new fatigues, and new ammo, along with other special items like beer and sodas. I never forgot the creativity employed to remind those in the rear of what they should be doing and I expect the experience lasted a lifetime for them.

In April of 1970 the battalion was alerted to participate in the invasion of Cambodia. When I heard that was going to happen, I really wanted to get back into a line unit. I tried but unfortunately that move was impossible, I was to remain the HHC Commandant. I was extremely frustrated that, after having chased NVA around the border area for months and not being allowed to cross the line to go after them, now finally Cambodia was no longer off limits.

I was given a pretty difficult task to organize and command the battalion convoy that would move our soldiers from An Khe to the Special Forces camp at New Plei Djerang. All of the line companies were air lifted and convoyed to my area on Camp Radcliff. New Plei Djerang had been chosen as the brigade assembly area because it had a landing strip long enough for C130's and therefore had enough room for all of the birds that would be required to lift the whole Golden Dragons Battalion into Cambodia.

We left Camp Radcliff early one morning around the 1st or 2nd of May in a long convoy made up of several serials. I believe I moved at least three of the line companies, Fox Force and some admin folks, most of the commanders had already flown into New Plei Jerang. We had a pretty good distance to cover through some questionable areas. My jeep was equipped with two radios and I had a driver and another soldier in the back seat. In addition to two M16's, and my CAR 15, we also had a Bloop with about 40 rounds of various types on board. I traveled back and forth between the several serials to keep tabs on everyone. There was only about a 15-minute gap between each element.

We took a couple of rest stops so the troops could get off the trucks, stretch their legs, and take a leak by the side of the road. Each time we did this I had security out to a couple hundred meters on both sides of the road. We had no enemy action but did suffer one bad incident. While loading back on the vehicles after a stretch break one of the bloop gunners discharged a round, which hit the back of one of his buddies. The round didn't go far enough to arm itself but it did lodge in his back close to his spine, or so it looked. The medics couldn't do anything but stabilize the wounded soldier and try to keep him still so the round wouldn't move or detonate. I called in a medevac and the wounded soldier was very carefully loaded on board and transported back to the evac hospital. I never did hear how he made out but I assume he was OK after the round was surgically removed.

I couldn't stay behind on an operation like this, so I finally cajoled a company commander to allow me to join his unit as a rifleman. I told him that if needed I thought that I could justify the trip because I needed to make sure that myt HHC guys were doing what was required to support the operation. After some hesitation, he agreed after I told him I'd wear no identifying name tag, or rank, that I would assume full responsibility for my actions, and I only wanted to stay for a short while; I couldn't afford to be AWOL from my HHC job for too long.

We did experience a really disgusting incident from some fellow Americans before we left Vietnam. There was a camera crew and reporter from one of the major news sources, it was one of the three major TV channels that came and encouraged our Black soldiers to refuse to go into Cambodia to kill their "Yellow Brothers". Somehow these assholes escaped detection by anyone in the command group. When we lifted off to make our initial assault into Cambodia, there were several Black soldiers who remained on the pad and refused to get on the birds. I don't know what happened to them or if the news crew even got on board.

I sat in my usual place in the door so I could watch what was going on; it was like being in a John Wayne war movie! The whole battalion lifted off together, I think well over 50 helicopters. As we gained altitude, I looked out to our side and saw several pairs of gunship escorts, like WW II fighters escorting bombers to their target. As we got close to our LZ, I could look ahead and see jets dropping ordinance on our landing zone; what a sight!

As we started to lose altitude, I could hear the familiar sounds of rounds being loaded into the chamber by every grunt on board and the air of nervousness and expectation. As we got lower, I looked below and could see figures running around on the ground and tarps being pulled off of anti-aircraft weapons of several sizes. Some of the enemy soldiers on the ground began to shoot at us with their AK 47s and light machine guns and the anti-aircraft guns began to get into the action. The pilot poured power into the engine, banked hard to the right and we started quickly gaining altitude as we turned away from our objective.

We returned to New Plei Djerang where we spent the night before making another attempt the next morning into a new area. I heard later that our first projected LZ was in fact an NVA Regimental Headquarters, which explained the large number of soldiers and automatic weapons I saw. I don't think we lost any birds but I did hear we had a few casualties on a couple of the helicopters. The next morning the battalion took off again, this time the assault was inserted into a cold LZ. After the battalion came out of Cambodia the battalion commander was relieved for aborting the first day's landing. Hard to believe!

We had no significant action, but did uncover a couple of huge weapons and supply caches. The battalion stayed in Cambodia for about 10 days before coming out and returning to Camp Radcliffe. I believe there were some minor skirmishes and more supply dumps uncovered. It was obvious the bad guys had been there in force and had left in a hurry when the invasion started. I guess we accomplished the mission, which was to disrupt the NVA logistics and troop replacement supply routes and thus take the pressure off the withdrawing US forces.

Aside from this adventure, the movement to An Khe, and the bunker building, my time as a REMF was pretty quiet. We were mortared and rocketed frequently; my area took several hits. Our BOQ hooch where I slept had some major damage done on at least one occasion. We had an area at the end of the building that functioned as a common area and club with a small bar. It was this place that took the hit from a rocket or mortar round, of course! We spent a couple of days putting it back together. I made an effort to improve support to the battalion in the forward area and often visited the firebases to check on my guys, to make sure they were in good shape and were being taken care of. There was just nothing like being back among combat soldiers.

My last few of weeks in Vietnam were memorable, even though I don't remember actually leaving the battalion. The battalion came out of Cambodia and returned to An Khe about the 16th of May, where I remained for another 6 or 7 weeks. The division mission had been to destroy the B-2 Front in Base Area 702. The B-2 front commanded all NVA activity in our II Corps area.

During this time, I was promoted to Captain on the 5th of June, 1970, the second anniversary of my graduation from West Point. I remember going to a briefing for an upcoming operation and being very thankful that I was leaving and wouldn't have to comply with the new Rules of Engagement (ROE). Because of the Mai Lai incident, the new rules were so restrictive troops couldn't return fire from a village without Vietnamese approval - even if they were taking casualties – impossible to get in anything short of a day or two! Somewhere in those last couple of days, I turned over my company. I think there were a couple of farewell parties in my area.

On my last day in An Khe I went to S4 to retrieve the gear I had left there when I arrived in-country a year earlier. Eventually, it came my time to out-process from the battalion and start my long journey home. I caught a bird to take me to Can Rahm Bay were I was to meet my Freedom Bird.

While there I ran into a classmate, he who commanded one of the units there and took me on a tour of the area. That night we went to a real officer's club and had a great steak dinner; to say I was somewhat envious would be an understatement.

DUTY! HONOR! COUNTRY!

20 - THE OTHER SIDE

In this chapter I'll try to shed some light on some of the other events of my time with Fox and HHC. It's really difficult for me to put these in chronological order so I'll just deal with them as they come to mind. Some were humorous, some not. But all reflect incidents and events in the life of a grunt that are not the normal experience.

CMMI INSPECTION   In a combat zone, particularly in those days, all kinds of things happened with equipment that was never officially reflected in any of the procedures proscribed by the Army. Stuff was lost, destroyed in combat action or accidents, or stolen from or by other units and never accounted for. One of the most popular ways to cover a loss was to list unaccounted for equipment by claiming it had been a "Combat Loss." This was an accepted resolution and was widely used to cover shortages. Of course, some of these actions would not necessarily produce the equipment or records normally required in support of a major inspection. Equipment accountability in Vietnam was an extremely difficult process. Units in the battalion were widely dispersed at most times; equipment was shared or loaned depending on the tactical situation and requirements. The environment with its heat, humidity, dust and rain was extremely hard on most equipment and many times things might be discarded in a firebase garbage dump, lost off of vehicles, or even stolen by locals or even other units. It was not always possible to adequately maintain vehicles to stateside standards and often times they, too, would just "disappear". Given this situation, logbooks and property books were almost impossible to maintain.

A BOY NAMED SUE   Before we all wound up in Vietnam, Johnny Cash had published a new song, "A Boy Named Sue," and it quickly rose on the Best Hit list. Somehow, Fox had procured a mascot monkey, without question a male, and due to his brash personality, he was given the name Sue. He never went to the field with us but was always tethered by a long lead to one of our bunkers; he even had a red scarf to wear. He and Will DeLong got very close; Will loved and doted on that monkey.

He was a real source of comic relief due to his actions and the fact none of the guys was reluctant to feed him a little beer from time to time. When we were on the firebase he was always the center of attention. I'm not sure what happened to him, I don't remember his being with us when we went to Lois, but for a while he was sure an important part of Fox.

RAT PATROL I believe it was sometime in October of 1969 that convoys coming out of Pleiku down HWY 14 to us and Fire Base Weit Davis were being ambushed by a .50 caliber machine gun mounted on the back of a captured American 5/4 ton truck. The .50 caliber M2 Machine Gun has been widely used during WW II, Korea, and Vietnam, and up to the present on the ground, in the air, and on the seas. The "Ma Deuce" as it was affectionately known, was a highly lethal weapon with a TREMENDOUS effective range that fired a devastatingly heavy round. Its max effective range is 2000 yards and max effective range when mounted on a stationary mount is 2200 yards. It had many different types of ammunition to include ball, tracer, armor-piercing and incendiary rounds. The Ma Deuce could decimate and shred a two and a half ton truck and any other thin-skinned vehicle found in the US Army, from a long way away. The two and a half ton, or "deuce and a half" was the standard ground vehicle used for transporting troops and supplies around the combat zone. Since there were no front lines in Vietnam, any convoy traveling between any two American controlled areas was subject to ambush, and the division was very anxious to eliminate this threat.

To make the situation even worse, it was rumored this truck and weapon were manned by two American deserters from the Marine Corps, one white guy and one black guy, who were known as Salt and Pepper. Needless to say, the American command structure was really anxious to find these guys and to kill them if they couldn't be captured.

The mission was given to the Golden Dragons; find those guys and destroy them. To accomplish this, Dragon and the S3 came up with an innovative idea. The best option appeared to be to use the convoys as bait but at the same time have them include the capability to effectively deal with the threat. That capability would be Fox, used not as a ground based recon platoon but rather as a jeep mounted "Rat Patrol." The name came from a very popular TV show of the 60's based on the exploits of a famous jeep mounted recon unit called the Rat Patrol that fought in the deserts of North Africa. We were to be a reincarnation of that unit.

We were issued four jeeps with upgraded engines that had a pedestal for an M60 machine gun and were to use these to run off of the roads on the flanks of a convoy to provide security and to react to and nullify the threat if ambushed. We had three guys to a jeep, maybe four, with a driver, a guy riding shotgun and then at least one, maybe two guys in the back with the machine gun. There was a radio on each vehicle as well as an M79 grenade launcher and a couple of M16's.

Everyone involved was also issued a set of goggles as we were running the jeeps with the windshields down. The goggles added a lot to the air of being the Rat Patrol. As I remember, we ran several of these escort missions without any real success. It was difficult because of the terrain and vegetation to run alongside of the convoy in many places. I was fortunate, we were never ambushed during one of my runs, or even fired upon during this time, and perhaps even more importantly, because the thin-skinned jeeps with the comparably weak M60 machine gun would have been no match for Salt and Pepper had we been unlucky enough to find them. But we did have fun running those jeeps over rough terrain at high speeds.

Finally Dragon decided that we needed to go into the area on foot to find their base camp and eliminate them. On a subsequent operation we discovered what appeared to be an NVA training area which included diagrams of the highway and local terrain as well as what appeared to be a depiction of the truck and its weapon. It was pretty complete with a large sand table depicting the terrain around the camp and the adjacent part of HWY 14, a covered training area, a mess area and sleeping accomodations for maybe 10 – 12 guys. However we weren't able to find any clues as to where the vehicle was being kept. I do remember that this site was a really scary place, a feeling I've recently discovered that was shared by Red Siner. As I remember the place was dark, maybe under triple canopy, and had a creepy, foreboding feel about it... like maybe we were being watched. As I remember this site was pretty big and showed signs of recent occupation. I think we were all relieved when I gave the word to saddle up and move out after destroying as much of as we could. This action may have forced the two guys and their vehicle to move as I don't recall any more convoy ambushes after this operation.

THE GREAT HAM CAPER One of the things that we looked forward to the most when coming out of the field and returning to the firebase was the battalion mess tent and some decent food after eating nothing but C rations. Once, when we arrived back at St. George after the evening meal some of the guys went to the mess tent anyway and asked the cooks if they could at least make some sandwiches. The mess team refused, they were done for the day and looking forward to some down time. As can be imagined, that didn't go over well with my dirty, tired, and hungry grunts.

If nothing else, recon soldiers are innovative and resourceful. When word came back to the bunkers that there would be no chow that evening, the guys decided that was a totally unacceptable situation. After dark, one of them, Ron Classen, decided to take matters into his own hands. Being the good recon soldier that he was, he snuck over to the refrigerators behind the mess tent, managed to get one open and looked inside. There in all of its glory was a large ham. Ron grabbed that, and a couple of loaves of bread, and quietly and quickly made his way back to the fox bunkers where he was treated as a hero when the guys found out what he had done. Everybody ate well that night.

The next morning there was a great uproar when the mess team reported to the kitchen to prepare the day's meal. When it was discovered the ham and several loaves of bread were missing, I suspect they went right to the battalion TOC and reported the theft of a large quantity of food. Of course there were no remnants to be found anywhere on the firebase, to include the Fox bunkers. The ham Ron had confiscated was evidently intended to be the main dish that day, and with its disappearance everyone was forced to eat C rations. I suspect that the Fox guys ate better that day; of course I have no first-hand knowledge of any of the facts.

THE PHANTOM SHITTER This is one of those incidents where to my knowledge the perpetrator was never discovered. Inside of St. George, there was a gravel path that ran across the north end and past the Dragon's hooch. One morning, someone out early found a large pile of human excrement on the path and in front of the Dragon's lair. It was quickly policed up and the search for the "Pooper" was unsuccessful. The same thing happened again for three or four days and to my knowledge the source of the poop was never discovered. The phantom shitter became a well-known and somewhat revered guy to many in the battalion.

MISS AMERICA VISIT Sometime in the fall of '69, while Fox was on an operation, we got word that Miss America and her entourage was going to visit Firebase St. George. That got everyone excited as we were scheduled to be back in for a stand down at about that time after many days in the jungle during the monsoon season. I also found out one of the other girls was Miss New York so I was excited about the prospect of meeting her as well. This visit would be a welcome break from the normal 1-14 curse of bad luck; we never had anyone famous come out to our firebase. Ah, our luck had finally changed.

The day before the scheduled visit we woke up and everyone was in a good mood. Everyone had breakfast and packed up early as were expecting to be told to move to an area where the birds could pick us up. We waited and waited and the word never came. A couple of radio calls to the TOC also resulted in no definitive word on when and where we were to be picked up. We were all getting a little anxious to say the least.

Finally Red told me that I had a call from the TOC. As I took the handset I fully expected to be given the info we needed to get back to St. George. Imagine the disgust and anger when I was told our mission was going to be extended; how in the hell could that happen? Telling the guys we weren't going in was one of the hardest things I ever had to do. The guys were so pissed I think it was a good thing we didn't run into the enemy that day, I think the guys and I would have gone on a real rampage. And, to make matters even worse, we were told we'd be going back the day after the visit of all of those beautiful young ladies. Dragon, to this day, perhaps with tongue in cheek, says that his decision to keep us out was made because he wasn't going to trust us around those gorgeous young women. We found out later he acted as the escort officer that day!

Fox Force did get some notoriety, however, even though we weren't physically present. While touring the firebase Miss America and her escorts passed our part of the bunker line. On top of one of the bunkers sat Sue, our mascot monkey, in his red scarf. The story goes that Miss America herself, upon spotting sweet, gentle Sue walked over to the bunker, all the while cooing and making cute noises as she approached. I was told that when she got close Sue jumped up on her shoulder. When Miss America moved to pet him Sue bit her on the neck and jumped off. I guess Sue knew how badly we all wanted to be there so she exacted some revenge for our absence.

Dragon has never lived down the fact he extended our stay in the jungle so we wouldn't be on the firebase when the gorgeous ladies arrived. Having gotten to know Dragon a lot better over the years, I suspect he really couldn't stand the competition of a bunch of young, swaggering studs in their red scarves. He wanted those ladies to himself and had the authority to make that happen.

BOILER MAKERS I don't remember the details but I did have the following experience related to me several times. It seems that after we returned to St. George after a mission a couple of my guys started drinking boilermakers, essentially a shot of whiskey with a beer chaser.

I've never been a whiskey drinker other than scotch, but that night the boilermakers sounded like a good idea. I was probably in one of my severe thirst modes so I put away several of those evil concoctions, so many, in fact, that my memory has gone blank on the events of the rest of the experience.

Evidently at one point I decided it was time to go to bed and somehow wound up in a small tent with one of the company First Sergeants who had an extra cot where I passed out. Sometime during that night we were mortared or rocketed . . . The story went that even though I was in a drunken stupor I must have been aware of what was happening. The First Sergeant related that I rolled off of my cot and began to low crawl across the wooden pallet floor. When I reached his bunk, with him still in it, I crawled up and over him, and then down the other side where I found a way under the tent wall.

I must have encountered the sandbagged blast wall because I started to crawl up the side. When I reached the top I must have passed out again, when the sun came up I was found draped over the blast wall, feet on one side and head on the other. The guys initially thought I was dead. I don't remember much of that day, but it was more than 40 years before I tasted another drink of bourbon.

UNBREAKABLE BONDS As stated earlier, Fox Force was a pretty tight knit organization in 1969, we had been through a lot together and had realized that everyone's survival depended on each and everyone else. That makes for a real closeness and band of brothers type of relationship. However, there is one story, one relationship, which kind of stands out from all of the others—the one between Charlie "Red" Siner and Larry "Diz" DesJardins. Their bond was truly special and unique.

Unbeknownst to all of us, before Vietnam, Red, Diz and I had all been stationed at Ft. Benning at the same time, although in different units, so there was no way we could have run into one another. Diz and Red met for the first time at Ft. Dix in June 1969 when they were in the replacement detachment awaiting shipment to Vietnam. While there, there was an incident when Red didn't answer to his name being called for a detail of KP which Diz thought was really cool. Everyone had just been issued new jungle fatigues and had not had the time to get name tapes and patches sewn on, so there was no way that the permanent party NCO could identify anyone by name. So when "Siner" was called Red just didn't answer. After a couple more tries the NCO went to the next name and that poor SOB got stuck with KP while Red, with Diz, just walked away when the formation was dismissed. That incident was the beginning of an incredible friendship.

Red and Diz wound up on the same bird going to Vietnam, and my guess is they were probably seat mates, as you naturally try to gravitate to someone you know when going into a trying situation. When the plane landed at Ton Son Nhut, a major air base outside of Saigon, they rode a bus together to the 90th Replacement Battalion at Bien Hoa Airbase where they awaited a unit assignment and transportation.

As luck would have it they were both assigned to the 4th Infantry Division and then to the 1st Battalion, 14th Infantry. Once assigned to the 1st/14th they were then both assigned to E Company and then to Fox Force along with a third new guy, Kenny McLacklan. That's quite a ride from Ft Dix to the jungles of Vietnam.

Red left Fox about the same time I did, early January of 1970. Diz stayed in Fox for about another month and then left to join the radar team on the firebase while Red had become the S3 Air for the battalion also stationed on the firebase, they were both done humping. For the remainder of their Vietnam tour they were together on the various firebases occupied by the battalion during that time.

Since they both had the same DEROS (Date Estimated Return From Overseas) date they left the field together to out-process from the battalion and division. As a final gesture, and because of his work as the S3 Air, Red arranged a traditional DEROS ride for the two of them. This was a tradition amongst grunts whenever it could be arranged, a wild final helicopter ride from the jungle location to the division firebase; the wilder and more dangerous the better. So Red, being the good friend that he was, arranged for a special ride in a Loach, a small and very maneuverable scout helicopter, for their final trip. Red sat up front with the pilot while Diz rode in back. The front was almost all Plexiglas so Red had a great view. Because of the internal configuration, Diz could see only out to the side so his perspective was a lot different.

The pilot was very accommodating because he and Red had worked together for a long time, and flew a hairy route above a river, climbing rapidly, auto rotating down, flying from side to side. When they finally landed at An Khe, Red thought he'd had the best ride of his life. Diz, on the other hand, was ready to do Red in because he had been scared to death by the experience. Not being a lover of scary rides like roller coasters, and because of his limited view out of the back of the bird, he'd had an entirely different experience.

They out processed together and rode the same Freedom Bird back to Seattle. Because they arrived at night, they had to spend the night is some barracks and wait until the hospital opened the next morning so they could take their separation physical before getting out of the Army. Red went to sleep almost immediately while Diz stayed up talking with the other guys. As a measure of "pay back", Diz had everyone move away from Red's bunk and then shouted "Incoming, Red" at the top of his lungs. According to Diz, Red levitated off the bed and hit the floor in a crouch looking about frantically for a place to hide until he realized what had happened. The cry of "incoming" was a signal that there were enemy rockets or mortars coming in to the location, a warning that no one liked to hear. Somehow Diz survived this experience.

The next day they processed out of the Army and then took the same flight to Chicago where they separated, Diz to go to Michigan while Red went home to New Jersey. This was the last they were to see of each other for 28 years. There wasn't much of an effort to reconnect, all of us were busy raising families and working, and it was just too hard to track folks through phone books. Many of us have since shared that frustration.

In 1998, Red tracked Diz to Port Huron, Michigan, called him and then flew up to reconnect. Shortly thereafter, thanks to Stag, others began to reconnect which led to our first reunion in 2000. Red joined but Diz wasn't yet ready to get back into Vietnam. Despite many urgings from Red, Diz didn't rejoin until the cruise in 2004. From then until now he's attended all of the reunions. When Diz remarried, Charlie was his Best Man. Today, given all of the shared experiences and memories, Red and Diz remain best friends with a bond that transcends all of those amongst the rest of us.

THE FAMOUS RIVER CROSSING During the month of September or October we were out on an extended operation during the monsoon season. We were tired, wet and miserable having been out in the rain for at least a week. Our skin was shriveling from being so wet, our feet were in bad shape, and we were tired of eating cold C rations. All we wanted to do was to get back to St. George where we would have shelter and hot chow and dry clothes. It sometimes took a couple of days to dry out our gear and bodies completely.

Our way home however, was blocked by a fast moving river that was normally just a small creek. It had become swollen because of all of the rain and now looked pretty formidable. Red heard on the radio one of the line companies, Delta I think, had lost a guy a couple days before to this same river. The guys were evidently trying to cross on a fallen tree when one guy slipped and went into the water. With the weight of his gear and the force of the water it was impossible to save him.

When we got to the river we halted on the bank, put out security, and I gathered my squad leaders and platoon sergeant to discuss the best way to get across. We decided not to risk trying to find a "tree bridge" and one of my squad leaders, Robin Sneeden, said he was a strong swimmer and would try to swim a rope across, secure it to the other side, and then we could use that to help us get across if the river wasn't too deep. Fortunately we were carrying some ropes.

So Robin stripped down to his fatigue pants, tied the rope around his middle and stepped into the water. The current quickly swept him off of his feet and he began to swim. After a couple of minutes he found that the current was just too fast and he yelled back to us to pull him back to shore. Even though he'd only been in the water for a short time, he was exhausted.

At that point Jimmy Harris, my Ranger qualified Platoon Sergeant, stepped forward and said he could get the rope across. Even though we'd all lost a lot of weight from all of the boonie humping Jimmy was still a formidable, muscular man. If anyone could get that rope across I figured he could. So he stripped down to his fatigue pants, entered the water, and began stroking quickly for the other side. For the first couple of minutes everything looked good and we were all feeling pretty good we'd soon get across that damned river and back to St. George. And then all of a sudden it looked as though Jimmy was tiring and the current was beginning to move him down stream.

I called for a couple of other guys to get on the rope so we could pull Jimmy back to our side. While these guys were coming up Jimmy suddenly was completely swept away almost pulling all of us on the rope in after him. More guys came forward to help with the rope and by this time Jimmy was barely visible; every once in a while we could see the water break as it passed around his head.

He had by this time become a dead weight at the end of the rope and it was getting harder and harder to pull him back to us. It's a good thing for us there were no bad guys in the area as our security pretty much went to hell as we tried to get Jimmy back. Progress was very slow due to the force of the current and his weight and I began to fear we might have lost him.

Finally we began to make progress and were slowly reeling in the rope and getting Jimmy closer and closer to the river's bank. After what seemed like an eternity we finally were able to bring him to shore and several of us went into the river to pull him up on the bank. At first glance things did not look good; he was initially lying on his back and there was no evident sign of life. Just as the medics came running up to begin to start CPR a little water dribbled out of his mouth, his eyelids fluttered, and he croaked in a low voice "Ran-n-n-n-ger". What a feeling of relief, we knew at that point that he would be OK.

While Jimmy and Robin were recovering from their ordeals I sent Danny Williams and a couple of guys down the river to find us a better crossing point; it was pretty obvious we weren't going to be able to get a rope bridge established. We got security re-established and everyone just hunkered down waiting for Danny and his patrol to return. Eventually they did, with word they had found a suitable fording point for us. We saddled up, moved down the bank, found the ford and made it across the river with no more problems. I think it was somewhat later that afternoon when we finally returned to St George, which looked to us at that point like an all-inclusive resort!

THE ST. GEORGE FLARE SHIP INCIDENT After finding the account of the flare ship on line I tracked down the pilot, Tim LaTour, who I discovered lived in Atlanta. Through a classmate of mine, Ron Adams, who also lives in Atlanta and who also served in the 10th CAV, I arranged for a meeting with Tim during an upcoming trip to Atlanta to see Margie's brother and my oldest son. I wanted to meet him and to shake his hand, and to express my condolences on the loss of his crewman Greg Rugenstein; they had risked all to come to our aid on that November night in 1969.

We had a great lunchtime meeting with Greg, Ron, Ron's roommate of those days who was a Cobra pilot, and Margie. I was honored to meet Tim and express my appreciation for what they had done that night. The flare ships had provided the only illumination we had as the D Company 81 mm mortars and the artillery battery were non-players, and I had all tubes from the 4.2 platoon firing HE because I didn't want to waste one on illumination.

Tim also related that he had communicated with one of the medics on duty that night at the Evac Hospital when he arrived with Tim. Tim had suffered a massive head wound; he'd been treated by a cosmetic surgeon who had tried to reconstruct his face, and had been given over 70 units of blood in the unsuccessful attempt to save his life; he died after a couple of days. One of the nurses who had attended him was so traumatized by the experience she developed Post Traumatic Stress

Disorder and wrote a book relating her experiences, including treating Tim. Unfortunately she has passed away.

I also learned that day that Greg's family had been told a pretty wild story about his death. The Army account was that Greg had caused the accident in the ship's cargo bay, that the flare had ignited and destroyed the bird, killing everyone on board. Greg had a daughter who read the same account that I did on line, and had contacted Tim in disbelief because they had been told that everyone on board the helicopter had been killed. Greg's wife had passed away believing the original story. Tim had assured her that the other three members of the crew had survived. I wrote a short note to his daughter to tell her of my side of the story, and to let her know that her Dad had died a hero while trying to save the lives of a lot of men he didn't know on the ground.

I relayed this story to my guys at a recent reunion (Aug 2017) and everyone was really affected on learning of another death on 6 November. They were also somewhat humbled to learn that Tim had just arrived in country and had volunteered for the mission that was to take his life, in order to protect theirs.

NEW YEAR'S EVE   After Christmas and maybe one more patrol, we received word that we were going to break down LZ Lois and the whole battalion would be moved back to Camp Enari for a New Year's Eve stand down and refit for a period of almost a week. This was the first break and relief from combat operations that the battalion had received since I joined them in July – six months of continuous patrolling and combat action. To say that this break was well earned by the Golden Dragons, and more specifically Fox Force, would be an understatement.

When we pulled into the battalion area at Enari we were moved into a small village of GP Medium tents that were complete with wooden pallet floors and GI cots; real luxury after our sodden sand-bagged bunkers or soggy poncho liners on the jungle floor.

I don't remember much of that week; I think it was my last few days with Fox. We were all given clean jungle fatigues, new boots if we needed or wanted them, and had opportunities for hot showers and haircuts. I know we began to feel almost civilized again.

New Year's Eve was a memorable occasion. I remember that there was a huge USO show that at one point featured an Australian band with a gorgeous blonde singer. I've seen a picture of her at one point where she was wearing what appeared to be a black negligee while performing, and then another where she was wearing a red scarf. I have no memory of how that happened and neither do any of the other guys

I've talked with. I'm sure that the memory loss was not caused by the infusion of too much alcohol into our brains.

At midnight the whole bunker line of Camp Enari lit up like a 4th of July fireworks show. There were flares going up as well as streams of tracers as guys on the bunker line celebrated. Back in our area a couple of my guys had a really good idea. Diz turned to Red with a hand flare in his hand prepared to fire, "Watch this Red!" They were in a tent, so it could not be fired vertically. Instead Diz held it out straight and horizontally and punched the end which drove the firing pin into the accelerant and the flare took off headed for an adjacent tent. Fortunately the sides were rolled up and the flare sailed right through and landed in a field behind the tents where it immediately started a fire. I think Red and Diz just ran off to get out of the area so they wouldn't get tagged by the MP's.

REST AND RELAXATION (R&R) That had been a heck of a trip to Hawaii in more ways than one. Neither Suzanne nor I knew anything at all about Hawaii or Honolulu, so she had picked a hotel of reasonable cost a couple of blocks back from the ocean. When my plane landed at Hickam AFB we were bused to FT DeRussey on Waikiki for briefings and processing. What a weird experience... we walked into the building through our waiting families but were prohibited from even touching them by rope barriers that kept us separated. I have no idea what the briefing contents were, probably the usual – don't break any laws, make sure you return on time, etc., etc. After about 10 minutes or so of this BS, we were finally released to greet our wives. What an emotional relief that was. To say that I was "wired" after the events of the previous month would be an understatement but, being back with Suzanne coupled with the tropical atmosphere of Hawaii, really helped me to throttle back a little.

We quickly grabbed a cab and went to the hotel she had selected. Don't remember even looking around as we headed to the room with only one thing in mind. When we woke up in the morning and I had a chance to look around, I was really disappointed, I couldn't see a beach, the ocean or Diamond Head. That sucked! So we checked out, hailed a cab, and I asked the driver to take us to a good hotel on Waikiki, albeit one that wasn't too expensive. We wound up at the Hilton Hawaiian Village, where they had super deals for guys on R & R from Vietnam. We were given a room on an upper floor of the Rainbow Tower, on the Waikiki side so we could go out on our lanai and look straight down the beach to Diamond Head. Now that was more like it. The support of the Hilton for R & R soldiers was nothing short of superb.

One night an electrical generator outside blew up with a sound like small arms fire. We were sound asleep and I awoke with a start, believing I was back at St. George. Suzanne had to quickly jump on me as I was low-crawling to the lanai, fortunately for her I was beginning to realize where I was and didn't try to kill her when she landed on me. It was a terrifying experience; I needed a couple of good Scotches to help me get back to a semblance of normalcy.

Another night we went to the hotel ballroom for a show put on by the legendary Don Ho; he even sang "Tiny Bubbles." At one point in the show, he asked all of the Vietnam guys to stand, we received loud applause from everyone there, a strange and proud moment.

Another evening we strolled down the beach to check out some of the other hotels. When we reached the Royal Hawaiian, the famous pink resort, we were captivated by the music and a huge Banyan Tree in the center courtyard. We decided to have a drink and walked in to look for a table. Surprisingly enough, I heard someone call my first name. Since I didn't expect to meet anyone I figured that some other John was being called. Shortly, someone walked up and gave me a hug, my Aunt Mary from California! She and some friends were sitting at a table under the tree and had seen us walk in. When asked why we were there they couldn't understand the reply; they had no idea most married soldiers in Vietnam met their wives in Honolulu for R & R. One of the guys at the table asked me if I was going to go back to Vietnam or would I go to Canada instead. When I told him that I would return, and then said that I enjoyed what I was doing when asked why, he became very silent and didn't say another word the entire time we were there. After about an hour and several more drinks, they left and went to their rooms.

We did a few touristy things like going out to Pearl Harbor and visiting the Arizona Memorial. That visit was more emotional than I had expected; I felt a real kinship with all of those great young Americans who were resting below me. Having survived the surprise attack on St. George, I could relate somewhat to what they had experienced; I felt really connected to those guys. I've been back there several times and still experience the same emotions. One day we rented a convertible sports car and drove around the island and back to Honolulu through the same pass the Japanese had flown through in 1941. Eerily enough, the car we were driving was a Datsun 1600 convertible, once again taking a Japanese machine through that pass and gazing down on Pearl Harbor.

On another day, Suzanne wanted to take a tour to see a waterfall in the center of the island. When we got off of the tour bus, I discovered I'd have to walk about a mile or so through a jungle area that closely resembled Vietnam. Even though we were on a well-defined walkway bordered by beautiful plants and flowers in Hawaii I became very uncomfortable… I had no weapon. I was certainly relieved when we returned to the bus and headed back into Honolulu.

I just wanted to relax, to enjoy my wife, and to enjoy the atmosphere of Honolulu. It was wonderful and ended all too quickly. Before I knew it, I was back on a plane headed back to the war zone.

RICHARD WARREN – GUNSHIP PILOT AND INSPIRATION

In the chapter entitled the Bunker Complex I related that the first fire support we received that day were two Army gunships; Huey Charlie Models based on the huey "slick". These were armed with a variety of weapons systems to include additional 7.62mm machine guns, various configurations of 2.75" folding fin rockets, and a .40mm grenade launcher mounted under the chin bubble.

In the chapter entitled "Together Again" I related a visit to a patriotic coffee shop in Mooresville named Pat's Gourmet Coffee Shop and run by by a man by the name of Richard Warren. These two sections are connected in that Richard was the pilot of one of the gunships!

I discovered this amazing fact when I went to Pat's a week or so after my FOX reunion held at my house in 2006 to see Richard. When I entered the shop he grabbed me by the arm and pulled me outside, "John, I have to talk to you! It's about the visit of your guys."

Aw shit I wondered to myself, had one of my guys broken something or "borrowed" one of the momentos in Pat's? No way could that be true; I was really at a loss to explain or understand Richard's sense of urgency.

When we got outside he turned and asked me if my Fox Force had been in a particular area in II Corps in early December 1969? "Yeah" I answered. And were we in deep shit facing an NVA unit incredibly bigger than we were? "Right again." "Do you remember who your first supporting fire came from?" "Not really" I answered, "I was kinda busy on the radio and pulling a trigger." "Well, that was me and my wingman!" Richard replied. And he told me that he was sure that he had supported us because after their first gun run his crewchief got on the intercom and asked, "Who are those crazy bastards down there wearing red scarves?" The location fit, the time frame fit, and the particulars of the incident fit . . . , here I was some 35 years later meetimg a man who was probably responsible for some of my guys and me being alive – what a small world.

239

I couldn't believe it! After more than 35 years I was face to face with someone who had probably saved the lives of some of my soldiers and maybe my own! Unbelievable! A couple of years later I was fortunate to go to Iowa to a small air museum where his bird was dedicated to be the center piece of the Vietnam part of the display. At that time I had the opportunity to meet his other crewmembers and even to sit in the door of that bird; what an emotional experience that weekend was.

This fact affected me in ways that I didn't realize at that moment. A year or so later Richard asked a couple of us to figure out a way to form a 501c3 non-profit organization, centered on his coffee shop, to be called Welcome Home Veterans. During the time that we were working on this Richard was looking more and more like he wasn't doing well. He and Pat had split up and he was living in an old, dingy house a block for the shop. Shorly after the non-profit status was awarded Richard passed away from Agent Orange related cancers in May of 2009. We thought at that point that he must have had a premonition of his impending death.

After he passed there were some issues between the coffe shop landlord and Richard's then ex-wife and the landlord shut us down. As the 501c3 status had been approved I was asked to join the Board of Directors which I was overjoyed to do, maybe by doing this I could begin to pay some of my debt to Richard for saving the lives of my soldiers and probably mine as well. A year or so later I was appointed to a new position as President of Welcome Home Veterans and saw it through a move from a small temporary site at the end of Main Street Mooresville to a much nicer and larger facility in the middle of downtown which we named Richard's Coffee Shop.

Richard's has become an incredible place; a place of comradrie, solace and healing. We continue many of the traditions that Richard had started like making Thursday free coffee for vets day, having each vet sign into our Book of Honor (we're now at almost 16,000) on their first visit, receive a key chain that commemorates the veteran's service as well as a warm and heartfelt "Welcome Home!" I have had guys come up and tell me that the atmosphere and comraderie of Richard's has literally saved their lives.

I have been honored to hold my position as President now for about six years, and will continue to do so for as long as I'm able.

DUTY! HONOR! COUNTRY!

21 - A DAY IN THE LIFE . . .

Life in Vietnam for the American infantry soldier was not one of constant combat, even though the potential was always there. There were no front lines so just about everywhere we went could be enemy country. For the average guy, many days went by without the sounds of bullets cracking overhead, no smell of gun smoke, and no sign of little guys in black pajamas or NVA khaki. But that is not to say that the off days were filled with pleasure and relaxation. Even if the day was quiet, the apprehension, and in some cases down right fear, was always present. Whenever the grunt was in the field, he could never feel safe. The environment could erupt around him at any moment in terrifying noises and smells. You had to be on your guard constantly, for if you ever let down for a second it could be your last. Being in the bush was not easy.

Vietnam was probably the last of the old technology wars for the infantryman. Although the M-16 was different than the M-1 Garand, most of the gear we carried would have been familiar to a grunt from Korea or World War II. The helicopter had its debut in Korea, and was certainly more prevalent in Vietnam in many more models than in the 1950's. Close air support was provided in many cases by Army helicopters rather than the original Army Air Force, and by the other services as well. Communications may have been better too. But, by and large, the grunt from the earlier conflicts of WW II, particularly in the Pacific Theater and in some ways Korea, could have adapted themselves to combat and life in Vietnam with little problem. The day was spent slogging through marshes or rice paddies, cutting their way through thick jungle or eight foot tall elephant grass which could leave nasty cuts, or climbing mountains… all with 100 pounds or more on his back. Grunts in Vietnam may have been the last of the American jungle fighters, a tough and resourceful breed born in earlier conflicts like the Philippines before World War II and the Pacific Theater during WW II.

The grunt's life was lived at the most primitive levels imaginable, at least on firebases and in the field. Those guys that managed to get "rear jobs" lived considerably better. The rear job was one that involved movement to the BN rear area that was located on the division's installation and allowed for sheets, mess hall meals and beds. There was also a Class VI or liquor store where the REMF's could buy all of the beer or hard liquor they wanted. There was also access to enlisted, NCO and officer's clubs as well as stores, theaters, barbers, dentists, doctors, etc. Rock bands from the US and the Philippines frequented the division areas, featuring performers of sometimes-questionable talent, but always with young women in tight and revealing outfits. Life in these jobs was certainly not on a par with life in "the world" (home); but it was considerably more comfortable and safer than being in the bush. However, every once in a while even those on division base camps were subjected to the face of war when the base camp was targeted by incoming rockets or mortars, or even scarier, sapper attacks by dedicated NVA commandos who targeted airfields.

Grunts in the jungles were removed from the life of their ancient cave man ancestors only by the type and amount of equipment carried. Life in the jungle sometimes even requiring living off of the land for food, certainly for water. This dark and sometimes tortuous countryside could be a forbidding atmosphere for even the most seasoned soldiers.

Grunts typically lived off of what they could carry in the way of food and water. Periodic resupply was usually available by helicopter if you were in an area where you were not afraid of giving your position away to the bad guys. At those times it was possible to restock supplies of C rations and occasionally receive somewhat hot "A" rations in mermite cans, an insulated container which held three vertical inserts. I'll try to explain the common items that influenced us on a daily basis.

CLIMATE – Vietnam was incredibly hot and humid with temperatures well over 100 degrees most days and normal humidity of 80 to 100%. I'm told that sometimes the temperature rose to 120 degrees and above. When in triple canopy jungle the environment was even worse as water was almost constantly dripping from the leaves. If we carried a wallet or other personal items they were always wrapped in a plastic bag. While there were no "baggies" as commonly found today, radio batteries were always received in plastic as were other items. These bags became extremely valuable, especially since the RTO's had first call so that they could protect their radio handsets. The body eventually acclimated to these conditions but we were always alert for signs of heat exhaustion or heat stroke in the field. There was not much difference between summer, fall, winter and spring. We also had a monsoon season with perpetual rain and cooler temperatures, particularly at night, which could be very uncomfortable, particularly if you were wet as well.

MEALS - "A" rations were regular food that you might find served in a mess hall in the rear area such as the BN firebase once in a while, or certainly in the bigger logistical bases or division camps. When sent to the field on a resupply bird, different foods were placed into three separate inserts in a container called a Mermite Can. These insulated containers usually contained meat and two vegetables. During my time in Vietnam the Army must have cornered the market on fatty hams, as that seemed to be the predominant meat served on the forward fire base, and hence to us in the field. Once in a while we would have steak or fried chicken. I did become turned off to any kind of ham for years after I came home, it was probably close to 30 years before I could face it again, even the type of glazed baked ham that my Mom made on Easter Sunday.

At one point the Army high command decided that the troops in the field deserved better service, and so directed that we be provided with ice cream on a regular basis. I'm sure that the mess crew in the rear tried their best, but it was hard to keep ice cream frozen in Vietnamese conditions. By the time it reached the grunt in the jungle it was a soupy mess, and was usually poured into a soldier's canteen cup for him to drink. But at least ice cream had been delivered, a reportable item required from battalion to brigade and division headquarters. Several times I sat in on the 1700 briefing, The Five O'clock Follies, on the firebase for the battalion commander and saw the stats of when each company in the field had been served, what flavor and how much.

Of course, once the mermites had been delivered to the field they had to be carried until they could be back-hauled. Because of that I often tried to get the bird to come back the same day so that we didn't have to deal with the ungainly containers in the thick jungles. Often times the "A's" were for the evening meal so we tried to get a bird out in the AM before we broke camp to continue our patrol.

Sometimes we were lucky enough to have some LRRP rations which were the first dehydrated combat meals developed for Long Range Reconnaissance Patrol units. The LRRPS were generally much more tasty than C's, but the disadvantage was that you had to add water, preferably hot, to reconstitute the meal. And they sure tasted better warm! If water supply was an issue, and you were forced to eat the rations in their dry mode, then one inconvenient after-effect was that they would swell in your stomach and cause great discomfort. This could also lead to severe constipation and/or gas, which were definitely maladies that you didn't want when humping the boonies.

Grunts normally carried the minimum number of cans of "C's" because of their weight. The favorite items were pound cake and canned peaches. Beans and weenies, beef steak and potatoes with gravy and spaghetti were always favorites, with ham and lima beans, known to the troops as ham and motherfuckers was always the least desired. If in a safe area, the meals could be heated with either a "heat tab" or more frequently, hotter and faster by burning pinches of C4. Most of us carried a hunk of the explosive with us for the express purpose of heating water for coffee or food. C4 burned quicker and hotter than the heat tabs which came with the rations, and didn't have the noxious odor of the tabs. And, it only took a pinch of the explosive to do what an entire heat tab could do.

C-RATIONS Commercially prepared packaged combat meals were used in the field and when hot meals were not available. These meals came in a case containing 12 different main course meals. Each meal was in its own cardboard box, which contained the individual items sealed in olive drab cans. A can opener (called a "P-38") was needed to open the cans. The accessory pack was sealed in a separate foil pouch.

> **This is the official Army Quartermaster's description of the C-Rations used in Vietnam**
>
> "The Meal, Combat, Individual, is designed for issue as the tactical situation dictates, either in individual units as a meal or in multiples of three as a complete ration. Its characteristics emphasize utility, flexibility of use, and more variety of food components than were included in the Ration, Combat, and Individual (C Ration) which it replaces. Twelve different menus are included in the specification.
>
> Each menu contains: one canned meat item; one canned fruit, bread or dessert item;
> one B unit; an accessory packet containing cigarettes, matches, chewing gum, toilet paper, coffee, cream, sugar, and salt; and a spoon. Four can openers are provided in each case of 12 meals. Although the meat item can be eaten cold, it is more palatable when heated.
>
> Each complete meal contains approximately 1200 calories. The daily ration of 3 meals provides approximately 3600 calories."

There were 4 choices of meat in each B group. Because there were several "vintages" of C's issued in Vietnam, more than 4 items may be listed in the B groups as well as the brands of cigarettes included in the accessory pack.

B-1 Units	B-2 Units	B-3 Units
Meat Choices (in small cans):	Meat Choices (in larger cans):	Meat Choices (in small cans):
Beef Steak	Beans and Wieners	Boned Chicken
Ham and Eggs, Chopped	Spaghetti and Meatballs	Chicken and Noodles
Ham Slices	Beefsteak, Potatoes and Gravy	Meat Loaf
Turkey Loaf	Ham and Lima Beans	Spiced Beef
Fruit:	Meatballs and Beans	Bread, White
Applesauce	Crackers (4)	Cookies (4)
Fruit Cocktail	Cheese Spread, Processed	Cocoa Beverage Powder
Peaches	Caraway	Jam
Pears	Pimento	Apple
Crackers (7)	Fruit Cake	Berry
Peanut Butter	Pecan Roll	Grape
Candy Disc, Chocolate	Pound Cake	Mixed Fruit
Solid Chocolate	Accessory Pack*	Strawberry
Cream		Accessory Pack*
Coconut		
Accessory Pack*		

Accessory Pack*

Spoon, Plastic	Cigarettes, 4 smokes/pack
Salt	*Winston*
Pepper	*Marlboro*
Coffee, Instant	*Salem*
Sugar	*Pall Mall*
Creamer, Non-dairy	*Camel*
Gum, 2 Chicklets	*Chesterfield*
Matches, Moisture Resistant	*Kent*
Toilet Paper	*Lucky Strike*
	Kool

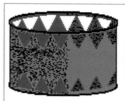 

How to make a C-Ration Stove

The small cans included in the meal were ideal for making a stove. Using a P38 pierce a series of closely spaced holes around the top and bottom rims of the can. This stove was satisfactory, but did not allow enough oxygen to enter which caused incomplete burning of the blue Trioxin heat tablet, causing fumes which irritated the eyes and respiratory tract. A whole heat tab had to be used.

A better stove was created by simply using the can opener end of a "church key" (a flat metal device designed to open soft drink and beer containers with a bottle opener on one end and can opener on the other commonly used before the invention of the pull tab and screw-off bottle top) to puncture triangular holes around the top and bottom rims of the can which resulted in a hotter fire and much less fumes. With this type of stove only half a Trioxin heat tab was needed to heat the meal and then the other half could be used to heat water for coffee or cocoa. A small chunk of C-4 explosive could also be substituted for the Trioxin tablet for faster heating. It would burn hotter and was much better for heating water.

.
A stove was usually carried in the back pack or cargo pocket and used repeatedly until the metal began to fail.

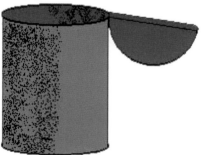

How to Heat a C-Ration Meal

Choose the meal to be consumed
1.   Open the can lid leaving at least 1/4 inch metal attached
2.   Bend the still attached lid so that the inside of the can lid is facing 180 degrees from its original position (inside up).
3.   Bend the edges of the can to form a handle
4.   Set meal on stove and heat to desired temperature, stirring frequently to prevent burning.

"Outstanding" Ham & Mothers

o   Open and heat a can of Ham and Lima Beans
o   When hot, add one can of cheese spread and stir until all cheese is melted.
o   Crumble 4 crackers into the mixture and blend thoroughly.
o   Eat when the crackers have absorbed all excess moisture.

How to make a C-Ration Coffee Cup

1. Obtain the B (large, dry) can from the C-ration meal
2. Follow steps 2 thru 4 in How to Heat a C-Ration Meal above.

Deluxe (reusable) Version*

1. Remove the top of the can completely.
2. Obtain 2 lengths of the bailing wire off of the C-Ration case.
3. Obtain a solid, sturdy stick about 4 inches long.
4. Notch out a groove around the stick near both ends.
5. Wrap each length of wire around both top & bottom ends of the can and twist the wire around itself leaving enough twisted wire to twist around the grooves in both ends of the stick 1 inch from the can creating a very nice handle.
6. Trim off excess wire.

* Thanks to "Doc" Byron Perkins for jogging my memory on this one

*The above information came from a web search for Vietnam C Rations at www.gruntfixer.homerstead.com. Spelling and sentence structure corrections were made by the author.

Many soldiers became C ration master chefs, devising recipes made from combining elements of several of the boxes and producing pretty good meals. Tasty stews were often concocted in the chef's steel pot. Almost every one of us carried hot sauce and garlic salt, which we got from home.

When not in the jungle, our battalion firebases normally had a mess tent manned by a mess sergeant and his team. Eating there was a real treat and welcome escape from C's. Sometimes we got real eggs for breakfast. Most of the time they were powdered because of their need for refrigeration. There was always plenty of hot coffee in the morning. Lunch meals were normally sandwiches; sometimes we could get hamburgers but no fries. Every once in a while we got chicken or steak with hot vegetables and mashed potatoes and gravy. A Kool Aid type beverage normally referred to as "bug juice" was supplied with ice when available.

Many of the mess sergeants became masters of making tasty soups either from the standard Army recipe cards, or from leftovers. Soups were really popular during the monsoon season when we were constantly wet and chilled.

Ice became a quest; I could never get enough. It was so hot and humid most of the time that cold drinks could command an exorbitant price in the villages. Even now I crave ice. My first memory of coming home was stopping at a barbeque restaurant on the way from the Atlanta airport to Columbus, Georgia with Suzanne. When my glass of quintessential southern iced tea arrived it was crammed with ice; the most beautiful thing I'd seen in months. Even now, more than 40 years later, I need a glass filled to the top with ice when I drink cold beverages, I don't think that I'll ever get enough or a drink that is too cold. Some things just stay with you.

WATER – Water was a necessity in the heat and humidity of Vietnam, sometimes it seemed that we could never carry enough, particularly in the beginning of a tour when the body was still acclimating. On a firebase there was usually enough water in lister bags or in a water buffalo, a 500-gallon water trailer. In the field, however, availability became a real problem. Most of us carried between three and five quarts when we left on a mission, but that went quickly. It was great when we could find a fresh flowing stream or clear pond for refills, but often we had to use the stagnant water found in rice paddies. These were normally covered with some kind of scum, often used as toilets by both water buffalo and the farmers. After scooping the surface away we filled the canteens and then added two Halazone tablets for purification. The combination had a taste that made it basically undrinkable

UNIFORMS - There were three different field uniforms. The most common was the US Army issued jungle fatigues, 100% rip stop cotton, which were comfortable, afforded lots of big pockets, were durable and dried quickly when wet. They also resisted ripping and tearing in the brambles and stickers of jungle wait-a-minute vines. Boots were again the US army issued jungle boot which consisted of a black leather lower portion and green nylon upper portion which allowed air to circulate and again dried quickly when wet. There was a thin steel plate in the sole to protect against punji sticks.

The other most popular fatigue styles were the tiger stripe pattern favored by a lot of Vietnamese units, and the American green and brown patterned camouflage style. These were both highly sought after as it tended to make the troops feel and look more menacing.

In my units we didn't wear any underwear. Undershirts just added another layer of warmth and stickiness which we didn't need, and the drawers tended to get wet from sweat and bunch up in the crotch causing "jungle rot" which itched and burned like mad. Very few soldiers wore personal fatigues with name and rank attached in our battalion because of the difficulty of tracking those through the field laundry units. We normally received bundles of clean uniform parts, and just went through those until we found a top and bottom that fit.

The uniforms quickly became filthy, wet and stinky. Putting on clean ones was a refreshing experience for at least 15 or 20 minutes. If we found a stream and it was in a safe area, we'd jump in and clean ourselves and our uniforms. During the monsoon season, the rip-stop material would eventually soften and rot, causing some problems depending on where the rip occurred. But they usually stood up well to the normal wear and tear of life in the jungle. The design and use of that material was probably one of the best decisions made during the war by military logisticians. Jungle fatigues were superb. But even these great uniforms became pretty gross when worn for 20 or so days.

BASIC LOAD – Over the jungle fatigues we wore our basic load of LBE (load bearing equipment) and ruck sack. The LBE was made up of the familiar web belt attached to a pair of suspenders made of the same basic material. The suspenders allowed you to unfasten the belt for easier breathing or better air circulation and still keep it, and the accouterments hanging from it, handy if needed. The suspenders had padded straps over the shoulders and points on the front to hang flashlights, first aid packs, or grenades. When this combination was first issued you also received a butt pack. This was a fairly small pack for extras like clothes, ammo, personal items and toiletries which fastened over the belt by a couple of sliding clips. It was useless in Vietnam.

We discarded the butt pack in favor of the much more versatile ruck sack which rode on a separate aluminum frame on the shoulders rather than pulling on them like the butt pack. The rucksack also had a lot more room and several different pockets so that you could better organize what you were carrying. There was a waterproof bag to insert into the biggest pocket so that you could at least attempt to keep things dry. One other major advantage of the ruck was that it could be shed easily and quickly, like when in enemy contact. The retained web gear would allow access to water, your first aid pack, etc. Ammunition for the M16 was carried in the issue bandoleers, which could hold seven loaded magazines. I wore two of these; one tied around my waste after cutting the strap and one as a bra after attaching the center of the strap to the middle magazine pocket with a safety pin.

MAIL - As in all wars mail from home was a real morale booster. During Vietnam writing was the primary means of getting information back and forth between the soldier and home. Some guys carried mini cassette recorders in their rucks and exchanged the small tapes with their families. These could become heavy, and useless if they got wet, so the predominant means of communication remained the hand-written letter.

Troops in the field sometimes had limited access to stationary and envelopes so we wrote on anything, like the flaps from C ration cartons. The message to home was written on one side, the address on the other, and "Free Mail" was written where the stamp was normally placed. This became a legal letter, processed through the APO (Army Post Office) and the US Post Office system.

Receiving mail was problematic, even though the Army tried its best. Some units moved around frequently and were hard to track. Mail would pile up until the unit was located and then several bags of it would be delivered at once. Getting mail in the field was always good, although packages containing cakes or cookies could be hard to deal with in that environment.

MARS TELEPHONE - If a soldier was lucky he might get a trip to the rear for some administrative reason and could get in line at the MARS (Military Affiliate Radio system) station. MARS was a telephone system, an operator in Vietnam would connect with a civilian HAM operator in the US to link a call to a personal phone in "The World." While hearing the voice of a loved one was always welcome, the conversation could be awkward. When one side was finished talking and wanting a response they would have to say "over" like on a tactical radio. This procedure allowed the HAM operator, who was the intermediary, to know when to switch from "send mode" to 'listen mode" between the connected parties.

Sundry packs – These were boxes of goodies put together by the Army in the US that were issued periodically to units, with the number of boxes delivered based on the unit's size. Fox was issued two at a time. The "SP Packs" contained candy, writing supplies, toiletries like shaving cream, razors and tooth paste, and the favorite item, cigarettes. I let my soldiers choose their items first so I normally wound up with the Chuckles (a gum drop like candy) and Red Dogs, another name for the Pall Malls, everyone's least favorite and unfiltered cigarette. I learned to love the Chuckles because of the sweet taste that could hide the nastiness in your mouth when I hadn't brushed my teeth for a few days. To this day I'll buy a package if I see them.

MALARIA PILLS – Malaria was a constant threat in Vietnam. If a soldier became infected he quickly became combat ineffective; the more severe cases were sent home. In its worst form the malady could provoke intense cases of chills and trembling accompanied by severe cramps and diarrhea. And worse yet, the disease could stay in your body for years. One large pill was taken weekly and a smaller one was supposed to be taken daily. The battalion headquarters was required to report to brigade on a daily basis that all troops had taken their required pills and that sleeves had been rolled down to prevent mosquito bites as dusk approached. Many guys had adverse reactions to the pills and tried to avoid taking them.

HYGIENE - Hygiene was at best difficult when in the field. The weather was always a problem, especially during the monsoons. During this 5th season, which lasted 4 to 6 weeks, the rains came every day. Sometimes the downpour could be so strong that you couldn't see 5 feet in front of you, most of the time it was just a relatively steady rain. During the dry season bathing in the field was rare. If the situation allowed I let my soldiers swim and wash up in streams; most of us carried a bar of soap for that occasion.

During the monsoons the temperature could drop dramatically at night, making sleep all but impossible due to shivering and being wet. We'd build low poncho hooches and wrap up in a wet poncho liner to try to stay as dry and warm as possible. The poncho hooch was made by stretching the four corners out as far as possible and tying them off on a nearby tree. The center head hole was tied off to keep water out and tied off directly above on a low hanging branch. The resultant structure was about 24 inches off of the ground and could shield you from the worst of the rain as you wrapped up in your poncho liner. The light and comforting poncho liner became a grunt's best friend as it could be warmed quickly by just body heat. It was one of the best and most popular items ever issued by the Army.

The calls of nature were answered in the most basic ways, by digging a hole then covering the waste; hopefully the soldier had some dry C ration toilet paper. Trees, bushes or just the side of a trail became handy urinals.

Most soldiers carried a toothbrush and toothpaste but the paste was seldom used in the field as it was feared that the bad guys could smell it. Often water was too scarce as well. Most of the guys would at least run a dry brush around their mouths in the morning.

After a couple of days, uniforms became dirty and sweat soaked, as did boots and socks. To say that a grunt became "ripe" in that situation would be an understatement. Most of us did not carry deodorant, again because of the smell, and we seldom shaved outside of the firebase.

A couple of pairs of clean and dry socks, wrapped in plastic bags, were a necessity no matter what time of the year. Our feet were our primary means of transportation so their good health was a real necessity.

INSECTS AND CRITTERS – As would be expected in a jungle climate, Vietnam was full of all kinds of unsavory critters. Mosquitoes were a constant irritant and carried the threat of malaria with them.

Another unwelcome guest found in streams and especially in rice paddies were leeches. They were horrible, blood-sucking critters that caused no pain but which could inflict horrible wounds that would take a long time to heal. Because these were open sores they often became infected and oozy. Every time we crossed a paddy, stream or river we would stop and check each other for leeches. We couldn't feel them, and if not dealt with, they would suck blood until they became engorged and fell off. The best way to get rid of them was with a drop of insect repellent on the head or the heat from a cigarette. It was not unusual to have several of these critters hanging from you at the same time, and invariably they attached themselves in the worst places. One of my guys in Charlie Company had a leech that crawled up inside his penis.

Another threat while moving through thick underbrush was disturbing a colony of red ants who often lived in the trees and bushes. When agitated or threatened they would cover a soldier in seconds and the bite was so painful that normally we would throw security to the winds in order to get rid of them. Soldiers would drop their gear and shuck their clothes in order to swat the insects off of their bodies. These ants were ferocious!

There were all kinds of snakes in Vietnam; two of the most common and most feared were the cobra and the bamboo viper. We once killed a cobra over 20 feet long and when we reported it, were told to skin it and send the skin back to be measured in hopes that we had a record. Bamboo vipers, on the other hand, were shorter bright green snakes that were even more deadly. Their venom was so deadly, it was said that, if bitten, you would only take two steps before you died.

In addition, it was possible to pick up all types of maladies from that environment; I came home with two such issues. One was an intestinal problem that would hit me monthly with severe cramping, gas and diarrhea that could last for four or five days and just about incapacitate me. The doctors couldn't diagnose the source and treated me for all kinds of intestinal parasites. None of those treatments really worked, but fortunately for me, the severity of the attacks lessened over time and eventually, after about four years, disappeared.

My other problem was a skin disease. Periodically my fingers would begin to itch intensely, little bumps would appear, and the surface layers would dry out so that I could pull the outer skin right off. This condition lasted for years, sometimes appearing to get better but then reappearing. I sometimes get a mild case to this day.

Upon reflection, life for a combat grunt in Vietnam was elemental in nature, and grim. I wonder now how we could have lived in such a primitive state. We were not much different than our fathers who had fought in the jungles of the Pacific Theater in World War II. Combat grunts from Vietnam are a special bunch. Not many guys who deployed to Vietnam ever experienced these hardships and the dangers of enemy action. At the peak of in-country strength during the war there were about 550,000 men in theater. Of that amount, on any given day, there were only about 10%, or 55,000 actually in the field! Any veteran who wears the blue and silver Combat Infantryman's Badge is a very special guy, a member of very small cohort of soldiers who actually placed his life on the line in close combat, while living like an animal.

DUTY! HONOR! COUNTRY!

22 – THE FREEDOM BIRD

After out-processing from the battalion and Division I went to Cam Rahn Bay by C130 to await transportation to The World. The company commander of the replacement company was a classmate who somehow linked up with me after I arrived. I remember him in clean jungle fatigues and spit shined jungle boots as he gave me a tour of his air conditioned office on our way to the Officers Club where we enjoyed a great steak dinner with a couple of cold beers. All I could think of during that entire time was "Man, what a great way to fight a war!"

I don't remember how long I was there before my flight, probably just a day or two, but I do remember rockets coming in one night and the extremely helpless feeling of running outside to a shelter made of a large culvert covered with sandbags. What a horrible feeling as we cowered in there, with no weapon. I didn't want to die on my last night in Vietnam.

Finally I was taken to the airfield to meet my Freedom Bird – I was going home! The new guys who had just deplaned were gathered in a group waiting for their bus transportation. We were a quiet group; nervously looking around for cover should we get shelled or attacked. I think we all expected to hear "in coming" at any moment. Most of us were also hiding bottles of booze we intended to consume once we had "wheels in the well" and were safely out of Vietnamese air space. We regarded the FNG's with a mixture of sadness and pity, knowing most of them were going where we had just left.

The interior of that big Freedom Bird was completely full of soldiers who were totally silent as we taxied down the runway and lifted off; no one dared breathe for fear of rockets or mortars stopping the liftoff. Even when we heard the wheels come up there was not a sound; not until the pilot came on the intercom, "Gentlemen, we have just cleared Vietnamese airspace; you are all safe now and homeward bound. Enjoy the flight and let us know if there is anything that we can do for you."

What a roar filled that plane, guys jumping up, slapping each other on the back, some grinning, some laughing, and some crying. And magically, if there were 200 of us on that plane, two hundred bottles of booze suddenly appeared. The stewardesses seemed genuinely happy to be flying home with a planeload of survivors and provided us with an endless supply of mixers.

My seatmate was a warrant officer; we became instant buds because he had flown with the "Black Jacks," the assault helicopter company that took us on our many combat assaults. We shared a lot of experiences and the fact that we'd travel together to our final destination as we were both headed for Atlanta was an unbelievable coincidence.

I don't have a clear recollection of the flight; I think we landed in Guam to refuel and then on to Hawaii, retracing our original flight of a year ago. We must have been pretty tightly controlled during the ground stops because I don't remember anyone buying more booze anywhere. But at least the "stews" were pretty generous with the little airline bottles as well as a few cases of champagne. I think we had a steak dinner on every segment of that flight.

Our destination on the mainland was the Seattle-Tacoma airport, SeaTac. There, those of us who were not getting out of the Army right away would catch our connecting flights to get home. I was proud to be wearing my summer uniform with my awards and decorations even though it had a couple of moth holes in one of the legs; I had served my country well.

My clearest memory of deplaning is of walking through a gauntlet of our fellow countrymen who were hurling insults, calling us baby killers, druggies, rapists and the like. I was shocked and really confused; I had no idea we were so unpopular at home. My warrant buddy and I looked straight ahead and walked as quickly as possible to clear this horde of assholes; we almost made it. Those idiots were so close they actually spit in our faces as they were hurling insults.

Suddenly I saw my buddy whirl and throw a punch at one of the longhaired protesters. I learned later this unfortunate human being had reached out and grabbed the pilot's arm while shouting derogatory spittle into his face. I saw a couple of other longhaired guys jump into the fray and then I must have gone into combat mode as I have no clear recollection of what happened next. My reactions took over and I must have waded into the protesters to back up my buddy. My next clear remembrance was of a cop, who came out of nowhere, asking if I was OK. I could feel that I had only a sore lip, a bruised cheek, and some very sore knuckles so I told him I was fine. I looked at my buddy and he was in about the same shape. He gestured towards the floor where a couple of longhairs were moaning and trying to get up, several others were being tended to by their friends. The flight crew who was walking behind us when the fracas started explained to the police what had happened. Fortunately one of them, I think, was also a Vietnam Vet. I guess they must have also called the medics as a couple arrived on the scene. As soon as the policemen were sure the injured were being taken care of and that we were OK, they grabbed our arms and escorted us to the gate for our Atlanta flight. They stayed close by until we boarded and advised us not to ever return to SeaTac. I have done my best to honor that directive!

I must admit that we were relieved to board that airplane. We asked the stew to bring us as many of the little booze bottles as she could. We must have been a scary sight; what a hell of a welcome home! We finally landed in Atlanta. I think we slept most of the way from SeaTac due to the booze, the 24 hours we had been up, and the adrenaline drain that followed our incident at the airport. As I remember, we landed late morning on a beautiful sunny Georgia summer day. Suzanne was there to welcome me home; it had been about 6 months since our R&R in Hawaii in early December of 1969.

But now I was home for good; no need to return to Vietnam.
On the way down to Columbus to get our things for the trip up to Rochester to see my folks I had an incredible experience. We stopped at a Barbeque place on the side of the road and when the iced tea I ordered arrived at the table I was totally mesmerized by the glass full of ice; boy, The World was a phenomenal place!

Vietnam returnees were given a 30-day leave before being required to report into our next duty station. We spent a couple of days with Suzanne's folks to enable me to recover from jet lag (and a nasty hang over) before we hopped in my Firebird and headed for Rochester to see my family; that was quite a home coming. It was good to be back with my folks and sister.

One day, we were sitting in our kitchen eating lunch when we heard a knock on the door. When I opened it, I was shocked to see Danny Williams, one of my Fox squad leaders; I think I'd forgotten Danny was also from Rochester, and I invited him in. We had a great visit for a couple of hours, my Dad treated him like a king, and when he left we talked about staying in touch. That was an empty promise because it was over 30 years before we saw each other again. At that time, I asked him why he had tracked me down at my folk's house and had then disappeared for so long. His answer really hit me: "I just wanted to make sure that you were home OK, Six."

During the time with my folks, we took a week to go to a place on Cape Cod Dad had rented, what a great time! We spent the day doing touristy things and eating at some fine restaurants. One night Suzanne and I must have been a little loud in our "getting reacquainted activities" for my Dad suddenly hollered out "Hold it down in there!" Breakfast was a little strained, as I remember, but all was soon forgiven.

Shortly after leaving Cape Cod we had to return to Columbus to collect what we needed for our next assignment. At the end of my 30-day leave, Suzanne and I left Columbus GA, pulling a trailer with my '68 Firebird 400 that I had bought at West Point, en route to Ft. Myer, Virginia, home of the 1st Battalion, 3rd Infantry "The Old Guard"; the Army's ceremonial unit stationed in the Military District of Washington. It was spit and polish and rigidly "old Army" as compared with the jungle combat environment I had just left. Talk about going from one extreme to another!

We initially lived in an apartment off base until quarters became available. We then were extremely fortunate to move to South Post, Fort Myer, a small independent area with neat little wooden quarters with big porches, our own gym, commissary/PX annex, gas station, theater, etc.

The only residents of this peaceful little enclave were Old Guard officers, company commanders and battalion staff. There was a gate that led directly into Arlington National Cemetery that was open all of the time. Our quarters backed up to what was then I95 on a built-up roadway so that our place was pretty quiet and serene. There was a tunnel next to our quarters that ran under the highway and to the Pentagon so we could visit the bakery there, etc. It was a great place to live. Since those days the area has been leveled and has become part of Arlington National Cemetery.

Although the time period between the jungles of Vietnam and Cambodia and the spit and polish of the Old Guard was only about a month, I don't remember having any particular problem adapting to the new environment. I was happy to be back "in the world", happy to be with my wife, and extremely happy to be in the Old Guard as an assignment, it was really an honor and meant that I'd done pretty well in my short Army career. My first son, John C. (Chuck) Hedley II was born at Ft. Belvoir's hospital during this assignment.

Initially I was assigned to HHC as an Assistant S3. During that time, I had to attend the Old Guard Charm School where I learned saber manual (my ceremonial side arm) and the "Old Guard Glide", a method of marching that ensured the soldier's head did not bounce up and down on the parade field or during ceremonies. During that time, one of my KIA classmates was returned to the US. I was called by the Pentagon Casualty Assistance Office and asked if I would escort the body home.

When I asked for a release from the battalion for the TDY required, it was refused because I had just been assigned and had too much to learn. I was also being investigated in order to complete my White House Security Clearance and and I told that also precluded me from leaving Virginia. The classmate had also been a Prep School classmate. I was really pissed and have never forgiven myself for not trying harder to take my buddy home.

After about three months in the S3 shop, I was offered command of Bravo Company, and of course I jumped at the opportunity. With this transfer, I had commanded three platoons and two companies in a little more than two years. I don't remember the date of the change of command, sometime in early October I think, but it was a happy day indeed. I really had no idea of the work ahead or the emotional price it would exact.

As a company commander, I was required to keep my unit proficient in four major areas. One was ceremonial; we held monthly parades to honor those retiring from the Army, plus performed in many other arenas that required us to look sharp and be experts at drill and ceremonies.

One of the highlights of this responsibility was performing in the first two years of a great musical event called "Spirit of America." This performance was written, staged and performed by The Old Guard and included performances by the Army Band, the Herald Trumpets, the Army Chorus as well as our own Drill Team and Colonial Fife and Drum Corps. This great music accompanied vignettes of the county's military history, with Old Guard soldiers dressed in period uniforms. One year I was honored to command the March On and March Off with my company.

I also participated in the "Torchlight Tattoo" performed weekly during the summer tourist season at the Jefferson Memorial. This was a scaled down version of the "Spirit of America" and was pretty well received by DC residents and tourists alike. I always felt it was a great honor to be able to participate in these events. One year we took the "Spirit of America" show to Norfolk, Virginia and performed in the Scope Arena, maybe its inaugural show. We were there for about a week for rehearsals and performances and were quartered at Ft. Story, Virginia where I shared a set of quarters with my officers. It was during this trip that I was honored to meet Mrs. Douglas MacArthur, who attended one performance, which always included as one vignette a reenactment of Gen MacArthur's return to the Philippines.

A second mission, the emotions of which I was not prepared for, was conducting Army funerals in Arlington National Cemetery. These experiences could be emotionally challenging as most of those who we buried were Vietnam casualties, and it was one of my duties to present the folded flag, which had rested on the soldier's casket, to the next of kin, usually a young widow. As the Company commander, I was responsible for the conduct of all officer funerals. Sometimes I would do two or three in one day, which required a clean and pressed uniform each time. Fortunately for me, I was authorized an orderly who occupied a room next to the company dayroom. In there he stored my extra uniforms, both greens and dress blues, and had an iron and ironing board and shoe cleaning equipment. Our shoes were made of Corfam, a shiny black plastic surface, as well as metal toe and heel taps and a large piece of iron attached to the inside of each heel so that we could perform a loud heal click when performing drill and ceremonies. The heel clicks also served as cues for parts of the funeral ceremony outside of the chapel.

Officers being buried were entitled to an infantry escort of one platoon of my company commanded by the platoon leader. In addition, the casket was carried on a caisson pulled by a matched set of horses with Old Guard drivers. The casket team accompanied the caisson marching on each side from the chapel to the gravesite. In addition to these units, the procession also included the Army Band, a color guard, and the Chaplain. The next of kin could walk or ride behind this procession. My duty was to get to the gravesite curb ahead of time so that I could render honors when the casket arrived and then accompany the casket to its bier while it was carried by my casket team. After the service, the three rifle volleys fired by a seven man firing team, resulting in a 21 round salute to the fallen warrior, and the playing of Taps by an Army bugler, it was my duty to receive the folded flag from the casket team and present it to the next of kin with the words "On behalf of a grateful nation and United States Army, I present you this flag in honor of your (husband's, son's. . .) service to his country." While doing this I usually knelt down on one knee and looked the next of kin in the eyes. I was not allowed to exhibit any emotion at this time but many times I cried inside as I saw the grief and sorrow. I found myself to be emotionally drained on funeral days, particularly if I had done two or three. Many times I thought, "There but for the grace of God . . ."

During this time I was the Officer in Charge of some notable funerals. I had the honor of burying the most well known hero of World War II, Audie Murphy. Not only had he been a war hero, but he also went on to be quite a movie star. There were a lot of other stars in attendance, I particularly remember John Wayne. I was also responsible for the funeral of Justice Black of the US Supreme court. A real unique experience was the burial of the crew of a World War II B-24 bomber that had been recovered in the Sahara desert when winds blew the sand aside. Remains of all 10 crewmembers were found on board; the military went to great length to find all of the family members, and the night before the funeral there was one hell of a reunion party, to which I was invited, as people got reacquainted after more than 25 years. I don't remember there being many caskets, maybe two or three, and they were buried together and the families had asked that there be only one headstone that listed all members of the crew.

One particularly difficult funeral occurred close to the end of my assignment. One of my platoon leaders received orders to go to Vietnam. When I learned this I spent many weekends with him at Camp A. P. Hill teaching him everything I knew about how to survive in the combat zone. I knew I had failed miserably when we received word that he was coming home, having been killed in an ambush only a couple of months after he arrived. I was crushed; I had tried so hard with him. We, of course, performed the funeral and presenting his flag to his Mom was one of the hardest things I had ever done.

A third mission was riot control training as the Capital streets were often filled with aggressive and destructive anti-war demonstrators. For a whole week we, primarily the NCOs, drilled the troops in proper techniques and formations. Fortunately we never had to "perform" on the streets—but we did have one deployment downtown where our mission was to protect the White House.

In the spring of '72, there was a huge demonstration planned. It was so big the pentagon deployed additional troops to the capital area. The Memorial Street Bridge was secured by a battalion of the 82nd as I remember. A battalion of Marines was quartered on the athletic field next to the gym on South Fort. The Marines pitched pup tents and practiced formations in the street in front of my quarters. All of our wives baked cookies, brownies, etc. to take out to them along with pitchers of lemonade and iced tea.

We were alerted to assemble in our company areas after dark for transportation downtown. We boarded buses that had been blacked out with thick paper over the windows. We were in fatigues with web gear and steel pots, with weapon and bayonet. When we arrived downtown we unloaded and the battalion split in half, two companies went to the Executive Office Building on one side of the White House, and the other two, to include my B Company, moved into the Treasury Building.

We had loaded our sleeping bags on the buses and these were now laid out in the hallways of the building so everyone could get a little sleep. When we awoke in the morning, we cleaned up, shaved, etc. in the rest rooms, and ate a breakfast from a line that had been set up on the first floor.

After eating we formed up and went through the tunnel that connects the building to the White House where we deployed as a single green line to protect the building and prevent its damage or destruction by the rioters. All of the companies emerged onto the lawn and we completely encircled the building. My soldiers stood there with bayonets fixed, each of them had a loaded magazine in their right front pants pocket, none of the weapons were loaded. I had two snipers who were locked and loaded and ready to fire, along with two RTO's, one to talk with battalion headquarters and one to speak with my platoon leaders. The President and his family were not in residence that weekend.

The White house was ringed on the curb by city buses parked as tightly as possible behind each other so as to provide a barrier to any rioters trying to get to the White House. Our mission was simple; stop anyone that got past the Secret Service guards. What was meant by "stop" was to shoot if required on command of the company commander. Shoot Americans, the same folks I'd served in Vietnam? Holy shit, what kind of a country had we become? Fortunately for us, the demonstrators never made it to the White House, so we were saved from having to make a horrible decision. To this day I don't know if I could have ordered my soldiers to fire on fellow Americans.

My fourth mission was to maintain my soldiers as effective and efficient infantrymen. This was difficult to accomplish given the time requirements of the first three missions. We were able to train for an afternoon once in a while, but infantry skill maintenance took a back seat during most of the year. In recognition of this fact, all of the rifle companies in the battalion were allowed to move to Camp A. P. Hill, south of Washington, for one month during the summer for concentrated infantry skills training, from the individual soldier to company sized operations. This month was almost like a vacation and eagerly anticipated by most of our soldiers.

During the period of 1970 -1972, the Vietnam War was still raging, so of course tactics and survival methods for that environment were the focus of our training. While I was the only combat experienced officer in the company, most, if not all, of my senior NCO's were combat veterans. Because of this I had a great organic source of experience on which to draw and didn't need much assistance from the battalion staff. I know I had to brief the S3 on what I intended to accomplish, but other than that, the only support I required was logistical from the S4 to include food, equipment, training materials and food for my mess team.

One of the great joys of company command in those days was that I had my own mess team, from a mess sergeant to cooks to soldiers detailed from the platoons for KP duties. I had a lot of control over what my soldiers ate and its quality. Outstanding food in sufficient quantity to satisfy hungry young infantrymen after a hard day's training was a high priority for me. While we were "in the field" while at A. P. Hill, most of the time was spent with the troops in one floor barracks. I did try, however, to have them spend as much time in the woods at night as possible. One of the glaring weaknesses of the American Army of those days was the inability to operate at night. With that in mind I had my soldiers run night navigation courses and night patrols to help them get over a soldier's natural fear of darkness when you can't see what's around you. In Vietnam the only night vision device that was usable in the jungle were our Model A1 eyeballs. The Starlight night vision devices were too big, heavy and cumbersome to carry when outside of the firebase.

While at A.P. Hill, we held refresher training in individual skills and moved up to squad, platoon, and finally a capstone company exercise at the end. This was a heck of a schedule for only one month.

About June of 1972 I received orders for my next assignment; attendance at the Armor Officers Advanced Course at Ft. Knox, Kentucky. The Advanced Course, normally conducted by each separate branch, was the next step after the Basic Course in the Army's organization of education. Normally I would have expected to return to Fort Benning for the infantry course, but in this case selection to go "out of branch" was regarded as an indicator that you were off to a good career start as the branches would send only their best officers to another branch's schooling.

This course required about a year and was designed to prepare captains for battalion and brigade staff duties. In addition, we were afforded a great opportunity to play with amphibious and main battle tanks; the 60-ton M60 A1 main battle tank and a really cool piece of equipment, the 15-Ton M551 Sheridan AR/AAV (Armored Recon/Amphibious Air Assault) vehicle. This was a real innovative fighting machine that had been introduced about 1968 and saw some service in Vietnam. It was amphibious and air droppable, and mounted a 152mm gun/launcher system that enabled it to fire HEAT (High Explosive Anti-Tank) rounds as well as the Shillelagh guided anti-tank missile. The HEAT rounds had a combustible shell casing, which burned in the breech and eliminated brass casings rolling around inside when in combat. This innovation, however, dictated a very slow rate of fire as the breech had to be checked to be clear of all remnants of the casing before another could be loaded.

When we went to the range to fire these weapons, the armor guys had a lot of fun with us grunts. Out of "professional courtesy" they allowed us to be in the tank commander's hatch first. When the main gun was fired, the recoil was so great that the first two or three road wheels would leave the ground throwing the TC into the commander's turret or even worse into the 50 cal. mounted at that position. There was great mirth and laughing as they watched their infantry brothers suffer bloody noses or black eyes since we weren't prepared for the recoil.

The Commandant of the Armor School was Major General George Patton IV, son of the famous WW II Commander of the famous Third Army. He looked a lot like his Dad and we all thought he tried to act like him as well. He was given to using racy language even during those times when we had our wives present for an occasion. The year was a great break and time to be with my family after four years of command. Although I thoroughly enjoyed my time there, it soon came time to leave and move on to our next assignment.

While at the Armor School, my assignment guys told me that it was time for me to go get some graduate schooling and instructor time, I'd had enough troop time and had to let other infantry captains command. I sure didn't like that advice; I loved being around soldiers, but agreed to an assignment teaching in the Military Art (history) Department at West Point. This slot had been arranged by one of my mentors, then a Professor from the Military Art Department. During our time at West Point, there were no academic majors other than the BS in engineering. Consequently there were few electives, only one a semester for the last two years.

My professor had been a Vietnam chopper pilot, specifically "C" Model gunships, and a guy I really admired. All four of my electives had been in Military Art and it was one of the few departments in which I'd done really well. This former Professor had arranged a slot in the department for me starting in 1975, and had also had me accepted at Stanford University in CA, as they were one of only two schools offering an MA in Military History. While I was really surprised at being admitted to Stanford with my less than stellar academic history, I had done well on the GRE's and my history studies. As I was preparing for this real adventure, I received some earth shattering information; West Point was going to admit women starting with the class of 1980… I could not be a party to that. I felt that the admission of women would change the mission and very nature of the academy that I was so proud to have graduated from, and I didn't want to see the resultant destruction. As a result I had to call my mentor and refuse the assignment to West Point, I don't remember how that call went or ended, other than he excused me from the job. I talked with Suzanne and we elected to go to Atlanta where I could study at Georgia State University and she could be close to her folks in Columbus.

The five years at Georgia State, two years studying and three years teaching, would prove to be a tumultuous time for me. I did well in grad school and survived the first RIF (Reduction in force), an involuntary separation from the Army of Regular Army Officers; some of my classmates were not so lucky. Our second son, Brian, was born during this time during a hurricane and soon thereafter Suzanne divorced me. I was crushed; I had lost my wife, my two sons, our house, and almost everything else we had owned. The only thing of value I managed to hang on to was my '71 Corvette T-Top.

For a while I was in the depths of depression and dirt poor, living in a BOQ at Ft. Gillem in Atlanta; an old style BOQ with a common bathroom and shower in the middle of the building. Sometimes I couldn't use the facilities because there was a guy standing guard outside the door while his girl friend took a shower. Also during those days I was dependent on one of the other ROTC instructors for transportation to work and back as I couldn't afford to drive my car. But eventually the divorce became final, my financial burden eased somewhat, and life became tolerable again. Amongst all of the bad things coming my way during this dark time of my life;, two good things did emerge; my Master's degree in Oriental History paved the way for my future Army and civilian careers, and I met my soon to be soul mate, Margie, the most wonderful wife and partner that any man could ever ask for.

Also during this time the Vietnam War officially ended on January 27th, 1973 with the signing of the Paris Peace Accords and the death of the last soldier in that war, LTC William B. Nolde. That event was to cause me one more unpleasant incident. I was in the outer office of the History Department's Dean when a guy I knew from some of my classes came up and gleefully announced that the "Illegal" war in Vietnam was finally over and that all of the Americans who had died in Vietnam had died for nothing and how happy he was about that. Well, I lost it and hit him as hard as I could. Not an auspicious end to a good experience in graduate school!

The end of the war also ended my quest to return to combat, a move I had tried to make happen several times. With Margie by my side, a new and wonderful phase of my life was about to begin.

DUTY! HONOR! COUNTRY!

23 – TOGETHER AGAIN

Sometime during the winter of 1999 – 2000, while living and working in Tokyo Japan, I received the following letter:

July 19, 1999
Dear John,

> *My name is Jimmy Harris. I am trying to locate a John Hedley that served with the 1st of the 14th 4th infantry division Co E in the year of '69 – '70. The recon team was called Fox Force. Hopefully this is you. If it is, would you please contact me by phone or letter. My number is 1-XXX-XXX-XXXX. I live at XXXXXX, Festus MO 63028. I was originally from Mississippi. I was SSGT Harris.*
>
> *I came across the address from Danny Stagner who also served with me. He lives in Albuquerque, New Mexico. He did not have a phone number to reach you. He was our Machine Gunner.*
>
> *I would really like to hear from you if you are the man I'm looking for. Thank you for your time.*
> *Sincerely,*
> *Jimmy Harris*

Holy shit, I was absolutely speechless as tears welled up in my eyes and long forgotten memories came rushing back into my mind.

I had tried for years to find Jimmy, kind of like my Holy Grail. We had spoken briefly a couple of times after we both got home; Jimmy was at Fort Campbell, KY, in the 101st and I was stationed at Fort Myer, VA, in The Old Guard. He was having real problems adjusting to life in the Stateside Army and wanted to get together to talk. As much as I really would have done that immediately, my first wife was pregnant with our first child and didn't want me to leave or to invite Jimmy to come to visit us. I regretfully told him the news and then never heard from him again. For years, I made cold calls to every Harris I could find in a Mississippi (where I knew he was from) phone book during those days before the internet and a computer in every home. I became really frustrated and eventually gave up trying after I retired from the Army and went to work for Raytheon in Japan. I thought that I would never be able to find SSGT. Jimmy Harris.

And then the letter arrived... evidently Charlie "Red" Siner was also in touch with Jimmy or Stag and found out I worked for Raytheon. Although they didn't know I was in Japan, they found an address for me. The address that they eventually came up with was, very fortunately, the address of the US office that supported us in Tokyo, and the letter eventually made its way to me. The stars must have been in alignment.

I wanted to call Jimmy immediately, but Margie pointed out it was only 2 or 3am where he was, and I should wait a couple of hours. Holy shit, after all of these years I had commo with Jimmy Harris, and she wanted me to wait? What torture! I did wait a while, I don't remember how long, but finally couldn't wait any longer. When Jimmy answered the phone, I immediately knew I had the right guy; I was finally back in touch with my Fox Force Platoon Sergeant. Unbelievable!! I don't remember how long we talked, it must have been for a couple of hours, and I promised I'd arrange a business trip home with a stop in St. Louis, close to where he lived, as soon as possible.

That call began recall of that year in Vietnam; I had virtually pushed it out of my mind for so many years. Pieces of memory came floating back, always disjointed and many times not in a recognizable context. I arranged for the trip, made the reservation through St. Louis for an overnight stay, and anxiously awaited the departure day; the time seemed to really drag.

Finally, the day came and I was on my way to CONUS and Jimmy Harris. I didn't sleep much on that flight, had a few drinks, and wondered what the meeting would be like. Would I recognize him, would he recognize me? Would our relationship really be as strong as I had imagined? What was I going to say after all of those years? The plane touched down during a rainy dusk and I'm sure that my heartbeat and blood pressure both increased! Since this happened before 9/11, folks could go to the gate to welcome arriving friends. As soon as I entered the terminal I recognized him, standing with his first wife, scanning the deplaning passengers looking for me. Our eyes met and it was instant recognition, the intervening 30 years just seemed to melt away. We moved toward each other and embraced, and the tears just started to flow from both of us, the emotional release was incredible! We must have been a sight for other folks passing by, two old guys hugging and crying!!

We spent all night talking about the old days and the intervening years, what had happened, where we'd been, what we'd done. There were a couple of bottles of liquor that were quickly consumed before we went down to the hotel restaurant for dinner. After returning to the room, we called Danny Stagner and had another long conversation. Danny was in touch with Red, they thought they might have a line on a couple of other guys, and we decided that it was time for a reunion with as many of the guys as we could find. Jimmy and I stayed up the rest of the night as I remember, maybe I went to my room for a couple of hours of sleep, and we then went to breakfast before my plane left for Massachusetts. What a hell of a time we'd had, it felt so good to finally be back in communication with Jimmy and at least a couple of my Fox guys.

After I got back to Japan, the emails started to fly and we decided to have our first reunion in Albuquerque, NM hosted by Danny Stagner, that summer of 2000. We didn't want to wait any longer to reunite. Since Margie and I were still in Tokyo, and this would be our first one, Margie decided that I should go alone so she wouldn't interfere with all of us guys reuniting after 30 years. That turned out to be a mistake, as I could have used her support in what proved to be a very emotional time.

I know that I was really nervous as I headed to that first reunion; the same questions arose as in my first meeting with Jimmy, would I recognize the guys, would I know their names, would they know me? How was this going to work?

I sat in the lobby of the hotel so I could watch folks as they arrived. Those that were coming for the Fox Reunion all had the same uncertain, apprehensive look on their faces. It was obvious that we were all suffering from the same doubts and uncertainties. But, it was absolutely amazing how quickly those first connections were made. If we couldn't remember a name or a face there was still something in the guy's bearing and expression that told everyone else that he was one of the Fox guys. I was honestly surprised at the depth of emotions that suddenly welled up in all of us; the tears were unbelievable.

As more guys came in, we gathered at the bar, a custom that would carry on for years. A couple of the guys had brought their wives and families, Ron Classen with his wife Mary and five kids, Dan Stagner with his wife Maria and two kids, Ron Shewell with wife Lucy and son, Gary Felton and Katie, Jim Cain and his sister, Gary and Patti Nelson, Jimmy and Susan Harris, Buck Buckelew with Chris, Erin and Fallon, as I remember. In addition, those attending without family members were Charlie Siner, Ken McLacklan, Bill Norton (my replacement in Vietnam when I gave up Fox) and me; it was an outstanding turnout for a first effort. It was an incredible weekend and we started traditions that would carry through until today. The reunions originally went from Friday to

268

Sunday because a lot of us were still working. Friday night became an informal pizza/sandwich night; Saturday mornings became our admin meeting followed by everyone going to dinner that night. Sunday we usually had breakfast together and then everyone headed for the airport or the road. For that first get together, the Stagner's hosted a meal at their house on Sunday. Maybe some of us left on Monday.

I do remember that during our first Saturday meeting we had to station Mary Classen by the phone in the meeting room so that she could call down for more tissues as they were needed; tears seemed to start for no reason as we talked and got reacquainted and began to talk about some of the incidents described in this book. It was kind of amazing how close to the surface everyone's emotions were. One of the things we decided at that first get together was that we'd get together for a reunion every two years in the future, there was just no way were we going to lose track of each other again.

It was really difficult for me to leave this gathering of men, and their families, that I had lead through some fairly hairy times. As I was leaving Stag's house to head back to the hotel, I had another real emotional experience. I don't remember who it was, but one of the wives came up to me with tears in her eyes, gave me a big hug, and said, "Lt. Hedley, thank you for bringing my husband home." Wow, I had never had that thought, and this wife's very emotional "thank you" just unleashed even more emotions and tears for me. When I got on the airplane the next morning to start back to Tokyo, I was drained, emotionally exhausted. I was lucky enough to share that flight with Ron Shula and his wife and son.

That was a fortuitous event, for some time before the next reunion, Ron passed away, the first guy we would lose to suspect Agent Orange-related problems after we started to get back together again. I unfortunately couldn't leave Japan for business reasons to go to the funeral, but I did write a letter to his family that I asked Red to read during the service. I was really depressed that I couldn't get back to the US for such a significant and emotional event.

Two years later we met in Orlando, Florida, and this time most of us brought our families along; Margie came with me from Tokyo. This was the first weekend in August of 2002, a time we had chosen during our inaugural reunion two years earlier. We had a great time in Orlando; the guys heard that Margie was craving Crispy Crème donuts, so on Sunday they had a dozen for her. That Sunday morning, I also made Bloody Marys for everyone. At that reunion, we guys really started to remember incidents that had occurred 33 years earlier, we waited until our families had gone to bed so that they wouldn't hear some of the worst stories. We were up until late in the evening and consumed a pretty good amount of adult beverages. We also decided at this event that two years was too long a time between reunions and from then on, we would meet on the first weekend of August every year.

The reunion in 2003 was held in Breckenridge Colorado. Because of a scheduled visit to Japan by the Raytheon CEO, I wasn't able to attend. It was at that reunion that "Bease" Beasely rejoined Fox. Bease had had a rough time medically having suffered a stroke and, I think, a heart attack such that he couldn't walk and was in a wheelchair. When the decision was made that the next year we'd celebrate with a cruise sponsored by Buck, Jimmy Harris challenged Bease to walk up the gangway a year later under his own power.

The year 2004 was a very special reunion in many ways. Al Buckelew, who was then the President of Princess Cruise Lines, hosted a get-together on the Emerald Princess's inaugural voyage on an Alaska cruise. He offered to let us invite any family members we wanted and the end result was that we had about 110 folks on board with 15 of us; what a phenomenal time. We were sailing from Seattle and gathered in a hotel the night before departure. I was sitting in the bar (surprise!) when one of my guys told me that I needed to come out to the reception desk because there was a real surprise awaiting me. As I walked out my knees almost buckled because there was Jim "Murf" Murphy with his wife and two beautiful daughters!! Holy shit, I really lost it because I thought Murf had died after being medevac'ed from St. George the night of the sapper attack. I had tried to check on my casualties by radio and message and the only feedback I'd received on Murf was that he was gone, no other details. For 34 years I carried the belief that I'd lost him that night, what a relief!! We went back to the bar and I drank a lot more!!

There were a couple other significant events during that weekend as well. I had gone to the airport with one of the guys to pick up Bill and Toni Strate when they arrived. Toni set what should have been an airline record for the amount of baggage required to support one week on a cruise ship, there must have been 10 – 15 pieces of luggage on the cart that Bill struggled with.

While waiting at baggage claim, I looked over at the waiting area and saw Charlie. When I went over to greet him a guy standing next to him asked me for a quarter… I was really caught by surprise. I tried to ignore him and talk with Red but the guy kept pestering me for a quarter. Finally, I guess when he could tell that I was getting a little exasperated he asked, "You don't recognize me do you?" When I acknowledged that I did not, he told me his name, Danny Williams. That was another shock. Danny had been one of my squad leaders and also, with Gary Nelson, one of my best point men. Danny left Vietnam sometime after I left Fox and went on to another assignment that he wouldn't talk about to any of us once we reunited. We had one other new addition on that cruise, Red's best friend Larry "Diz" DesJardins. Diz had been one of my snipers and we were all glad to welcome him back to the unit.

A real highlight of the trip was Bease. Since Jimmy had challenged him the year before to walk onto the ship under his own power, Bease had been working hard on his physical therapy. When we showed up at the ship, Bease was standing and walking with a cane; he made it up the entryway under his own power to the encouragement and cheers from all of the rest of us. What an accomplishment. Bease had a great cruise, dancing with as many of our wives as he could and walking most of the time with just his cane. During those times when he needed his chair, Danny Williams, his squad leader in Vietnam, pushed him around. At one point Charlie, after taking a lot of guff about no longer having much hair, and the fact that what was left was no longer red, decided to get his hair dyed back to its original color. Bease thought that a really cool idea so he did the same, after having his head shaved into a Mohawk cut. The night of the last formal on board I got a call in my cabin from Danny, Bease wanted to walk into the dining room with me. I have a picture from that event that is one of my most treasured possessions. When Bease passed away a year or so later, he had asked that his funeral flag be given to me rather than to his sister. I had no idea that would happen and fought my way through another very emotional moment.

In 2005 we met in Denver, CO and then in 2006 we had a reunion at our house in Denver, NC. We had a total of 62 people show up for that event, a really great turnout. On Saturday morning I took all the guys up to Pat's, the coffee shop in Mooresville run by Richard Warren, a Vietnam veteran gunship pilot. Richard had a very welcoming vet centric facility that had become a real hangout, particularly for Vietnam guys. I had asked Richard if I could bring my guys in before he opened on Saturday morning for the live music get together.

We all put on our red scarves and headed up to Mooresville. When we walked into the shop Richard had two tape decks playing; one playing Vietnam era music and the other a recording of the "wop, wop, wop" of Huey helicopter blades; these sounds were a real emotional welcome. Richard warmly welcomed all of my guys and his assistant, Cheryl Ann, circulated giving all of my guys a hug, a kiss on the cheek, and a very warm "Welcome home." My guys were really affected by this warm and welcoming atmosphere; I saw several of them with tears in their eyes. After about 45 minutes I gathered everyone together, we posed for a picture outside of the shop, and then said a warm goodbye to Richard and Cheryl Ann, and headed back to Lake Norman.

We had a hell of a reunion. Will Delong's Mom, sister, niece and brother all came which really made me uncomfortable to begin with as I wasn't sure how they would react to me as I held myself to be responsible for Will's death. I should never have worried; they proved to be the most understanding and loving people that could ever be imagined in a situation like we had. As a matter of fact, Will's sister Paula, Paula's daughter Amber and granddaughter McCartney hardly ever missed a Fox Force function after that reunion. I never ever thought that I'd experience such acceptance from the family of a man who died because of a stupid mistake that I should have been able to prevent. I was really upset to learn that Will's Mom had never received the letter that I had written to her after the accident. Paula and Amber could not have been more loving, or more forgiving of me for the loss of Will; and finally after many years I made a trip to Ohio to pay my respects to Mom De Long and to offer a personal apology for my lack of supervision that fateful day. Mom gave me a big hug and told me not to feel guilty, followed once again by Paula and Amber. I can't adequately express how I feel about those ladies, or how much I love them for trying to lighten my burden.

In those days there was a lot of alcohol consumed at our reunions. Robin Sneeden showed up for the first time and brought with him a commercial frozen Margarita machine and gallons of mix. I had a keg of beer and a case or two of wine available, all of which contributed to a very lively time. Diz's swimsuit wound up being raised on our flag pole after some horse play in the lake. We had a wonderful dog named Bubba Gump, who had been rescued from New Orleans after Hurricane Katrina, who discovered that he really liked beer and margaritas. He would walk around the edge of the pool and knock over a drink glass or can of beer, and proceed to lap up the spill. The next morning it was obvious that poor old Bubba had a doggie hangover when he passed out on the side of the pool in the hot sun. We placed a sign on him asking folks to not contribute to the delinquency of our dog. Poor Bubba, it took him a couple of days to recover.

It was during this reunion when we showed slides from the guys to show our families what Vietnam had been like for us. We also began to talk openly in their presence about some of the incidents and experiences; I think that this was a good move for everyone.

The following year we met in San Antonio, and this was the first time that The Dragon and his wife Lois joined us. Earlier that year, through the efforts of Charlie Siner, we reconnected with Col (R) Victor M. Robertson Jr. who had been our first battalion commander in 1969. After talking with him on the phone for the first time, Margie and I drove down to Fort Jackson outside of Columbia, SC to meet him after a 37-year separation. It was a great meeting; Dragon and his wife were very happy we had reestablished contact and were really interested to hear about what was going on with the unit. It was an incredible experience for me, I thought the world of our Dragon while in Vietnam, he'd made a real impression on me and had taken really good care of my guys even though he sent us out on some hairy missions! I couldn't believe our luck in finding him after so many years.

I had taken him a picture of an event when one of the Assistant Division Commanders came out to the field to visit Dragon and Fox. In the picture Red is not wearing his steel pot and Lois questioned The Dragon on how could he allow that to happen, and why were we wearing red scarves in the field? Red later explained that I had ordered him to take off his pot so his red hair would stand out and he could draw fire away from the rest of us! Lois asked the Dragon if he had given us permission to wear our scarves in the field, and Dragon said that he hadn't. He looked at me in a questioning way and I told him we did it all of the time and that I had never asked for his permission. At that response I received a kind of disapproving look from Mrs. Dragon.

Dragon and Lois made a real impact on all of us and became invaluable members of the group. Unfortunately, we lost Lois, but all of the guys rallied around to support Dragon in any way that we could. Margie and I continue to go to Fort Jackson every five or six weeks to shop in the commissary and PX, and to have lunch with The Dragon.

Once again, as Buck remembered: *I didn't know at the time but Firebase Lois was named after the wife of Lt. Colonel Victor Robertson Jr the Battalion Commander or Dragon (1/14th is the golden Dragons).*

Almost 40 years later I would have the honor of meeting her – an incredible woman. I think Dragon would agree, that she would have been an excellent Dragon herself – she definitely was a woman in command.

The next year, 2008, we went to Nashville and the Grand Ol' Opry. That was a great weekend with a lot of time around the pool drinking beer and enjoying the great weather. The music was superb as was the food. The Fox Force beer cooler was Diz's bathtub so he made a

273

lot of trips back and forth through his open window to keep everyone supplied.

In 2009 we made a pilgrimage to Washington, DC primarily to visit the Vietnam Memorial, "The Wall." While there we also visited several other memorials as well as made a visit to Arlington National Cemetery to watch a changing of the Guard, a very impressive and moving ceremony. I was able to arrange a tour of the guard's barracks under the tomb for my folks because of my prior service in The Old Guard. That was a very moving experience both days, to see The Wall and to go to Arlington; it was almost like a pilgrimage. We were allowed to have a private ceremony at the apex of the wall and many of us laid wreaths in honor of departed comrades. Red's older brother, a Hamburger Hill survivor from the 101st remembered his buddies as did a good friend and Marine aviator did the same for a bunch of guys he knew. It was a very meaningful weekend. General Petraeus, then commander in Iraq, saw a bunch of us in red scarves sitting around the hotel lobby one afternoon and came over to say "Hi". I told him who we were and he thanked us all for our service in Vietnam.

2010 was a great year; we held our reunion at Schofield Barracks on the island of Oahu in Hawaii, with the 1st Battalion -14th Infantry, 25th Infantry Division. I had heard that the battalion was going on another deployment to Iraq and had contacted the battalion commander to see if I could bring my folks out to Schofield to present our red scarves to his current recon platoon so we could share our heritage with the young guys and let them know that they had support from some old guys who had also gone where they were headed – into Harm's Way. The CO, LTC Andy Ulrich, even though he had no idea who I was, was very supportive and encouraged us to make it happen.

On the 19th of May, on the parade field in front of Division Headquarters at Schofield Barracks, my guys tied red scarves around the necks of their counterparts in the battalion's recon platoon. There were 13 of us, including Dragon, and two families of guys who had died from Agent Orange related cancers since our return. We formed up on the parade field in front of the entire battalion and the Division Band, with Chad Classen (son of Ron) as our color bearer (we used the special Fox Force colors presented to us by Colonel and Mrs. Robertson), and tied our scarves around the necks of our counterparts, I was proud to honor Lieutenant Allan Sara, the Platoon Leader. As we tied the scarves on the young guys, they in turn presented us with a beautiful red scarf embroidered with the battalion crest and the date of the ceremony. The wives of two of our departed brothers tied scarves on the appropriate soldier as well.

When we had completed the ceremony for the scout platoon, Jimmy presented an honorary scarf to the Battalion Command Sergeant Major and I did the same to Andy Ulrich. Instead of handing it to him, he asked that I tie it around his neck as we had for the recon guys; I was proud to do so. As each of us completed our part of the ceremony, we moved to the front of the reviewing stand. When all the presentations were complete, Andy gave the command to "Pass in Review", then left the reviewing stand, ran onto the field, replaced the battalion XO as Commander of Troops, and lead the 1st Battalion, 14th Infantry in review past the reviewing stand to honor us. What an incredible feeling, what an honor, finally what a "Welcome Home" for my guys. After the ceremony, Andy treated us and the battalion to a Luau at the Hale Koa, the military hotel on Waikiki Beach. In addition to these events, we had a good time staying in downtown Honolulu, just a block from Waikiki. My guys still had their recon skills, as they were able to find all kinds of places that served adult beverages. I would guess that we had almost 50 people participating. LTC, now Colonel (Ret), Andy Ulrich is a great guy and remains a true friend of Fox and me to this day; it's an honor and privilege to know him.

From 2011 to 2016 we went back to Albuquerque and back to Lake Norman, to St Louis, and then to Ohio on the Lake Erie shore, Columbus Ohio for Diz and Angie's wedding, and then back to Columbus Ohio again for the whole group. Rockie Lynne, a phenomenal performing artist, veteran, supporter of active and former soldiers, and kind of a guardian angel for Gold Star Families, joined our reunion in St. Louis with his wife Susan. Rockie performed for us one night, especially highlighted his patriotic veteran-respect songs, and had many in the audience in tears by the time he finished. During these years we had a couple of other weddings, Jimmy and Lauri Harris and Dan and Beth Williams. I was incredibly honored to be Dan's best man, and the ceremony was performed on a floating chapel as we motored down a river in Florida.

The yearly family reunions are wonderful events, particularly when they're held in a place that all of the guys can get to. When that happens we have three generations of many families present as our kids have started having kids. My hope and dream is that this multigenerational group will become so tight and so close that our kids will continue to get together with their kids after all of us are gone.

In addition to the August family reunion, we have a yearly pheasant hunt in Nebraska that is a guys-only event. In 2005, Ron Classen, who lived in Humphry, Nebraska, started inviting the guys out to go pheasant hunting. The initial date chosen was in February around Martin Luther King's holiday, so that all those who were still working could use a long weekend. Most years, the weather was brutally cold and not real suitable for hunting, but the hardcore old recon soldiers went out anyway. Ronnie passed away in 2008 and all of us that were able to gathered in Humphry for his funeral. We acted as his pallbearers and also folded the casket flag that I presented to Mary. After the reception, all of the Fox guys gathered outside of the church and had a toast to all of our guys, those who had passed, those who could not attend, and those of us gathered for the sad event. The townspeople of Humphry were really impressed that the Fox guys gathered from all over the country to say goodbye to one of their own, and as a result of witnessing the bonds that held us together, and still connected us to Ronnie, took us into their hearts.

Fox decided that we needed to keep going to Humphry in the winter for the Ron Classen Memorial Fox Pheasant Hunt. The Humphry townspeople made all of the arrangements, provided transportation, and took care of everyone's needs. Word of what was happening got to an incredibly generous local man named Mike Wilke. Mike had not known Ronnie and knew nothing of Fox until the story was related by one of his friends in Humphry. Mike, who was a successful farmer, among other things, decided to take things into his own hands to ensure that the Fox guys were well treated.

Mike owned a lodge on his ranch about 20 miles from Humphrey that was equipped with bedrooms, a kitchen, a fully stocked bar, and all of the other requirements for a great weekend. He decided that he'd invite Fox to his lodge where he could host them and take care of everything. Not only was the lodge and all of its benefits provided, but Mike and his family provide all of the food and did all of the cooking. In addition, he provided recreational activities like a hot tub, access to weapons and, for the last three years, an air show conducted by local pilots.

There is an Old Soldiers' Home in Norfolk, NE about 30 miles away that also has a military memorial area. Mike has funded incredible memorials and tributes to Ron Classen and to Fox Force that will be there long after we're all gone. Because of their generous hearts and love of veterans, particularly Fox, Mike and Lois Wilke have become an integral part of the Fox family, as have many of the residents of Humphry. I find myself at a real loss for words that would adequately express my deepest appreciation for what he, and others in Humphry, have done for all of us. In addition to Fox, Mike has also supported my non-profit in Mooresville, NC, Welcome Home Veterans. I was proud to host Mike and his wife Lois, for a visit in 2016. Everyone at Richard's Coffee Shop is very thankful for his more than generous support.

These last 16 years with the guys from Fox and their families have been an incredible ride. Never, in those days of cutting through jungles, climbing mountains, and slogging through rice paddies while being shot at would I have ever imagined a time like this. We banded together in order to survive, we bonded as only men who share infantry combat can. But I don't think that any of us foresaw what would happen in the future. All we wanted to do was to survive our tour and get back to the world; for most of us that meant getting out of the Army and returning to civilian life. For two of us, Robin Sneeden and me, it meant serving for many more years. I would think that all of us reflected back on our time in Vietnam from time to time, to not do so was virtually impossible. But certainly in our early days there wasn't much thought of reconnecting. As stated earlier, I spent a great deal of time trying to find Jimmy Harris, but finally gave up. It took a couple of guys like Red and Stag to do the detail work and to try to track some of us down. Once the initial connections were made, the process snowballed, and today many of us are intimately connected with our past. Sincere thanks to those two guys for sparking these reunions, thus making sure that we've all stayed connected.

POSTSCRIPT

On August 3-6, 2017, Margie and I attended our yearly Fox Force Reunion, sponsored this year by Phil "Rosco" and Kathy Worley at the Wakulla Springs Lodge in Wakulla Springs, Florida. What an absolutely incredible event! I think that for the first time ever, we were in a location that facilitated us all hanging together for the entire weekend; there was no other place to go nearby for sightseeing or other activities. We thus spent more time together than we normally experience which was a really good thing.

However, what truly made this a special weekend and makes this reunion stand out among almost all of the others, were two events created by our own folks. One was a song written and composed by Lisa Thorson, the special partner of one of our guys Gene Charny, entitled "Brothers The Day We Met" and performed in a professional arrangement by our own "Murf" Murphy. Lisa is a professional vocalist and composer who teaches music at the college level. Murf has a rich and emotional voice that was perfectly suited to performing this anthem dedicated to the men of Fox. There were not many dry eyes after Murf's performance; we are all indebted to all involved with the performance of this song for producing such a beautiful result.

The second event of the weekend that made our gathering so special was the presentation of a four hour video about Fox produced by Steve Surgalski, the boyfriend of Shannon Murphy, one of Murf and Kathy's daughters. Steve, nicknamed "Grasshopper" by many in Fox, had recorded all of the reunions and some of the pheasant hunts since the 2006 reunion at our house. The core of his presentation, however, were personal interviews that he and Shannon did with each one of us during our trip to Hawaii for the scarf presentation. Around this structure Steve wove pictures of Fox in Vietnam and since then, as well as archival footage available on the web of US soldiers in the combat zone, all set to music of the time and ending with Lisa's song. The end result of his years of effort was a product whose historical and emotional value and impact cannot be easily described. Words like "phenomenal," "incredible," "emotional," or "awesome" just do not do it credit or adequately express its impact. We watched two hours on Friday and two on Saturday, and most of us had problems absorbing it all. It is an invaluable historical document that will last as our legacy for generations. Once again, there are no words that I know that can adequately express my most sincere thanks and admiration to Steve and Shannon for this documentary filled with love and history.

REFLECTIONS Producing this book has been a multi-year effort for me, with many stops and starts, and many long gaps when I did nothing at all. Part of the reason was that many of these incidents were hard to think about. And once the memories were back, it was difficult to write about them in any meaningful way. A lot of the reason for some of the delays was intense introspection caused by remembering the events that we all experienced. Two incidents in particular have caused me a lot of thought.

Did I select the best possible place for us to night laager two nights after the battle at St. George when we found ourselves surrounded on that hilltop? Shit, I almost got many, if not most, of my guys killed that night… had it not been for my guardian angel in the form of Puff that appeared without notice. I wonder what would have happened if my strobe light hadn't worked? I had carried the light for months but don't remember testing it after it was issued; I wasn't sure that it would work. What if it hadn't?

Did I do the right thing by refusing to spend the night in the field near the bunker complex? Should I have put my guys at risk and complied with the order even though we weren't prepared or really able to defend ourselves, especially in the dark? What tactical objective would have been accomplished? If I had decided to stay, and if we had survived, maybe we would have killed a lot more of the bad guys the next day. A more likely scenario is that a whole bunch of really pissed off NVA would have come looking for us that night and many of us wouldn't be attending reunions.

The responsibilities of a small unit leader in combat are huge. When that small unit operates on its own, many times outside the range of communications and/or artillery support, and no help is possible, then those responsibilities become even more consuming if you allow them to weigh on you. If you screw up, the results can be catastrophic as there aren't two more platoons of a full infantry rifle company alongside to help out; there is no one else. That kind of "loneliness" in itself is a heavy load and adds urgency to any decisions made; we didn't have much hope of rescue. Add to that the relationship that I had with all of my guys and the responsibilities became even more intense. Even in those days the Fox guys were my family.

As I look back on those days from a vantage point of 48 years later, it's sometimes hard to believe that we lived at the base level that we did. We had no creature comforts, we had no direct communication with our loved ones at home, and we were reviled by our countrymen for what we were doing. The grunts in Vietnam put up with a lot, and on most occasions performed well if not heroically.

As I've read through the battalion's ops logs to try to give myself some kind of a time line, more often than not I was struck by how cold and emotionless the entries were. An entry that Recon spent the night at such and such a coordinate in no way details how physically uncomfortable that might have been. I didn't allow my guys to dig in because of the noise that would create, so we basically rolled up in our poncho liners and slept on the ground. There were rocks and roots to contend with, to say nothing of mosquitos, fire ants, spiders and leeches. There is no mention in the log of just how scary it was to sleep in the jungle at night with little to no vision and all sorts of strange noises. Were those animals or bad guys?

There is no mention in the logs that the guys may have gone to sleep without being able to eat anything warm, or maybe eat anything at all. And if it was the monsoon, as it was for us for about two months, how miserable is it to try to sleep when you're cold and wet, and being pummeled by rain?

And if you're the commander these feelings or fears can be magnified, for you're responsible not only for your own life, but the lives of up to 30 other guys as well. There were many nights I spent poring over a map before the sun went down so as to be familiar with the terrain around me in case we had to move in the dark. The logs don't reflect the discomfort of open and oozing wounds on your arms or legs, or jungle rot. They don't mention the discomfort of ringworm or the intestinal issues that result from having to drink rice paddy water. They don't mention the physical discomfort of being filthy, of having to live in the same uniform for days without being able to take it off or wash it, to say nothing about not being able to wash your body or adequately brush your teeth.

We lived in a land where the temperatures could get to 120 degrees and the humidity close to 100% and we had no air conditioning, in the field or the base camp. During the monsoon it actually got cool at night and that was miserable if you were wet. When back at a battalion base camp like St. George or Lois we slept in sandbagged bunkers with little to no ventilation that we shared with rats and six or seven of our smelly best friends. It was a great day when you could shave, take a shower, really brush your teeth, or put on a clean uniform. In the division rear you might get to sleep on a cot in a room with a wooden floor and walls, but still there was no AC and the only ventilation was provided by a desk fan or the screens that doubled as windows.

There was nowhere in country where you could feel safe, there were no lines that separated us from the enemy and no real "rear areas". If you were in a 'rear area" you might not have to worry about being sniped at, ambushed or stepping on a booby trap, but you were always susceptible to rockets, mortars and even sapper attacks. If you were on a highway the risk of booby traps and ambush were always present. So there was no real rest or peace of mind for a year.

Yet by and large the American soldier performed with great competence and valor, at least in the world that I lived in. None of my guys threatened to frag me, at least that I know of, and we all got up in the morning knowing that we could get killed that day for no real reason, and the country did not intend to win our war. My soldiers had the same sense of duty, dedication and fought with the same valor as did our dads of the Greatest Generation

As I reflect back on all of this, I marvel at how my Fox guys lived and performed the way they did. I'm sure that the battalion duty logs do not reflect every time that we got shot at, or every time that we saw bad guys. And yet there were no slackers in Fox, there were no incidents but one where anyone refused to do what we were asked to do. There was never any hesitation in the face of the enemy. My Fox guys were superb!

I consider myself to have been blessed to have been able to serve with them. While Vietnam was maybe not the most enjoyable period of my life, I wouldn't have missed the experience for anything. I really enjoyed command, and must admit that I enjoyed that rush of adrenaline of combat. There's no feeling or psychological high like it; I really felt alive when the possibility of death was so close. I enjoyed being an independent small unit infantry commander. I feel a real sense of satisfaction that I brought most of my guys home, and at the same time feel incredible guilt about Will and maybe Sergeant Allen at St. George, both of whom were friendly fire casualties. I sincerely hope that what I've written helps my families understand some of what their loved one experienced while serving in Vietnam. It was a distinct honor and privilege to have served with all of them. And I hope that for those not a part of the Fox Family, that my efforts in recounting our service will help them to better understand Vietnam Veterans and motivate them to give a heartfelt "Welcome Home!" to any Vietnam Vet they see.

DUTY! HONOR! COUNTRY!

24 - EPILOGUE
THE FINAL CEREMONY

As I look back over the past fifty years I find that my life is like a living book, a work in progress that already contains many chapters that have been defined by jobs, events and experiences. Many of my life chapters correspond to a large degree with the chapters I've written for this book in an effort to record my memories of part of my life as a soldier and veteran. My six months in command of "Fox Force", the Reconnaissance Platoon of the 1ˢᵗ Battalion, 14ᵗʰ Infantry (The Golden Dragons) in the Central Highlands of South Vietnam in 1969, remains one of the most pivotal and significant times in my life. In that context I recently experienced a very emotional event, one that was neither planned nor foreseen, but which will effectively close my relationship with the active recon platoon of the Golden Dragons, and thus sadly end one of the most meaningful and rewarding chapters of my life's book.

Normally when Marge and I go to Hawaii most every winter I coordinate ahead of time to stop by 1-14 Inf. stationed at Schofield Barracks with the 25ᵗʰ Infantry Division to meet the command group and to talk with the current recon guys in an effort to keep our history and legacy alive. I've done this every year since a scarf exchange ceremony in 2010 and have always found it to be an extremely rewarding experience. The young soldiers of today are motivated and professional, and it's always an emotional high for me to be around them whenever I can be.

In 2010, I took my guys and our families, as well as several families of those guys who we've lost, to Schofield Barracks to present red scarves to the then active duty recon platoon before an upcoming deployment to the Middle East. Our intention was to share our chapter of the unit legacy with those young soldiers, and to show that there were old guys who had walked in their boots, even though ours were jungle boots, and had gone before them into harm's way. That whole day was such an incredibly meaningful event to me that I started returning every year to be able to interface with the Command Group and my new Fox guys.

Almost every time I went there were new guys in the platoon, and often a new battalion commander.

When in Hawaii in 2016 I did not make my usual prior arrangements for a visit as I'd heard that the battalion was scheduled to be deactivated and I wasn't sure of their status. On our last day on the island, while staying with a classmate, Dutch Hostler, who kindly allowed me to borrow one of one of his poems as an incredible illustration of what I've tried to do with "Saddle Up!" We decided to go to Schofield Barracks to the Post Exchange and I thought that I'd take a chance and stop by 1-14 Inf to see what was going on.

I was happy to find the battalion still active, so after introducing myself to the HQ CQ (Charge of Quarters), I met the current command group and others from the battalion staff. We had quite a discussion in the battalion commander's office about what's currently happening and also of our Fox Force history, the scarf exchange, and my yearly visits. I met the battalion XO and Command Sergeant Major, and suddenly a Sergeant First Class came running into the office and gave me a big hug, he'd been in new Fox during the 2010 ceremony. The folks I met were extremely welcoming and very interested in our history; I think it must be a welcome change when an "old guy" stops by!

I had made no prior arrangements to talk with the recon guys so felt keenly disappointed that I'd missed that opportunity. I was asked to accompany the Battalion Commander and the Command Sergeant Major on a tour of the building to help them identify important mementos from the Vietnam War that they should save. When I made a move to leave because I thought that I had been there too long I was told that I could not yet go outside! We walked around some more and finally a soldier showed up with the headgear for the Battalion Commander and the Command Sergeant Major. Finally I was given the OK, so I said my good byes and offered my thanks to them. I went out the door, unexpectedly accompanied by the command group, and was very surprised to find the recon platoon in formation alongside of the Golden Dragon statue.

At that time I was invited to speak with those soldiers; to say the least I was taken a little aback, and found myself at a loss for words; I didn't think this opportunity would happen. I took command of the formation, put them at ease, and talked with the soldiers for a few minutes about my pride in our shared experiences in recon, and how much in awe of them I was due to the operational climate they were living in. Looking into those young faces I could almost see the faces of my guys in Vietnam. After a few minutes I was prepared to leave so I turned the formation back to the platoon leader, but was then asked to remain in front. At that time the guidon bearer came forward, presented the guidon to the platoon leader, who then presented to me the unit guidon of the Recon Platoon! Wow, what an honor, I was speechless and almost lost control of my emotions . . . couldn't do that in front of those soldiers! I think that all soldiers understand what it means to be presented with the guidon or colors of a unit in which you've served, especially one you've commanded in combat. I was also presented with a framed picture of Jimmy Harris, Red Siner, and me from Vietnam which had been on the door of the platoon leader's office since 2010... nobody knew who the guys in the picture were!

So that's the good news. The sad news is that I did learn that the battalion would be deactivated which means it will no longer be an active unit; it essentially disappears from the Army. The cause, I was told, was sequestration and the resultant lack of funding. The date was Oct 16, 2016. The battalion commander invited me and my guys to attend the deactivation ceremony, and maybe even participate! I was honored by the invitation and really looked forward to attending. Unfortunately, however, the date was changed to one that I could not make so I missed the deactivation ceremony and the casing of the battalion's colors. I was extremely disappointed by this unfortunate turn of events.

The platoon guidon has an honored place behind my desk in my bunker or "man cave". Many emotions and remembrances well up inside me whenever I look at that blue banner; respect and love for those who served under it, immense pride in the accomplishments of my guys during the time we served, a deep sorrow for those who lost their lives and a real sense of sadness that I will no longer be able to visit the active unit. It was an incredible honor to have commanded that very special Fox Force in combat. I can't adequately describe the sense of pride that I have that this revered guidon was presented to me for safe keeping and that I can share it with my guys. Like our red scarves, the guidon represents so much more than a mere piece of blue cloth. I owe my deepest and most sincere thanks and appreciation to LTC David Krzycki, the last commander of the Golden Dragons, for making this happen. He sure made an old soldier proud!

The deactivation of the Golden Dragons represents a definite end to one of the most meaningful chapters of my life.

GOLDEN DRAGONS, SIR!

THROUGH THE EYES OF WAR

I'VE SEE ENOUGH TO SIT AND CRY,
LOOKING UP TOWARDS THE SKY

SEARCHING OUT THE TRUTH INSIDE,
NOT KNOWING IF I'M GOING TO DIE.

NOW THERE'S BLOOD AROUND MY FEET,
WAR, AGONY, AND WORST DEFEAT.

IS ALL THIS REAL WITH DISBELIEF,
THAT HEAVEN AND HELL SHALL CROWD MY FEET.
FOR THE PAIN I'VE SEEN, MUCH LESS I FEEL,
OF DYING MEN, CRYING IN THE FIELDS.

LOOKING NOW TOWARDS THE SKY,
SO PEACEFUL, SO BEAUTIFUL, SO VERY MUCH ALIVE.

BUT AS I GLANCE UPON THE GROUND,
THINGS JUST SEEM TO TURN AROUND.
SO UGLY, SO MISERABLE, SO VERY MUCH OF DEATH.
THAT ENDS A LIFE WITH A WHIMPERING BREATH.
WHAT HOPES AND DREAMS OH LORD, HAVE WE LEFT.

WONDERING NOW IN MY MIND,
OF OUR GOD THAT'S SO DEVINE.
MUST THE DEVIL LEAD US BLIND,
PLACING OUR LIVES ON LIMITED TIME.

NOW I ASK YOU LORD FOR ALL I SEE,
HOW DO WE FIGHT FOR WHAT YOU TAUGHT US TO BE.
FOR TRIALS AND TRIBULATIONS ALL AROUND,
HEAVEN IS WHERE I AM BOUND.

OH LORD! SHOW ME NOW THE PARTING OF THE SEA,
IN HEAVEN NOT HELL, I SOON WILL BE.

B.D. HAGUE, SGT, USA 1968-1972
1/5 (M) INF. RECON, 25TH INF. DIV, 1969-1970